# WESTERN ARBITRATION

*The Arbitral Chain*

Arthur J. Gemmell

University Press of America,® Inc.
Lanham · Boulder · New York · Toronto · Plymouth, UK

Copyright © 2008 by
University Press of America,® Inc.
4501 Forbes Boulevard
Suite 200
Lanham, Maryland 20706
UPA Acquisitions Department (301) 459-3366

Estover Road
Plymouth PL6 7PY
United Kingdom

All rights reserved
Printed in the United States of America
British Library Cataloging in Publication Information Available

Library of Congress Control Number: 2007942932
ISBN-13: 978-0-7618-4006-0 (paperback : alk. paper)
ISBN-10: 0-7618-4006-0 (paperback : alk. paper)

∞™ The paper used in this publication meets the minimum requirements of American National Standard for Information Sciences—Permanence of Paper for Printed Library Materials, ANSI Z39.48—1984

# Contents

| | |
|---|---|
| Acknowledgements | v |
| Introduction | vii |
| 1. Commercial Dispute Resolution Without Litigation | 1 |
| 2. The Arbitration of Greece and Rome | 33 |
| 3. The *Lex Mercatoria* | 59 |
| 4. The Arbitral Chain and the Common Law | 87 |
| 5. Chinese History and the Arbitral Chain | 113 |
| 6. The Modern PRC and the Arbitral Chain | 141 |
| 7. Chinese Arbitral Enforcement Practices and the Arbitral Chain | 175 |
| 8. The Sinicization of the Expedient | 195 |
| Table of Public Laws/Statutes and Rules | 207 |
| Table of Authorities | 213 |
| About the Author | 217 |

# Acknowledgments

Since the genesis of this book was my doctoral dissertation, I wish to thank Professors S. Sucharitkuk, S. Clavier, and J. Sylvester of the Golden Gate School of Law. Each was always there, always supportive, and always upbeat about the progress of my work. Their extensive knowledge of International Law was surpassed only by their warmth and eagerness to help.

My appointment as an International Law Scholar by Dean Donald Polden and Asst. Dean Elizabeth Powers within Santa Clara University School of Law's Center for Global Law and Policy aided my research efforts and gave my research the weight of a wonderful law school. I am, in addition, grateful to Santa Clara Law Professors Beth Van Schaack and Jiri Toman for their scholarship, support and friendship. I am so fond of them all.

Dean Joseph M. Moless of the Lincoln Law School of San Jose has been a constant supporter and cheerleader throughout my academic pursuits.

I am especially grateful to my LL.M classmate Wei (Alex) Zhang and his law partner, Yuwu Liu, for the help they provided in arranging various interviews during my trip to China. Without their help, this book would have lacked the depth of scholarship of my 'on the ground' research.

My thanks to the interviewees in China who gave so generously of their time, insights and candor. I have listed them alphabetically. Their anonymous comments remain just that: anonymous.

My special thanks go to Zheng Rungao whose perceptions and challenges helped guide my thinking as to Chinese history and Chinese arbitral practice.

Whenever I found work on this book to be tiring—at times, even exhausting—I was uplifted by two heroes: my sister, Janet and her son, my nephew, Robert. Both lost battles to cancer. I love them both for their courage, for their good humor in the face of terrible illnesses, and for Janet's good sense to have married Larry, with whom she raised a remarkable young woman, my niece, Andrea.

My wife, Barbara, put up with my gnome-like existence for the many months it took to write this opus. For your encouragement and unflagging support, thank you.

Throughout the many edits, rewrites, and frustrations of this work, my 'boys' were always there to cheer me on. The 'boys' are my sons, Keith, Ken, and Kevin, and my grandsons, Cole, Caden, and Keith. What terrific 'guys' they are and how fortunate I am to be their *Poppa*. I hope they take comfort in the joy and delight they brought to my life.

Good humor that helped carry me along was always supplied by my boon pal and fellow graduate law student, Ted Biagini. I always tried to better his humor but his younger mind was always too comedically agile.

Of course, any errors or omissions are mine, and mine alone.

## Persons Interviewed

| | |
|---|---|
| Cao, Lijun | CIETAC, Beijing |
| Chen, Frank | Chen & Co., Shanghai |
| Huang, Wen | CIETAC, Shanghai |
| Liu, Yuwu | King and Wood, Beijing |
| Lu, Lawrence | CIETAC, Shanghai |
| Sommers, Amy | Squire Sanders, Shanghai |
| Su, Glenn | Jones Day, Beijing |
| Tan, Johnson | Jones Day, Beijing |
| Tong, Ang Yong | Robert Wang & Co., Shanghai |
| Wang, Cheng Jie | CIETAC, Beijing |
| Wang, Hongsong | Beijing Arbitration Commissison |
| Wang, Peter | Jones Day, Shanghai |
| Yan, Chu Cong | Beijing Arbitration Commissison |
| Ye, Ariel | King and Wood, Beijing |
| Zhang, Wei | King and Wood, Beijing |
| Zhang, Xiaojian | Peking University School of Law |
| Zhang, Zhiyong | Peking University School of Law |

# Introduction

Seasoned businesspeople, especially those engaged in international business, are keenly aware of the fact that no matter how pleasant their pre-arrangement business courtship has been, post-arrangement disputes may indeed occur. Some disputes may be benign and settled amicably by the parties. Other disputes, however, provide the parties with only an unsated resolution due to prolonged and costly litigation entered into subsequent to the parties' inability to resolve their international commercial dispute peacefully. If businesspeople, caught up in the euphoria of 'making a deal,' fail to provide for amicable dispute resolution, then prolonged and costly litigation—regardless of how distasteful—may become the only solution available.

In order to avoid 'scrambling' once a material dispute occurs, time, energy, and effort should be expended 'up front' to ensure that, regardless of the form that the business arrangement takes, the documents creating the arrangement reflect an agreed-upon method of dispute resolution. A leading arbitral practitioner cautions, "Most corporate lawyers are focused on completing the transaction at hand and add boilerplate language on arbitration at the last minute."[1] This monition is especially relevant in the international arena wherein parties have been acculturated with different socio-political-cultural norms, are familiar primarily with their own business practices, and are, all too frequently, only superficially acquainted with their business partner.

Unwanted, yet undertaken, litigation is far too often the failure of a businessperson's and his or her lawyer's not having explored the foreign dispute settlement options or mechanisms available to resolve business disagreements. It is for this reason that this book has two target audiences: individual members of the international legal scholastic community, and academic libraries where this book should provide a resource for their teaching and scholarship. But while legal academics will find this book of value, the additional academic target audience is the commercial-legal community of business executives and lawyers, as well as law and business students who, in a relatively short period of time, wish to visit a law/commercial library and learn about arbitration, arbitral history, and arbitration's place in the Chinese legal landscape. To this end, this book seeks to avoid the density of expression ofttimes found in sombre, legal, academic tomes.

Few will take umbrage with the apodictic proposition that sustainable foreign investment and bi-lateral trade are of worldwide economic importance. Globalization has spawned an untold number of daily international commercial transactions. As disputes arose from these transactions, states fretted that their domestic court system would be unable to deal with foreign commercial disputes expeditiously and equitably. Hence, nation-states have, for the most part, accepted international commercial arbitration as the preferred vehicle for private commercial dispute settlement. The number of signatories to various international and regional arbitration conventions attests to the support established by commercial, political, and judicial interests throughout the world for this method of peaceful dispute resolution. The UNICTRAL Model Law on International Commercial Arbitration, NAFTA, and the New York Convention are illustrative.

This is not a book on "how-to do arbitration in China." There is already ample material on this subject in a library's legal or commercial sections. Rather, the book attempts to make a comparative analysis between the foundations upon which Chinese and Western arbitral systems were built. Therefore, one will find rooted throughout the book the proposition that an understanding of the international arbitral system enriches and sustains commercial intercourse while serving as a truly viable avenue for commercial dispute resolution. Granted national arbitration systems are not without their flaws, yet they remain for the most part institutions of commercial peace—buttressing, promoting, and ensuring commercial harmony.

Since legal rules and arbitral practices are commonly passed on from antecedent legal eras, it is important for meaningful long-term trade, this book contends, that international businesspersons, their lawyers, as well as students, absorb the dispute resolution history of the nation within which they intend to do business. Only then will commercial parties 'see' prospectively the backdrop against which their disputes will be played out.

*Introduction* ix

The notion of *arbitral chain* is a term that has been coined for use in this writing. The arbitral chain describes the process through which arbitration was developed over the years. The term will occur repeatedly as a metaphor for the linkage of one arbitral age with subsequent arbitral eras. Once linked one with another, how did successive eras accommodate, assimilate, or modify that which had been forged before them?

The Chinese and Western arbitral systems serve as the book's focal points. As used in the book, the Western arbitral eras include those of the Greeks, the Romans, the Law Merchants, the English and the Americans. The book determines that there was an arbitral chain that linked the eras of the West's arbitral past with its arbitral present. Were there similar links that fashioned the Chinese arbitral structure? Were the links forged from China's legal history? From Western arbitration traditions? Or are the links a composite of both? Stated another way, to what extent did Western and Chinese arbitral legal histories influence the development of their modern arbitral practices? Whether Western or Chinese, is a nation's arbitral history substantially or marginally reflected in its contemporary arbitral scheme?

If one will permit a bit of metaphorical license, this book will deal with those seeds of international commercial arbitration that were planted during selected western, national, and Chinese arbitral eras. Some seeds blossomed into the international treaties and agreements that govern today's international commercial arbitration arrangements. Other seeds found roots and grew into the international commercial arbitration tribunals upon which the commercial world relies to 'adjudicate' disputes—and to do so under predictable procedural and substantive rules.

At one point in my business career, I joined Fujitsu America, Inc. (FAI) as a Senior Vice President. Anxious to learn Japanese commercial culture and thereby become a more effective executive, I found a virtual gallimaufry of books on the subject. I immersed myself in various readings about the Japanese "commercial way" and read about the alleged uniqueness of the Japanese business culture: customer commitment, the drive for commercial perfection, bushido, Japanese women in the workplace, the inclusion of foreign executives in a Japanese inner circle, and exquisite politeness.

Many trips to Japan and years of experience convinced me that most of what I had read was simply a rehash of commercial stereotypes overlaid with a helping of unenlightened caricatures. Japan, like any other nation with broad economic ties, had its own unique facets. However, the alleged unique commercial characteristics that I found in the 'business' literature had little to do with the way of the samurai. Rather, Japan's commercial exemplars were, it turned out, simply modifications of and adoptions to twentieth century commercial realities.

It has been be the unflagging commitment of this book not to engage in such trite stereotyping. Nations' and their investors' 'high stakes' commercial activities deserve better.

This book examines how private commercial discordance was and is expeditiously and peacefully resolved.

Chapter One provides the reader with an introduction to commercial arbitration. Chapters Two, Three, and Four explore the arbitral chain as it was forged in the Western legal-historical experience. Chapters Five, Six, and Seven examine whether or not the arbitral chain was forged in the Chinese experience. The book ends with Chapter Eight, entitled "Sinicization of the Expedient." Rather than being shackled by an arbitral chain, China, as a matter of expediency, picks and chooses from the world's arbitral practices and sinicizes the expedient. The book concludes with thoughts on the implications for the international commercial player who is doing business in China.

It will be the goal of this book to contribute research and scholarship so that, having once read it, the international businessperson, lawyer, and student will better understand the relationships between the antecedents of international commercial arbitration and how these historical antecedents are being played out in China today.

# Note

1. L. Schaner, quoted by J. Toth, *International Arbitration: Enforcing or Contesting Awards*, available at www.martindale.com/pdf/c2c/magazine/2006_Mar/C2CO306_GP_Jenner (last visited May 2, 2006).

## Chapter One

# Commercial Dispute Resolution Without Litigation

This chapter is intended to introduce the 'newcomer' to commercial arbitration by providing a general understanding of what is, perhaps, the most successful peaceful dispute resolution process available in the commercial world. Arbitral practitioners and scholars will find little helpful in this particular chapter. For those on the opposite end of the arbitral learning curve, however, the following might be likened to an orchestral overture before the main characters take center stage, as indeed they will as this book unfolds.

One additional word regarding the focus of this chapter: the world of commercial arbitration encompasses what is euphemistically referred to as private and public arbitration. Simply put, public arbitration is the dispute resolution process between national entities. Private arbitration is, on the other hand, a dispute resolution process between two private commercial parties. As we shall see later in this chapter, however, private arbitration might also include the resolution of a dispute between a private commercial party and a governmental entity. The focus of this chapter, however, will be on private arbitration.

Within the commercial business environment, disputes whether current, foreseeable, or inevitable are typically managed through one or more of four alternative dispute resolution (ADR) schemes: negotiation, mediation, conciliation, and arbitration.[1] Each scheme is extra-judicial in that private parties, while oftentimes using legal tools, do not avail themselves of litigating in the courts in order to resolve their disputes. Rather, the parties, to one extent or another, avail themselves of either the time and efforts of each other or those of a neutral third party. Each approach has its advantages and disadvantages; however, the success of the ADR choice rests, in no small measure, on the commitment by the parties to the scheme's success.

*Negotiations*, typically, do not involve a third party. Each side to the dispute tries to resolve their mutual difference(s) by coming to the bargaining table and attempting to fashion an agreement through compromise, capitulation, or concession. Simply, the parties try to 'hash things out' between them. If the parties find themselves unable or unwilling to agree to agree, their options include turning to another ADR alternative or litigation. If the parties opt to stay with ADR, they might wish to bring in a third party who can act as an arbitrator, a conciliator, or a mediator.

The advantages to a negotiated settlement are substantial. Instinctively, it makes sense that an agreement brought about by the good efforts of the disputants might very well be a more long lasting solution than one imposed by a third party. Furthermore, the costs associated with negotiations and the attainment of a subsequent settlement are substantially lower than the expenses that would have been incurred if a more elaborate ADR scheme were invoked. Cheap, fast, efficient, indeed; however, a negotiated settlement might sometimes turn out to be fatally shortsighted and myopic. Unsophisticated bargainers from each side may temptingly reach for a settlement that on its face appears adequate to the occasion. A more experienced third party/ADR specialist might well recognize the limitations of the 'solution' and attempt to take the parties in a direction that more likely assures a result with longer staying power and with enhanced implications for each side.[2]

## Mediation-Conciliation

Should negotiations fail, rather than leap into litigation, the parties might turn to a third party whose charter includes the steerage of the parties through their conflicted waters into the safe harbor of settlement. The neutral third party is, typically, referred to as either a mediator or a conciliator and his navigational tools are known as either mediation or conciliation. What is the difference? Depending on the reference in which one searches: some or none.

*The Guide to WIPO Mediation* refers to the two processes synonymously, "Mediation, also known as conciliation in many parts of the world. . . . In the commercial world, interest in it has increased sharply in recent years."[3]

Rather than mediation, the United Nations Commission on International Trade Law (UNCITRAL) refers to this process as the "conciliation of disputes arising out of or relating to a contractual or other legal relationship where the parties are seeking an amicable settlement of their dispute. . . ."[4]

The Permanent Court of Arbitration follows the UN taxonomy and has promulgated a set of *Permanent Court of Arbitration Optional Conciliation Rules*.[5]

Regardless of whether the process is labeled as mediation or conciliation, the fact is that the differences are, according to the French arbitrator Charles Jarrosson, merely subtle—differences of degree rather than of nature.[6] Of the two, Jarrosson posits that mediation is the more proactive. Conciliation, according to Jarrosson, is regarded as more passive since the conciliator plays a more facilitative role than does a mediator. A mediator's role is typically that of an active facilitative intermediary, whereas a conciliator is likely to be more of an evaluative mediator.[7] Whether mediation or conciliation is employed, the advantages of this approach to commercial dispute settlement are significant when juxtaposed with the cost and length of litigation.

Unlike litigation, mediation/conciliation is entered into voluntarily; the parties control the entire process under which an attempt to resolve their dispute will be pursued; and the entire proceedings are conducted in an informal manner. The mediator/conciliator has no vested stake as to how the resolution is achieved or the form that any resolution ultimately takes. The mediator/conciliator's sole responsibility is to act as an honest broker by shuttling those communications between the parties that the parties would rather have a third party convey.

This writer has, on more times than one has fingers and toes, used the good offices of the Federal Mediation and Conciliation Service when an impasse occurred during the collective bargaining process. There were often matters that management could or would not wish to reveal in a public forum before an entire union negotiating committee. Moreover, the same was true, at times, for the union's professional negotiators. Nevertheless, communication could and did take place thru a Federal mediator and more often than not the facilitative efforts of the Federal mediator caused a settlement to be reached and a strike averted.

At times, there were occasions when an emotionally charged impasse had been reached at the collective bargaining table and a work stoppage detrimental to both sides was about to take place. Often, an experienced mediator was able to pull from his/her 'bag of tricks' solutions that had worked for other parties under similar circumstances and help avoid what had appeared to be the inevitabilities of a prolonged and damaging strike.

The obvious disadvantage of either mediation or conciliation is that the solution attained, if indeed a solution is attained, is not final and binding on the parties. Furthermore, prolonged attempts at mediation/conciliation could have the effect of anchoring the parties even more solidly to their positions. Consider the Microsoft-Dept. of Justice litigation. There, and virtually without precedent, a federal *district* court judge appointed a federal *appellate* court judge to be the mediator in the dispute before the district court. Unfortunately, the Microsoft-Department of Justice mediation failed. The mediator, Judge Richard Posner, revealed in a press release that, "twenty successive drafts of a possible consent decree, evolved over the past months. . . ."[8] The failure of Judge Posner's meditative efforts and the failure of twenty consent decrees, no doubt, hardened the positions of the parties when the litigation before the district court resumed.

So, if and when the time comes and all good faith efforts at dispute resolution through negotiation, conciliation, or mediation have failed—what then? Clearly, resort to the courts is an option. However, more and more commercial parties are turning to commercial arbitration as an alternate to the courts.

## Characteristics and Appeal of Commercial Arbitration

Martin Hunter, the eminent arbitrator and scholar of Nottingham School of Law, put forth a very seductive proposition as to why international arbitration is so appealing to commercial parties. Hunter maintained that arbitration clauses were in commercial contracts because, "corporations and governmental entities engaged in international trade are simply not willing to litigate in the other party's home court." In addition to the possibility of judicial chauvinism on the part of national judges, Prof. Hunter puts the matter in more practical terms, namely, there is no reason to play an away game unless it is absolutely essential.[9] Sports aficionados will quickly pick up on Prof Hunter's reference: playing an 'away game' in international sports means playing before hostile crowds in unfamiliar ballparks, in front of fans who speak in an unfamiliar tongue. In international litigation, the 'away game' analogues might be hostile courts, unfamiliar rules of procedure, all done in a language requiring translators and local counsel.

In addition to the practicalities described by Prof. Hunter, the commercial predisposition toward arbitration has been judicially reinforced, notably by the U.S. Supreme Court. In a decision concerning an international agreement in which trademarks were essential elements of the purchase and sale of business, the Court overturned decisions by the district and appellate courts that had stayed an arbitration and ordered the arbitration clause be enforced. The Court was obviously supportive of arbitration in stating

> uncertainty will almost inevitably exist with respect to any contract touching two or more countries, each with its own substantive laws and conflict-of-laws rules. A contractual provision specifying in advance the forum in which disputes shall be litigated and the law to be applied is, therefore, an almost indispensable precondition to achievement of the orderliness and predictability essential to any international business transaction. Furthermore, such a provision obviates the danger that a dispute under the agreement might be submitted to a forum hostile to the interests of one of the parties or unfamiliar with the problem area involved.[10]

In view of the commercial and judicial bent toward arbitration, it might be helpful, before going further, to concretize a definition of arbitration upon which this writing will consistently rely. The American Arbitration Association (AAA)'s definition is as good as any. AAA pronounces commercial arbitration as, "the submission of a dispute to one or more impartial persons for a final and binding decision. Through contractual provisions, the parties may control the range of issues to be resolved, the scope of relief to be awarded, and many procedural aspects of the process."[11]

Arbitration can, as we saw, be distinguished from other forms of dispute resolution. Mediation is a process wherein "the emphasis is not on who is right or wrong or who wins and who loses, but rather upon establishing a workable solution that meets the participants' unique needs."[12] Arbitration, however, and by its very nature, does, at the end of the day, pick who is right and who is wrong; who won and who lost; one side over the other.

## The Appeal of Commercial Arbitration

Commercial parties as well as their legal counsel need always keep in the back of their minds that commercial arbitration is a legally sanctioned dispute resolution process. Its existence is not simply predicated on the wishes of private parties desiring an avenue for dispute resolution. Commercial arbitration exists *because national law and national courts permit commercial arbitration* to exist if commercial parties have agreed to arbitrate a dispute before them or agree to arbitrate a dispute that might occur in the future.[13] Sir Michael Kerr, as Lord Justice of Appeal, in an advanced legal seminar paper averred, "The necessary powers to give binding effect to the legal consequences of arbitration, which is the whole *raison d'etre* of the arbitral process, is invariably vested in the national courts by legislation. . . . In the ultimate analysis the effectiveness of the private process must therefore rest upon the binding and even coercive powers which each state entrusts to its courts."[14]

Most developed countries have arbitration regimes that permit the resolution of commercial disputes between commercial parties if the parties have:

1. included an agreement to arbitrate disputes within a commercial contract between them or
2. consummated an *ad-hoc* agreement calling for the resolution of their dispute that arose after their commercial contract had been entered into.[15]

When national courts are not utilized, commercial parties will often seek arbitration under the auspices of a 'private' arbitral organization specializing in commercial dispute resolution. Noted national and international arbitration organizations include:

- The American Arbitration Association
- The Japan Commercial Arbitration Association
- The Singapore International Arbitration Center
- The Stockholm Chamber of Commerce
- The International Chamber of Commerce
- The World Intellectual Property Organization

- The China International Economic and Trade Arbitration Commission
- The Hong Kong Arbitration Center

Of the above, one of the most utilized institutions to settle private commercial disputes, over the years, has been the International Chamber of Commerce (ICC), headquartered in Paris. Utilizing its Rules of Arbitration, the ICC rendered 325 arbitration awards in 2005; a total of 521 Requests for Arbitration were filed.[16] The ICC, it should be noted, is not an arbitral body; rather it is a membership organization within which is the International Court of Arbitration that is not a court *per se* but rather an administrative body whose Secretariat administers arbitrations under ICC Rules. Even though the ICC's parlance might be a bit confusing, any confusion has not been a barrier when it comes to usage by commercial parties. The ICC's popularity stems in part from the fact that it enjoys worldwide membership, hence, making its arbitral facilities easily available to parties. The ICC is also known in the commercial arbitral world for its administrative soundness as well as its general *laissez-faire* attitude toward the parties once a tribunal is formed.[17]

If commercial parties find a certain beneficial confidence in arbitration, and its usage confirms they do, engrained within the arbitration process must be certain attributes that have withstood the test of time and upon which the parties have come to rely. The advantages of commercial arbitration (over litigation) most often cited by practitioners include:[18]

1. The confidentiality of the proceedings and awards
2. The reduced cost of arbitration versus the costs of litigation
3. The neutrality and or expertise of an arbitrator in a neutral location
4. The flexibility of arbitration and the parties' ability to control:
   a. the selection of the arbitrator;
   b. the substantive and procedural rules by which the arbitration will be conducted, as well as
   c. the language the proceedings will employ; and
   d. the speed with which an arbitration might be conducted and a judgment rendered.
5. The enforceability of arbitration

A few words follow on each of the above.

## Confidentiality

Unquestionably, one of the perceived advantages of arbitration is the belief that a commercial entity's 'dirty linen' will not be hung out in public for all to see. Unlike litigation, which takes place in the glare of the public judicial arena, arbitration is conducted behind closed doors. Indeed, the UNCITRAL Rules declare that, "Hearings shall be held in camera unless the parties agree otherwise."[19] While it might be possible in a court proceeding to keep certain materials confidential, the fact of the dispute itself is in the public arena, as are the courtroom proceedings.

Awards which might bring public relations nightmares to the 'losing party' are rarely published (if at all) and, usually, only with the consent of the parties. But lest one adhere to the belief that the confidentiality of arbitration is inviolable, consider the following statement from the High Court of Australia.

> Despite the view taken in *Dolling-Baker*, . . .[20] I do not consider that, in Australia, having regard to the various matters to which I have referred, we are justified in concluding that confidentiality is an essential attribute of a private arbitration imposing an obligation on each party not to disclose the proceedings or documents and information provided in and for the purposes of the arbitration.[21]

Parenthetically, it must be noted that the basis for the Australian court's position was not etheric. The court relied on US judicial holdings, writing, "Indeed, in the United States, the decided cases are inconsistent with the proposition that confidentiality is a characteristic of arbitration proceedings."[22]

It is true that, for the most part, arbitral awards are held confidential. However, it must be recognized by practitioners that confidentiality may very well fall to a nation's public policy interests, the interests of stock exchanges, liquidators, and securities regulators.[23]

To wit, an English court, while giving a nod to the notion of an "implied obligation" as the basis for arbitral confidentiality, went on to write,

> If it is reasonably necessary for the establishment or protection of an arbitrating party's legal rights vis-à-vis a third party . . . the award should be disclosed to that third party in order to found a defence or as the basis for a cause of action, so to disclose it would not be a breach of the duty of confidence.[24]

In a similar vein, the Supreme Court of Sweden held, "[The] duty of confidentiality does not apply without a separate agreement thereon," hence, an arbitration award was not vitiated by the publication of an arbitration award by one party without the knowledge of the second party.[25]

A close reading of the Rules of the International Chamber of Commerce[26] provides little solace to parties as to the confidentiality of matters brought before the ICC under its Rules:

> Under Appendix I- Article 4, the Chairman or the Secretary General of the Court may authorize researchers undertaking work of a scientific nature on international trade law to acquaint themselves with awards and other documents of general interest, with the exception of memoranda, notes, statements and documents remitted by the parties within the framework of arbitration proceedings.
>
> Under Appendix I- Article 6, the work of the Court is of a confidential nature that must be respected by everyone who participates in that work in whatever capacity.
>
> Curiously, the work of the court appears to be considered confidential but the award and materials that come out of the arbitration are not similarly regarded under the rule.
>
> Article 20-7 is permissive only requiring that the Arbitral Tribunal *may* (emphasis added) take measures for protecting trade secrets and confidential information.

In the United States, the most cited case on arbitral confidentiality is *United States v. Panhandle Eastern Corp.*[27] in which the defendant oil company sought a protective order preventing the United States from obtaining documents relating to an ICC arbitration in which it was involved. The court held, ". . . the ICC's rules regarding confidentiality, do not apply to the parties to arbitration proceedings or to the independent arbitration tribunal which conducts those proceedings."[28] The court sided with the federal government's request for the defendant to produce the requested documents.

Similarly, an arbitration tribunal, in a dispute between the Government of Indonesia and a hotel investor, maintained that disclosure of the fact that an arbitration took place between the parties was not confidential. The tribunal held, "Finally, as to the 'spirit of confidentiality' of the arbitral procedure, it is right to say that the Convention and the Rules do not prevent the parties from revealing their case. . . ."[29]

So, while the matter of confidentiality is frequently touted as one of the virtues of arbitration, in fact, care must be taken by the parties to ensure that their national law, the arbitral organization they choose, and their agreement to arbitrate all line up properly if they wish confidentiality to be maintained. The confidentiality obligation imposed by the major arbitral institutions varies considerably. Thus, the parties to an arbitration need to be sure that their arbitration clause stipulates the confidentiality obligations they wish to require of each other.

Finally, and perhaps not of concern to business persons, the confidentiality of arbitral awards make scholarly research on commercial arbitration quite difficult—as the writer of this book can attest.

## Costs and Delays

Dickens's fictional court case, *Jaundyce and Jaundyce*, involved an inheritance battle so protracted that when it was finally concluded the legal fees had eaten up virtually the entire estate. Beside the financial gluttony of lawyers, Dickens also addressed his criticism to the Court of Chancery,

> This is the Court of Chancery, which has its decaying houses and its blighted lands in every shire, which has its worn-out lunatic in every madhouse . . . which gives to monied might the means abundantly of wearying out the right, which so exhausts finances, patience, courage, hope, so overthrows the brain and breaks the heart, that there is not an honourable man among its practitioners who would not give—who does not often give—the warning, "Suffer any wrong that can be done you rather than come here!"[30]

Dickens' words are no mere cavil; rather he takes to task the piggery of those who would not only eat from, but deplete, their client's trough. One can only speculate whether or not Dickens would have permitted arbitration to be offered as a more expedient solution in *Jaundyce and Jaundyce*. Of course, inheritance issues are, typically, proscribed as arbitral matters. But, were this not the case, the more ardent supporters of commercial arbitration might have convinced Dickens of arbitration's cost efficiency in both absolute and relative terms. On costs, Born has written, "[A]rbitration has long been lauded as a prompt inexpensive means of dispute resolution."[31]

Although commercial arbitration can indeed be a low-cost dispute resolution process, arbitration can, under different circumstances, be rather expensive. Again, Born: "but international arbitration is also not infrequently criticized as both slow and expensive. . . . [T]he truth is less clear cut and lies somewhere between those extremes."[32]

After all, an arbitrator or a tribunal of three arbitrators must be paid; the body administering the arbitration must be paid; and the costs associated with litigation such as expert witnesses, attorneys' fees and so forth all need to be paid. As de Vries has pointed out, "[T]he advantages attributed to domestic arbitration—speed, economy, and informality—are reversed in international disputes . . ." because of distance, difficulties of communications, language, and related problems.[33] Not surprising then that in 1998, a survey found that 81% of non-US lawyers felt that arbitration was *more* expensive than litigation in national courts.[34] Carbonneau contends that the entry of more and more lawyers into the arbitral fray was the catalytic agent that has transformed what had been a parsimonious route to dispute resolution to one replete with formalism, contentiousness, and cost. Expert witnesses, extensive discovery, and all the 'benefits' of a common law trial have, in no small measure, extirpated the simple roots of arbitration and in its place replanted what can be, depending on the dispute, quite a lengthy and expensive process.[35]

Routh provides cost estimates for the fees that one might expect to pay for the use of an arbitral tribunal.

> [I]f you assume a claim of $1,000,000, the AAA would charge $5,000 for its services as the appointing authority and administrator. The I.C.C. would charge $16,800. The I.C.C. generally has a more thorough review process, however, which probably improves the quality of the awards. The London Court of Arbitration charges $2250 plus time and expenses for administration plus approximately the amount the arbitrator would normally earn in his or her profession. The Japanese Commercial Arbitration Association would charge approximately $12,350, while the British Columbia Arbitration Centre would charge approximately $3,360 plus additional fees per quarter ($350 per party) as administrative fees.[36]

The International Chamber of Commerce has on its website an arbitration cost calculator. Insert a few numbers and an estimate for the cost of an arbitration is provided.[37] So, if one were considering the costs to arbitrate an amount in dispute of ten million dollars, with three arbitrators the ICC's cost estimate is $304,025—a large amount in absolute dollars but a small percentage of the dispute at issue.

A fascinating sidebar regarding the cost, confidentiality and speed of arbitration concerns the Fujitsu-IBM arbitration. From conversations this author had over the years with a number of executive colleagues, this arbitration had most of the features to suggest that it was, indeed, representative of commercial arbitration between large industrial disputants.

The writer was, at the time, a Senior Vice President with Fujitsu America, the US subsidiary of Fujitsu Ltd. of Japan. And while not directly involved in the arbitration, many a night was spent over sake and sushi dinners during which frank conversations with the writer and Fujitsu employees close to the arbitration took place. Except for dates, the remainder of this discussion is anecdotal—but derived from first hand sources.

In July 1985, IBM filed a demand for arbitration with the American Arbitration Association (AAA) charging Fujitsu Ltd. with violations of IBM's intellectual property rights in their operating systems software. On September 15, 1987, after *more than 26 months of arbitration* between IBM and Fujitsu, the arbitrators handed down an opinion that, with the concurrence of the parties, was published.

Procedurally, the arbitration commenced rather formally with hordes of lawyers and standard courtroom tactics being used by both sides. Over time, however, a more relaxed atmosphere came to pass with arbitral sessions held in a hotel in Palo Alto, California. The arbitrators selected by the parties included a computer expert and an ADR expert.

Even though the award took 26 months to be delivered, it was impressed upon me that the full cost of arbitration would likely have been less expensive than if adjudicated in the courts. And, while no report has ever been made public about the cost of the arbitration, figures the writer heard bandied about were in the millions of dollars in legal fees.

In hindsight, litigation between the parties could have dragged on for years, not just 26 months, and, undoubtedly litigation would have increased all costs to the parties, e.g., attorneys' fees, employee time, and travel. Thus, Fujitsu may have very well been correct that, in their estimation, they saved money by utilizing arbitration in their dispute with IBM.

Two other cases, while perhaps at the extremes when discussing delays and costs, are, nonetheless, illustrative. An arbitration between Advanced Micro Devices and Intel lasted ". . . from 1987 until 1992, involved 355 days of hearings, 47,000 pages of reporter's transcripts, and 2500 exhibits."[38] *Pilkington v. PPG* began in 1985 and lasted until 1992. It was the first arbitration in London that lasted almost 300 hearing days. Legal fees were estimated to run over sixteen million pounds.[39]

Arbitration can also be used to provide 'cover' to one or more of the disputants when costs are secondary to other more primary matters. Hunter relates an example of such an occurrence while serving as an arbitrator in the Gulf region. An award for less money than would have been levied in arbitration was rejected by one of the parties, a government minister, who pointed out to Hunter that were he to accept the settlement on the table he would be excoriated by hostile political enemies. If he lost at arbitration, however, he could simply have the Ministry of Finance draw a check and then complain publicly about the incompetence of the arbitrators.[40]

The real fascination within Prof. Hunter's tale is the difference in the mind set between private parties and public parties to arbitration. The ease with which the government minister accepted a higher cost to his nation's coffers in order to avoid political recrimination is telling. In the private commercial world, it is beyond this writer's ken to imagine a corporate executive turning down an opportunity to settle a dispute for less than a projected arbitration award while assuming that a call to the entity's CFO would produce a check, and a call to the entity's public relations gurus would generate a press release proclaiming the arbitrator's incompetence. Should such an occurrence transpire, only one word comes to mind to describe the subsequent corporate reaction: severance.

## Neutrality of Arbitration

Commercial arbitration, especially in the international arena, is often preferred over litigation because arbitration represents an alternate way to minimize the possibility of localism by the sitting national court. As Born put it, arbitration is a way of "mitigating the peculiar uncertainties of transnational litigation."[41]

Unquestionably, local parties are at an advantage in a local court given their knowledge of the intricacies of their courts which, Weiss said, "may cause unfairness to one of the parties," and given the complexity of international litigation, neutral predictability is an attribute that businesses desire.[42]

In the commercial arbitration *milieu*, the likelihood that arbitral neutrality is part and parcel of the 'legal' system should not be presumed. Prof. Barrington writes of the Pakistani Supreme Court's decision in *Hubco v. WAPDA*. There the court took jurisdiction away from an ICC tribunal in London over allegations of corruption. The court held such matters were not arbitral but were matters of public policy and for courts to decide. Barrington asserts that this case is illustrative that arbitration, "still very much depends on the attitude of the courts of the parties involved. . . . The decision, as it stands, has thrust Pakistan law squarely back into the 1950s, putting it at odds with modern arbitration rules and jurisprudence the world over."[43]

Nevertheless, the international business community still prefers international commercial arbitration to litigation since, by agreeing to arbitration in a neutral forum under favorable choice of law provisions, business people hope "to avoid having disputes judged in the national courts of the opposing party."[44] According to Park, the nightmare business people hope to avoid is having to engage in "judicial proceedings . . . in a foreign language before a hostile judge of a country where political influence makes a fair trial problematic."[45] The parties' ability to select procedural and substantive rules, as well as the arbitral seat helps, as Knull and Rubins put it, "to insulate themselves to some degree against the uncertainty of differing choice of law systems around the world."[46]

However, if what Carbonneau suggests is true, that "arbitration has become a privately-funded and privately-supervised parallel court system for both international and domestic disputes," then does the veil of neutrality get pierced by the entity with the bigger pocketbook?[47] Can the aspiration to neutrality be marred by the 'guy with the biggest stick?' Perhaps not, as the tales of certain Middle Eastern arbitrations demonstrate. Two commercial entities, in two different disputes arbitrated against the wealth and oil of Abu Dhabi and Saudi Arabia. How was it that commercial entities successfully made their cases against powerful nation-states in two distinct arbitral settings?

There are in International Law two Latin phrases that are used to describe the nature of a nation's law: *jure imperii* and *jure gestionis*. When a nation-state acts *de jure imperii,* it is said to act as a government or a sovereign and, for the most part, the acts rendered under this principle are accorded governmental immunity from jurisdiction by foreign courts. The same does not hold for those governmental acts deemed as private or commercial in nature. When a government acts in a commercial capacity or as a commercial entity, its acts are considered acts *de jure gestionis* and, consequently, do not enjoy the same immunity from foreign jurisdiction as do acts *de jure imperii*. Thus, when a nation-state enters into a commercial contract with a private commercial party, the nation-state will, often, give up its sovereignty and agree, like any other commercial party, to submit any dispute(s) that may occur to arbitration.[48] That's what occurred in the Abu Dhabi and Saudi arbitrations.

The issue before the arbitrator in the "Abu Dhabi" arbitration,[49] concerned a dispute over an oil concession contract that had been granted and, subsequently, revoked by the Sheikh of Abu Dhabi. The arbitrator, Lord Asquith, acknowledged that, consistent with the agreement between the parties, Abu Dhabi law should govern. However, he rejected the parties' agreement and concluded that the sheik was

> an absolute, feudal monarch . . . [who] administers a purely discretionary justice with the assistance of the Koran; and it would be fanciful to suggest that in this very primitive region there is any settled body of legal principles applicable to the construction of modern commercial instruments.

Asquith, therefore, held, that the terms of the contract "invite, indeed prescribe, the application of principles rooted in the good sense and common practice of the generality of civilised nations—a sort of 'modern law of nature'." Although Lord Asquith conceded "English municipal law [was] inapplicable as such," he determined that "some of its rules are . . . so firmly grounded in reason, as to form part of this broad body of jurisprudence" and, indeed, are "principle[s] of ecumenical validity" and "mere common sense."[50]

In a dispute involving the interpretation of a concession agreement between Saudi Arabia and Aristotle Onassis regarding the transport of oil, the arbitrator in the ARAMCO case[51] decided that ARAMCO's rights would be unable to be "secured in an unquestionable manner by the law of force in Saudi Arabia . . . [and that Saudi laws] must be interpreted or supplemented by the general principles of law, by the custom and practice in the oil business and by notions of pure jurisprudence."[52]

So, while two commercial entities were able to fend off two state Goliaths, the framing of the awards by the arbitrators remain teaching tools as to how neutrality can go astray in a commercial arbitration setting. In these cases, the arbitrators concocted a unique arbitral stew topped with one dash cynicism for domestic law and one part disbelief as to the Islamic parties' ability to enforce rights. Is it no wonder, then, that 'Western' forms of commercial arbitration have, to this day, been a grudging addition to the Islamic arbitral menu on which 'neutrality' might not be a featured entrée?

## Flexibility of Arbitration

International lawyers refer to the national law governing arbitration as the *lex arbitri*. The UK's *lex arbitri* is as good an example as any of how a nation's arbitration law supports—indeed, virtually advocates—the use of arbitration. The U.K.'s Arbitration Act of 1996 at Section 1(a) declares that subject to a public policy exception, "the parties are free to agree how their disputes are resolved" and at 1(b) that courts "should not intervene except as provided."[53]

The Act governs such matters as how an arbitration is commenced; certain procedural and evidentiary requirements of an arbitration; and the challenges to an arbitration award.[54] Importantly, the Act provides substantial discretion to the parties to address their commercial needs and precludes, as do most national arbitral laws, the arbitration of family law, criminal law and offensive public policy matters.[55]

It is worthy of repetition that arbitration exists because national law permits arbitration to exist; if there is consent of the parties to arbitrate. And if the parties consent, they can fashion the arbitrator's scope; they can frame the issue that the arbitrator will decide; they can determine the contours of the arbitral award; and the parties can decide the rules under which they choose to be governed. In a decision that could have been rendered by any number of commercially astute national courts, the California Supreme Court wrote, "In private arbitrations, arbitrators, unless specifically restricted by the agreement to follow legal rules, may base their decision on broad principles of justice and equity. . . ."[56] The court went on, "In particular, because arbitration is a creature of contract, the parties by agreement may expand the arbitrator's arsenal of remedies to include novel and creative equitable remedies."[57] And in what is perhaps the most famous phrase to come out of this decision, the court boldly proclaimed that, "remedies available to a court are only the *minimum* available to an arbitrator (unless restricted by agreement)."[58]

But all the praiseworthy components that reinforce the girders of flexibility get cast asunder if one of the parties to a dispute either resiles from or does not agree to arbitrate. *One's commercial rights exist in the arbitral arena to the extent that the other disputant agrees to permit them to exist.* Consent is not necessary to have one's *legal* rights enforced in court; consent is necessary, however, for *arbitral* rights to be enforced, including the manner and before whom such rights will be 'arbitrally' adjudicated. Of course, a party might express its displeasure over being hailed into an arbitral 'court.' However its consent to arbitrate cannot be withdrawn. The party may opt not to participate in the arbitration hearing. Nonetheless, the rules of the leading arbitral institutions permit a valid arbitration to go forward even with the abstention of a disputant. Obviously, such conduct foreshadows the litigation that will likely follow the conduct of the one-party arbitration.

## Enforcement of Arbitration Awards

> "The arbitrator's decision should be the end,
> not the beginning of the dispute."[59]

Parties to an international commercial arbitration need to consider a variety of issues surrounding the enforcement of international arbitral awards. After all, having spent considerable time, effort, and money in obtaining a favorable arbitration award, the parties want assurance that, whatever the outcome, there will be both finality and enforcement of the award's terms. As de Vries wrote, "The effectiveness of arbitration in providing a final and binding resolution of international commercial disputes depends upon a legal framework for court enforcement when a party defaults. True arbitration, or arbitration proper, in the international context, contemplates a binding decision with the legal effect of a final judgment of a court."[60]

A note of caution: it is an all too common occurrence for phrases like the 'recognition' of a foreign judgment and the 'enforcement' of a foreign judgment to be bandied about as if the terms were synonymous. They are not. The *recognition* of a foreign judgment is a determination by a court that additional litigation is unnecessary since the matter has been well settled in a foreign court. Lawyers refer to this action as giving *res judicata* effect to the foreign judgment. *Enforcement*, on the other hand, is an affirmative use by a court of its power to compel a defendant to comply with an arbitral judgment rendered abroad.[61] This section will deal only with the enforcement of arbitration awards.

Whether or not an arbitration award will be enforceable is of vital importance to commercial interests. A commercial party, more likely than not, knows beforehand that a judgment obtained in a foreign court will be subject to the vagaries and uncertainties of foreign law when the enforcement of an award received is sought. To use the United States as an example: for all the support the arbitral process receives from governmental 'on high,' the nation is not a party to any bilateral or multilateral agreement regarding the enforceability of foreign judgments. In addition, there is no federal statute dealing with the enforcement of foreign judgments.[62] Any attempts for the enforcement of a foreign judgment in the United States are a matter of state and not federal law. With the conclusion of The Hague Conference on Private International Law in June 2005, there is cause for optimism that the adoption of a convention dealing with foreign judgments might very well become a part of U.S. law.

Staying with the United States as an exemplar, a commercial party can find comfort, however, in knowing that an arbitration award received abroad will find U.S. mechanisms available for enforcement under both treaty and statutory regimes. Statutorily, the disposition of foreign arbitration awards falls under the umbrella of the Federal Arbitration Act, primarily at § 2 dealing with the enforceability of domestic and foreign judgments.[63] In addition, the United States is a signatory to a treaty, now examined, that deals exclusively with the enforceability of arbitration awards.

The document most credited with the enforcement of international arbitral awards is, unquestionably, the New York Convention. Di Pietro and Platte write that the New York Convention[64] "stands as a landmark between the ancient world and the new one." They go on, "Thanks to the New York Convention, arbitration has overcome the uncertainty of the past. . . ."[65]

Hunter concurs suggesting that, besides avoiding the previously referenced 'away game', "The other positive feature of arbitration lies in the treaty obligation for enforcing arbitration awards across national boundaries."[66] The treaty to which Hunter refers is the New York Convention.

Adopted in 1958 and entered into force in 1959, the New York Convention requires courts of each contracting state to:

1. apply . . . the recognition and enforcement of arbitral awards made in the territory of a State other than the State where the recognition and enforcement of such awards are sought, and arising out of differences between persons, whether physical or legal.
2. apply to arbitral awards not considered as domestic awards in the State where their recognition and enforcement are sought.[67]

Thus far, there have been over 130 countries that have ratified the Convention, including all the major trading powers of the world.[68]

The Convention permits states to subscribe to the Convention while declaring either or both of two reservations:

1. "[A]ny State may on the basis of reciprocity declare that it will apply the Convention to the recognition and enforcement of awards made only in the territory of another Contracting State.
2. It may also declare that it will apply the Convention only to differences arising out of legal relationships, whether contractual or not, which are considered as commercial under the national law of the State making such declaration."[69]

The reciprocity reservation permitted under the Convention, has, in no small measure, been instrumental in permitting states to ratify the Convention, knowing full well that the Convention will be applicable only to states that recognize each other's foreign judgments.

In addition, the commercial reservation assures subscribing states that matters strictly domestic, such as family or inheritance law, will not be subject to the Convention.

Paradoxically, it is the volume of states that have ratified the Convention that represents a major stumbling block for modifications to the Convention. Any amendment proposed to enhance the effectiveness of the Convention requires ratification by *each* member state.[70] One can imagine the difficulty of getting over 130 independent nations to agree on wording for any amendment proposed.

Technological developments also create problems for the parties to the Convention. In an age where e-commerce and electronic communication are pervasive, the Convention requires that, "Each Contracting

State shall recognize an agreement in writing. . . ."[71] However, the Convention narrowly defines an agreement in writing as including an arbitral clause in a contract or an arbitration agreement, signed by the parties or contained in an exchange of letters or telegrams.[72] So, while e-mails were not contemplated by the drafters, the writing provision has not been interpreted as a *conditio sine qua non* and, for the most part, has been managed through multi-lateral measures (e.g., The European Convention) or through national arbitration statutes that take into account the world's streamlined methods of communication.[73]

While there are a number of Conventions[74] dealing with the recognition and enforcement of international arbitration awards, one other deserves mention: the International Center for Settlement of Investment Disputes (ICSID). The ICSID was established under the *Convention on the Settlement of Investment Disputes between States and Nationals of Other States*—better known as the "Washington Convention." The ICSID is an autonomous international organization. However, it has close links with the World Bank. All of the ICSID's members are also members of the Bank.[75]

The Washington Convention is in force in more than 150 countries and through ICSID provides for the management of arbitration between private investing entities and member states.[76] What makes the ICSID unique is that it provides for its own enforcement. An ICSID award, when rendered, is recognized and enforced by the member states as if the award were a final judgment of the members' national courts. The awards are directly enforceable and *not* dependent on other international conventions, such as the New York Convention.[77]

The New York Convention requires that an arbitration award be recognized as follows:

> Each Contracting State shall recognize arbitral awards as binding and enforce them in accordance with the rules of procedure of the territory where the award is relied upon, under the conditions laid down in the following articles. There shall not be imposed substantially more onerous conditions or higher fees or charges on the recognition or enforcement of arbitral awards to which this Convention applies than are imposed on the recognition or enforcement of domestic arbitral awards.[78]

New York Convention signatory states, then, must recognize arbitration awards as binding and enforce awards in accordance with *their particular rules of procedure*. While the procedural rules cannot be more stringent than those applied to domestic arbitral enforcement rules, if domestic rules are stringent and difficult to enforce, Article III *does not* make the enforcement of foreign awards any easier.

Under the New York Convention, the only grounds for *refusal to recognize and enforce an award* are:[79]

1. Incapacity of the parties to perform
2. Lack of due process, specifically: notice
3. Arbitral award went beyond the scope of the arbitral submission
4. Either or both the composition of the arbitration tribunal or the arbitration procedure were faulty.
5. The arbitration award was not yet 'binding' on the parties or the award had been set aside at the place of arbitration.

As is the case with many international agreements the New York Convention also permits a country to refuse to recognize an arbitration award that is "contrary to the public order of that country."[80]

These exceptions to enforcement under the New York Convention represent interpretive challenges for the international legal practitioner since terms such as 'due process' and 'incapacity' are subject to a myriad of judicial constructions by the courts of the various signatory countries.

*Contrast* the New York Convention's exceptions to enforcement with the paucity of enforcement exceptions under the Washington Convention:

- Article 53 declares that the parties are bound by the award and that it shall not be *subject to appeal or to any other remedy except those provided for in the Convention* (emphasis added).
- Article 54 requires every Contracting State to recognize the award as binding and to enforce the pecuniary obligations imposed by the award as if it were a final decision of a domestic court.[81]

Despite its flaws, the New York Convention is brief and written with a great deal of clarity. It is "the most widely utilized means" for enforcement of foreign awards.[82]

The Convention provides a simple and effective way to obtain recognition and enforcement of both arbitration agreements and arbitration awards since, under Article V, the Convention limits the grounds for judicial review. "It is mainly due to the provisions of the New York Convention that arbitration has become a very attractive alternative to traditional litigation."[83]

Thus far, this writing has dealt primarily with the Euro-Anglo arbitral world and will later deal extensively with the law within the People's Republic of China. However, the issue of enforcement is so important to the commercial world that at this juncture, we might take an instructive opportunity, steer off our arbitral road a bit, and take a brief journey to another part of the legal-arbitral world—the Islamic Middle East where enforcement of arbitration awards is, at best, spotty.

A critical economic and geo-political region whose activities are of substantial world consequence, it is neither the region's size nor its population that gives the region its economic distinction. The major economic driver behind the importance of this part of the world is oil, with the Middle East's possessing over half of the world's proven oil reserves.[84]

Second only to China, the Middle East was the fastest-growing region in the world. In 2004, the Middle East enjoyed an economic growth of six percent (versus the U.S. rate of four percent, for example).[85] With relatively high oil prices, as well as a weaker dollar, there seems to be no prognosis indicating a substantial moderation in the region's economic growth, absent unthinkable military activities in an already troubled and tremulous area.

When doing business in the Islamic Middle East, care must be taken by international lawyers in the drafting of enforcement provisions in their arbitration agreements. Should a Muslim and a non-Muslim contract with each other under principles other than the Koranic Law (the *Sharia*), then a Middle Eastern court could or would invoke the 'public order' provision of the New York Convention and refuse to enforce the foreign award.[86]

Although a number of Middle Eastern states have become signatories to the New York Convention, there exists something of a duality between form and substance. Since the ARAMCO decision, the Saudi position, "may be extreme, legislation tends to create all kinds of typically procedural problems to arbitration. This is done either for special contracts of some commercial significance, like those related to agency and distribution, or in a more general manner. . . . Whether rejected openly by legislation or hampered by administrative means, the uselessness in Lebanon of an arbitration clause . . . is true of Bahrain, of the UAE, of Kuwait, of Jordan, and Oman. The list is not comprehensive."[87]

This attitude carries over into enforcement, as well. Prof. Mallet writes, "[T]here is a long string of statutes allowing setting aside arbitration awards granted internationally, by freezing them, subjecting them to various appeals, or simply ignoring them."[88]

As evidence, Mallet cites various legislative decrees in Algeria, the UAE, and Kuwait. He also quotes an unnamed but 'well known' English barrister who spoke of Oman, "since the commercial judicature was constituted in its current form, more that ten years ago, there has been no case where direct enforcement of a foreign arbitral award has been granted."[89]

Prof. Roy is more optimistic about those states that have acceded to the New York Convention. She points to Kuwait and Syria writing that, "In fact, Kuwaiti enforcement of international arbitration awards was routine prior to its adoption of the New York Convention."[90] As for Syria, she writes, "Syria . . . enforces all non-Syrian arbitral awards, whether or not the award was made by a New York Convention signatory. The New York Convention prevails over traditional Syrian law in all cases of non-Syrian arbitral award enforcement."[91]

But as for Saudi Arabia, Roy is more in tune with the critics.

> As Saudi Arabian law and policy is diametrically opposed to the rules and laws of many member nations, Saudi Arabian courts may find it easy to reject non-domestic arbitral awards pursuant to New York Convention Article V(2)(b).[92] In essence, Saudi Arabia may not be required to enforce any more non-domestic arbitral awards than it did prior to its 1994 accession to the New York Convention.[93]

## Shortcomings of Commercial Arbitration

If parties to a dispute believe that the matter at hand would best be resolved in the courts, there are certain safeguards available in litigation that are not available in arbitration. In the legally developed world, most states and governments utilize distinct rules of civil procedure and rules of the court. Parties have the capacity to know before they enter the judicial fray the procedural requirements that will be imposed on them. No such procedural certainty exists in arbitration. Procedural certainty may come with the selection of an arbitral institution before or after a dispute commences or in the discretion that parties give an arbitral tribunal to determine procedure 'on the fly' so to speak.

If there have been judgments rendered in a common law jurisdiction in similar cases, those cases might very well be used by the presiding court given the reliance of common law courts on precedent. Alternatively, if the parties' case were unique then the decision rendered might create precedent in subsequent similar cases. No such precedent exists in arbitral 'jurisprudence.'

Justice Douglas in *Bernhardt v. Polygraphic* well summed up the competing legal practices one might encounter when attempting to determine the arbitration-litigation calculus:

- The change from a court of law to an arbitration panel may make a radical difference in ultimate result.
- Arbitration carries no right to trial by jury that is guaranteed . . . by the Seventh Amendment
- Arbitrators do not have the benefit of judicial instruction on the law; they need not give their reasons for their results; the record of their proceedings is not as complete as it is in a court trial; and judicial review of an award is more limited than judicial review of a trial.
- Whether the arbitrators misconstrued a contract is not open to judicial review.
- Questions of fault or neglect are solely for the arbitrators' consideration.
- Arbitrators are not bound by the rules of evidence. They may draw on their personal knowledge in making an award.
- Absent agreement of the parties, a written transcript of the proceedings is unnecessary.
- Swearing of witnesses may not be required.
- And the arbitrators need not disclose the facts or reasons behind their award.[94]

Finality is often lauded as an advantage of commercial arbitration; it comes at a price, however. The obverse side of the arbitral coin reveals the institutional, judicial, and legislative restrictions put on one's ability to appeal an award. For example, in addition to the Washington Convention's enforcement requirements mentioned above, the Arbitration Rules of the World Intellectual Property Organization mandate that the parties, "waive their right to any form of appeal or recourse to a court of law or other judicial authority."[95] Knull and Rubins raise the question of whether or not it is time to offer an appeal option from arbitration and support the legitimacy of their query, in part, by pointing to a survey of 606 corporate lawyers from some of America's largest corporations who chose not to opt for arbitration given the difficulty in appealing an arbitral award.[96]

A substantial amount of leeway is impliedly granted in the way an arbitrator conducts matters in his/her 'courtroom.' But, an arbitrator lacks those coercive powers that may be necessary to support the arbitral process. Under the US Federal Arbitration Act, an arbitrator can issue a subpoena for documents and testimony.[97] However, an arbitrator's subpoena power alone cannot compel the testimony of witnesses. An arbitrator's subpoena is not self-executing, hence, the subpoenaed party may simply ignore the subpoena that might ultimately be enforced through a court proceeding. Furthermore, an arbitrator only has discovery powers to the extent granted either by the parties or under the rules of an arbitral organization agreed to by the parties. Under the rules of some of the major arbitration institutions such as the ICC's Court of Arbitration, the London Court of Arbitration, and the American Arbitration Association, the arbitrator or tribunal is given broad power to determine if and how much discovery will take place.[98] All fine and good for parties accustomed to litigation in the United States, but for those parties from civil law countries, discovery can be a bewildering process whereby documents which had never been envisioned as becoming public come to light in an arbitration 'courtroom.'

Traditional litigation may be more helpful to disputants in multi-party disputes. Arbitration is a process requiring the mutual consent of the parties to submit their differences for a final adjudication by a neutral third party. Arbitrators lack the legal authority to join parties without their consent. While it might be possible for the parties to agree to join multiple parties should a dispute come about, such an agreement should be legally pristine in order to avoid litigation over the issue.[99]

As for class actions, the ICC Rules are silent and, consistently refer to the arbitral parties in the singular. However, if one were predisposed to find a basis for multi-party dispute resolution through arbitration in the *UNCITRAL Model Law on International Commercial Arbitration (1985)*, one could find such reliance if a generous and broad reading of the *Rules* were employed. As for class actions and the judiciary, the U.S.

Supreme Court, in the rather fractured decision of *Green Tree Financial v. Bazzle*, seems to have tilted the playing field toward an acceptance of class actions being settled through arbitration.[100]

Depending on one's point of view—or whether one's ox has been gored—it may matter little or greatly that the arbitral system does not employ a jury. The decision maker is one person or a tribunal—a creation of the parties who may be expert in the matter, a fact that might provide consolation to some and *angst* to others. In a sophisticated commercial dispute, the parties might very well want assurance that the decision maker in their case brings an understanding of the technicalities of their dispute to the forum. On the other hand, in a commercial dispute involving a person of modest means versus a commercial party of substantial means, the claimant might wish for a jury in order to obtain a 'sympathetic' and not a 'reasoned' judgment.

If provided for under domestic law or under the rules of the arbitration society under whose auspices the arbitration is being conducted, arbitrators might possess the authority to grant injunctive or provisional relief when necessary; however, an arbitrator's power is limited to the parties before her. For example, an arbitrator might very well enjoin ongoing intellectual property violations under the American Arbitration Association's International Dispute Resolution Procedures rule: "At the request of any party, the tribunal may take whatever interim measures it deems necessary, including injunctive relief and measures for the protection or conservation of property."[101] Similarly, the UK Arbitration Act permits an arbitrator to grant provisional relief if the parties had beforehand agreed to give the arbitrator such power.[102] In contrast, however, under Greek or Italian law, an arbitrator is precluded from providing interim relief.[103] Consistent with relevant domestic law, a court of competence, unlike the limited power possessed by arbitrators, might provide injunctive relief against the disputants and against third parties as well.

Sanders considers a "major drawback" of arbitration to be the subsequent action by the losing party to set aside an award after an arbitral decision has been rendered.[104] Such an action can take a number of years and result in substantial costs to the 'winning' party. Even if the award is successfully set aside, the dispute is not over since the matter will need either to be re-arbitrated or re-litigated unless the parties through fatigue or exhaustion finally settle the matter.[105]

An illustration of Sanders' concern involved the Swedish shipbuilder, Gotaverken Arendal AB (the large Gothenburg shipyard) and the buyer of three newly constructed tankers, the General National Maritime Transport Company (later succeeded by the Libyan General Maritime Transport Organization).[106] Libyan General refused to take delivery or pay their outstanding balance because 1) contract provisions prohibiting the use of components made in Israel had been violated, and 2) certain technical specifications had not been met. Gotaverken rejected these arguments and initiated arbitral proceedings in accord with the contract.[107]

The dispute was submitted to the International Chamber of Commerce (ICC) for arbitration in Paris. The arbitration tribunal rejected Libyan General's claims.[108] When Libyan General would not voluntarily comply with the arbitral ruling, Gotaverken sought enforcement in the Swedish courts. Libyan General opposed this request on the ground that it had already begun appeal proceedings in France as it had petitioned the Court of Appeal of Paris to set aside the arbitration award. When the Swedish court denied Libyan General, it instituted an appeal to the Swedish Supreme Court requesting the ICC award be held in abeyance until the proceedings before the Court of Appeal of Paris had been decided.[109]

As it turned out, the French court refused jurisdiction since the parties had not selected French procedural law and their commercial transactions had nothing to do with French law. That the arbitration took place in France was not persuasive. The award was considered foreign and thus free from appellate review.[110] The Swedish courts recognized the award and enforced the award even though the award could be characterized as a "stateless or a national award."[111]

So, to recap, an arbitral award was made under the ICC rules in France. Enforcement was sought in Sweden by the 'winning party.' The 'loser' of the award appealed in French courts and in parallel sought a stay of enforcement in the Swedish courts. All the while, legal fees mounted and both parties attempted to go about their respective business while litigating about arbitration matters already decided and in a manner that the parties themselves had selected.

And so, with this base line knowledge of commercial arbitration in place, we can now move on and begin to examine the processes that forged the links of the *arbitral chain*. The search for an arbitral chain begins with the Greeks since, in this writer's era, elementary schools taught that, "Everything started with the Greeks."

## Notes

1. This list is not exhaustive but reflects the most utilized ADR schemes. Other ADR mechanisms include: med-arb, mini-trials, fact-finding panels, etc. See generally, KATHERINE V.W. STONE, PRIVATE JUSTICE: THE LAW OF ALTERNATIVE DISPUTE RESOLUTION, 5-8 (Foundation Press 2000).

2. See generally, ROGER FISHER AND WILLIAM URY, GETTING TO YES: NEGOTIATING AGREEMENT WITHOUT GIVING IN, (Bruce Patton, ed., Penguin Books 2 ed. 1991) and Michelle Maiese, *Negotiation,* available at www.beyond intractability.org/essay/negotiation/ (visited July 19, 2006).

3. Unattributed author, *The Guide to WIPO Mediation,* WIPO ARBITRATION AND MEDIATION CENTER Publication No. 449(E), at 1, updated 2004.

4. *UNCITRAL Conciliation Rules,* 1980, Article 1(1).

5. *Permanent Court of Arbitration Optional Conciliation Rules, July 1, 1996.*

6. Cited in Dr. Jose Pascal da Rocha, *Mediation: Effective alternative to dispute resolution,* available at www.Proconsensus.blogspot.com (visited July 27, 2006).

7. *id.*

8. http://www.pbs.org/newshour/bb/cyberspace/jan-june00/posner_4-3.html (visited July 24, 2006).

9. Martin Hunter, *International Commercial Dispute Resolution in the 21st Century: Changes and Challenges*, NEW ZEALAND INSTITUTE FOR DISPUTE RESOLUTION available at http://www.e-arbitration-t.com/papersadr/paper_international.pdf (visited July 7, 2006).

10. *Scherk v. Alberto-Culver,* 417 U.S. 506, 516 (1974).

11. From the website of the American Arbitration Association http://www.adr.org/index2.1.jsp?JSPssid=15784, (visited February 2, 2006).

12. D. Hoffman, *Mediating Life and Death Decisions,* 36 ARIZ. LAW REV. 821, 848 (1994).

13. Arthur von Mehren, *A General View of Contract,* 7 INTERNATIONAL ENCYCLOPEDIA OF COMPARATIVE LAW, 52-56 (1982).

14. Quoted in D. Underhill, *Do State Courts Have a Useful Role to Play in International Arbitration?* www.intiarbitration.net/pdf/statecourts_Spenser Underhill_Feb03.pdf (visited May 9, 2006).

15. Richard Hill, *Primer on International Arbitration* http://www.oikoumene.com/arbprim.html (visited July 22, 2006).

16. http://www.iccwbo.org/court/english/right_topics/stat_2005.asp.

17. M. Polkinghorne & Jean-Claude Najar, *An Introduction to ICC Arbitration in Australia,* 3 BOND L. REV. 46-50 (1991).

18. R. GARNETT ET AL., A PRACTICAL GUIDE TO INTERNATIONAL COMMERCIAL ARBITRATION, 11-14 (Oceana Publications 2000).

19. Article 25 (4), *UNCITRAL Arbitration Rules* (1976) (Adopted by the General Assembly on December 15, 1976)

20. *Dolling Baker* was an English Court of Appeal case upholding the confidentiality of arbitration and can be found as cited at *Dolling-Baker* [1990] 1 WLR 1205 at 1213; [1991] 2 All ER 890 at 899.

21. *Esso Australia Resources Ltd v. Plowman* 183 CLR 10, 30 (1995).

22. *Esso*, at 56.

23. GARNETT, at 14.

24. *Hassneh Insurance Co. et al. v. Stuart J. Mew*, Queens Bench Division (Commercial Court), 22 December 1992. 2 LLOYD'S LAW REP. 243 (1993) found in TIBOR VARADY ET AL., INTERNATIONAL COMMERCIAL ARBITRATION 495501, (West Group 2003).

25. *Bulgarian Foreign Trade Bank v. A.I. Trade Finance Inc.* Supreme Court of Sweden, October 27, 2000. Mealey's Int. Arb. Court Documents-Doc. No. 05-001127-101 found in VARADY at 504-509.

26. *Rules of Arbitration*, International Chamber of Commerce (1998) http://www.iccwbo.org/court/english/arbitration/rules.asp (visited June 2, 2006).

27. *United States v. Panhandle Eastern Corp.*, 118 F.R.D. 346 (D. Del. 1988).

28. *The United States v. Panhandle*, at 350.

29. *Amco-Asia Corp v. Republic of Indonesia,* 23 I.L.M. 351 (1984).

30. CHARLES DICKENS, BLEAK HOUSE, Chapter One, available at http://dickens.thefreelibrary.com/Bleak-House/1-1 (visited August 12, 2006).

31. GARY BORN, INTERNATIONAL COMMERCIAL ARBITRATION IN THE UNITED STATES, 8 (Kluwer 1994).

32. BORN, at 8-9.

33. Henry P. de Vries, *International Commercial Arbitration: A Contractual Substitute for National Courts,* 57 TUL. L. REV. 42, 61 (1982).

34. H. Verbist & J. Erauw, *Resultats de l'enquete concernant l'arbitrage et le monde des affaires*, 5 REVUE DE DROIT DES AFFAIRS INTERNATIONALES, 689,707 (2000) cited in W. Knull & N. Rubins, *Betting the Farm on International Arbitration*, 11 AMERICAN JOURNAL OF INTERNATIONAL ARBITRATION No. 4 at fn. 29 (2000).

35. Thomas Carbonneau, *National Law and the Judicialization of Arbitration,* in INTERNATIONAL ARBITRATION IN THE 21ST CENTURY, Lillich & C. Brower, eds., 126 (Transnational Publishers 1993).

36. Charles Routh, *Dispute Resolution-Representing the Foreign Client in Arbitration and Litigation*, SF24 ALI-ABA 1. 8 (Nov. 2000).

37. http://www.iccwbo.org/court/english/cost_calculator/cost_calculator_test.asp (visited July 31, 2006).

38. Donna Sadoway, *Advanced Micro Devices v. Intel: Do You Really Want to Arbitrate?* 10 SANTA CLARA COMPUTER & HIGH TECH L.J. 239 (1994).

39. Richard Hill, *Dispute Resolution in Telecomminications*, May 1995, available at www.oikoumene.com/arblaw (visited on June 3, 2006).

40. Martin Hunter, *International Commercial Dispute Resolution in the 21st Century: Changes and Challenges*, NEW ZEALAND INSTITUTE FOR DISPUTE RESOLUTION, available at http://www.e-arbitration-t.com/papersadr/paper_international.pdf (visited on July 7, 2006).

41. BORN, at 2.

42. Elizabeth Weiss, *Enforcing Foreign Arbitration Awards*, 53 DISP. RESOL. J. 71-2 (1998).

43. Louise Barrington, *HUBCO v. WAPDA: Pakistan Top Court Rejects Modern Arbitration*, 11 AM. REV. INT'L ARB. 385, 385 (2000).

44. *Id*.

45. William Park, *National Legal Systems and Private Dispute Resolution*, 82 AM. J. INT'L L. 616, 621 (1988).

46. W. Knull & N. Rubins, *Betting the Farm on International Arbitration: Is it Time to Offer an Appeal Option?* AM. REV. OF INT'L ARB. 531 Vol. 11 No. 4 (2000).

47. Carbonneau, at 127.

48. *Verlinden B.V. v. Central Bank of Nigeria*, 461 U.S. 480, 487 (1983).

49. *Petroleum Development Ltd. v. The Sheikh of Abu Dhabi*, 18 I.L.R. 144 (1951).

50. All the quotes regarding this arbitration are from C. Brower & J. Sharpe, *International Arbitration and the Islamic World: The Third Phase*, 97 AMJIL 643, 645 (2003).

51. *Saudi Arabia v. Arabian Am. Oil Co*, 27 ILR 117 (1963).

52. Brower & Sharpe, at Fn.16.

53. *Arbitration Act*, 1996 CHAPTER 23.

54. The above list is NOT exhaustive but merely illustrative.

55. CLIFFORD CHANCE, ENGLAND AND WALES, 148 in ARBITRATION WORLD (European Lawyer Reference Series).

56. *Advanced Micro Devices v. Intel Corp*, 9 Cal. 4th 362, 364 (1994) (hereinafter *"AMD"*).

57. *AMD*, at 400.

58. *AMD*, at 390-1.

59. *Moncharsh v. Heily & Blasé*, 3 Cal. 4th 1, 10, (1992).

60. *de Vries, at 47.*

61. BORN, *at 936.*

62. BORN, *at 938.*

63. *Federal Arbitration Act*, 43 Stat. 883 (1925), 61 Stat. 669 (1947), codified as 9 U.S.C. §§1-16.

64. Formally, *The United Nations Convention on the Recognition and Enforcement of Foreign Arbitral Awards (New York 1958)* (hereinafter *"The N.Y. Convention"*).

65. DOMENICO DI PIETRO & MARTIN PLATTE, ENFORCEMENT OF INTERNATIONAL ARBITRATION AWARDS 13 (Cameron May Ltd. 2001).
66. Martin Hunter, *International Commercial Dispute Resolution in the 21st Century: Changes and Challenges*, New Zealand Institute for Dispute Resolution http://www.e-arbitration-t.com/papersadr/paper_international.pdf (visited July 7, 2006).
67. *The N.Y. Convention*, at Article 1, § 1.
68. Statistic available at http://www.eisil.org/index.php?t=link_details&id=596&cat=641 (visited on August 16, 2006).
69. *The N.Y. Convention,* at § 3.
70. DI PIETRO, at 16.
71. *The N.Y. Convention,* at Article II, § 1.
72. *The N.Y. Convention* at § 2.
73. DI PIETRO, at 73.
74. For example: the Panama Convention, the Amman Convention, the European Convention, the Moscow Convention, etc.
75. *Convention on the Settlement of Investment Disputes between States and Nationals of Other States,* commonly called *the 1965 ICSID Convention* or *the Washington Convention*. Information regarding the ICSD can be found at http:www.worldbank.org.
76. DI PIETRO, at 17
77. *id.*
78. *The N.Y. Convention*, at Article III.
79. *The N.Y. Convention,* at Article V 1 (a)-(e).
80. *The N.Y. Convention*, at V 2 (b).
81. From The World Bank website at http://www.worldbank.org/icsid/basicdoc/partB-section06.htm#04 (visited February 5, 2006).
82. Richard Mosk & Ryan Nelson, *The Effects of Confirming and Vacating an International Arbitration Award on Enforcement in Foreign Jurisdictions,* 1 THE INTERNATIONAL ARBITRATION NEWS, Number 2 (Summer 2001).
83. DI PIETRO, *at 17.*
84. Unauthored, *Middle East Crude Oil Production and Exports,* XLVI MIDDLE EAST ECONOMIC SURVEY NO. 40, (October 6, 2003).
85. *Middle East's economic prospects remain bullish for 2005,* THE DAILY STAR, January 11, 2005.
86. Article V (2) gives a national court the authority to refuse to recognize an award on the grounds that the subject matter is not arbitrable in the "enforcement" state or that an arbitration award is contrary to public policy.
87. Chibli Mallat, *A Comparative Critique of the Arbitration process in the Arab World,* 1 LEBANESE REVIEW OF ARAB ARBITRATION 3, 5-7 (1996).
88. Mallet, at 5-7
89. Mallet.

90. Kristin Roy, *The New York Convention and Saudi Arabia* . . . 18 FDMILJ 920, 936 (1995).
91. Roy, at 938.
92. The public order exception of the Convention.
93. Roy, at 954.
94. *Bernhardt v. Polygraphic Co. of America,* 350 U.S. 198, 203-4 (1956).
95. Article 64 (a), *WIPO Arbitration Rules*, WIPO Publication No. 446.
96. Survey cited in D. Lipsky & R. Seeber, *The Appropriate Resolution of Corporate Disputes* in W. Knull & N. Rubins (2000) *supra*, n. 48 .
97. *Arbitration Act*, at § 7.
98. J. Rubinstein, *International Commercial Arbitration: Reflections at the Crossroads of the Common Law and Civil Law Traditions*, 5 CHI J. INT'L L. 303, 304 (2004).
99. R. Fischer and R. Haydock, *Drafting an Enforceable Arbitration Agreement* 47 in THE ARBITRATION PROCESS, D. CAMPBELL, ED., Kluwer Law International (2001).
100. *Green Tree Financial Corp. v. Bazzle,* 539 U.S. 444 (2003).
101. Article 21, International Dispute Resolution Procedures, Amended and Effective 1 May, 2006.
102. *U.K. Arbitration Act,* at section 39.
103. A. REDFERN & M. HUNTER, LAW AND PRACTICE OF INTERNATIONAL ARBITRATION, 393 (Sweet & Maxwell 2004).
104. PIETER SANDERS, QUO VADIS ARBITRATION? 7 (Kluwer 1999).
105. Sanders, at 7.
106. I.C.C. Awards Nos. 2977, 2978, and 3033 (1978).
107. For an in-depth review of this case, see Edward Okeke, *Judicial Review of Foreign Arbitral awards* . . . 10 N.Y. INT'L L. REV. 29 (1997); Pippa Reid, *Delocalization of International Commercial Arbitration* . . . 10 AM. REV. INT'L ARB. 177 (1999); V. Ditek, *The Choice of Applicable Law in International Arbitration,* 9 HASTINGS INT'L & COMP. L. REV. 235 (1986); W.L. Craig, *Some Trends and Developments in the Laws and Practice of International Commercial Arbitration,* 30 TEX. INT'L L.J. 1 (1995)
108. *General National Maritime Transport Co. v. Societe Gotaverken Arendal* (1980) D.S. Jur. 568 (Cour d'Appel Paris).
109. Judgment of Aug. 13, 1979, Sup. Ct., Swed. The decision is translated into English in J. Paulsson, *The Role of Swedish Courts in Transnational Commercial Arbitration,* 21 VA. J. INT'L LAW 211, 244-48 (1981).
110. Okeke, at 37-38.
111. Craig, at 22.

## Chapter Two

# The Arbitration of Greece and Rome

We begin to explore the notion of an *arbitral chain* with an examination of arbitration as developed and practiced by the Greeks and the Romans. We do not endeavor in this chapter to make the reader a *savant* as to the ways of arbitration in 'ancient times.' Rather, we begin to test the working hypothesis of this book that an arbitral chain was in fact created over time by successive arbitral eras. There is no better place to start this exploration than by looking at arbitral dispute resolution as practiced by the Greeks and the Romans—two systems that contributed so mightily to the development of the civil and common law.

### Greek Arbitration

Menander, the delightful Greek comic, spins a tale in his play, *The Arbitration*, about two ordinary folk—Daos, the shepherd, and Syros, the charcoal burner—who find themselves in the middle of an argument. Having once agreed to arbitrate their dispute with virtually any man serving as the arbitrator, they proceed to stop a stranger, Smikrines, and ask Smikrines to arbitrate the dispute between them.

> SYROS [to SMIKRINES]: Would you please good sir, spare us a little of your time?
> SMIKRINES: Spare time? What for?
> SYROS: We have an argument. . . . We're looking for a fair man who would arbitrate.

SMIKRINES [before agreeing to arbitrate asks]: Will you abide by what I shall decide?
SYROS: Yes, we will.

The issue before Arbitrator Smikrines was the ownership of trinkets that had been taken by Daos from a newborn that Daos had initially found; the newborn was later given by Daos over to Syros. Both Daos and Syros asserted ownership of the trinkets.

Each side presented its case and, after questioning each party, Smikrines decided for Syros, holding that Syros had taken up responsibility for the child's welfare whereas Daos only had an interest in the child's trinkets. Smikrines admonished Daos, "My god, I'll not decide it goes to you who are defrauding it, but to the man who's helping and resisting all your plans to swindle it." Daos complied with the arbitration award and turned the trinkets over to Syros while lamenting over his agreement to select Smikrines, "Why did I entrust the case to him?" Over the verdict rendered, Daos uttered, "What scandalous injustice! God!"[1]

It is evident, based on a close reading of the play, that Menander was familiar with arbitration given the facility and precision with which he captured; the method by which the arbitration was agreed; the spontaneity of the arbitrator's selection; the lack of procedure during each side's testimony; the ease with which the arbitrator cross-examined the parties; the speed with which the verdict was rendered; the fact that the award was rendered not on the law but on what was right and just—what we would refer to, modernly, as *equity*; and the compliance with the award by the losing party (albeit a begrudging compliance).

Given the recently explosive ubiquity of arbitration in the commercial world, it would be understandable if one came away with the impression that arbitration is a process of recent vintage. But, Menander's yarn is hardly modern and one can only guess at how much older arbitration is than Menander's tale of Daos and Syros. Wolaver writes that the place and time "man first decided to submit to his chief or to his friends for a decision and a settlement with his adversary, instead of resorting to violence and self-help or to the public machinery available, is not known."[2] Kellor chimes in, "Long before law was established, or courts were organized, or judges had formulated law, men had resorted to arbitration for the resolving of discord, the adjustment of differences, and the settlement of disputes."[3]

For Benham and Barton, their study of "primitive" peoples' ADR techniques was both instructive and "humbling" when their studies revealed ADR practices that, by today's standards, are considered cutting edge.[4] Binding and non-binding arbitration, summary jury trial, minitrial, and mediation were all found prominent in Benham and Barton's examination of dispute resolution in the ancient cultures of Japan, Polynesia, and Africa.[5]

Martin Domke, attempting to better chronicle the study of commercial arbitration, set the date of the first recorded arbitration at 2550 BC. Domke then proceeded to generalize that, "All through early history, whenever and wherever commerce reached a high degree of development, arbitration was resorted to for the settlement of disputes between buyers and sellers."[6] The great Oxfordian epigrapher, Marcus Tod, wrote of an arbitral decision to fix boundaries between two warring Sumerian cities that was found on a local *stela* indicating the award had been rendered about 4000 BC.[7]

Domke's observation is both insightful and instructive. Clearly, until an economy reaches a high degree of development within which competing economic forces come into play, its legal system will be relatively benign and confined to local jurisdictions. We see this notion borne out in the substantial growth of trade in Classical Athens thanks in part to the Athenian emphasis on developing products almost exclusively for trade: clothing, metal works, and pottery, for example.[8] Greek nobles built ships and encouraged commerce. Greek merchants then traveled extensively throughout their world of the day peddling Greek-made wares. Greek colonists "spread Greek civilization and made it supreme in the Mediterranean."[9] In fact, Demosthenes contended that the pervasiveness and utility of *coda* and commercial treaties (*symbola*) was such, that laws governing commercial disputes "are everywhere identical."[10]

While we are not sure exactly when Greek arbitration first came into use, Dowell writes there were legally binding arbitrations before 404 BC and that arbitral practices had universal acceptance among Greek states.[11] In addition to arbitration, various papyri and literary texts reveal that mediation, and adjudication were complementary parts of a dispute resolution system working together throughout the Greek world from the earliest times.[12]

And, while there was Hellenic acceptance for arbitration in general, an even loftier endorsement was given. In particular, Aristotle wrote,

Equity is justice that goes beyond the written law. And it is equitable to prefer arbitration to the law court, for the arbitrator keeps equity in view, whereas the judge looks only to the law and the reason why arbitrators were appointed was that equity might prevail.[13]

The law court and judge referred to by Aristotle have different meanings from those used in similar, modern legal terms. The law court, or *dikasterion,* as Aristotle would have used the term, referred to an assembly of citizens who heard judicial cases and executed legislative and executive decisions. The judge, or *dikast,* was a member of the *dikasterion.*[14]

Arbitration came into its own as Athenian law passed through three stages:

1. The *Themis*: defined as law that had been divinely sanctioned and revealed, embodying moral order and world harmony.
2. The *Thesmoi*: a collection of holy customs set into writing. Over time, the codifications (the *nomoi*) were freed from religion and became a secular basis for law.
3. Ultimately, the accumulated growth of these bodies of law formed the Codes of Draco and Solon.[15]

Besides codifying the laws of Athens that ultimately defined its democratic institutions, Solon demonstrated his endorsement of arbitration by personally arbitrating disputes between landowners and debtor peasants. In a circumstance not unlike today, land had accumulated in the hands of large credit landowners who demanded that any loans granted to the peasantry be secured by land or personal freedom. Solon, as arbiter, decided to maintain the extant land system, but put into desuetude the obligation that a debt be secured by land or personal freedom. King and LeForestier suggest that Solon's decision, essentially freeing the peasant majority, encouraged them to become the seed of Athenian democracy.[16]

Further evidencing Solon's support for an arbitral system, Demosthenes praised Solon's multifaceted approach to justice. For those without either the personal or the financial resources, Solon, according to Demosthenes, urged that they not use the court system. "Solon, who made these laws did not give those wanted to prosecute just one way of exacting justice from the offenders for each offense but many. . . . [If] you have no confidence in yourself and are too poor to risk a 1000 drachma fine: bring a *dike*[17] before the arbitrator and you will run no risk."[18]

After the reforms of Solon, Pisistratus appointed thirty judges to travel throughout the Attic townships (*demes*) and conduct arbitrations in order to minimize the judicial powers that had theretofore been exercised by aristocratic families.[19] *Demes* were small Athenian districts or regions. Each *deme* had its own assembly and so important was the *deme* in a citizen's life that one was identified by the demotic rather than the patronymic (*i.e.*, "*X*" of Thorikos rather than "*X*" son of Laertes).[20]

Aristotle explained the rationale behind the assizes of Pisistratus.

> For the same reasons he instituted the local justices, and often made expeditions in person into the country to inspect it and to settle disputes between individuals, that they might not come into the city and neglect their farms.[21]

This system of thirty visiting judges has been characterized as "*Deme* Justice."[22] After Pisistratus, the thirty were recalled and replaced by a Board of Forty sitting in Athens—forty because there were four judges picked by lot from each of the ten Attic tribes.

We contend that comparisons in law need never be exact as long as they are within a magnitude of capacity for cogent comparisons to be made. In the arbitral context, it is fascinating to consider that in the thirteenth century, a system of traveling judges was introduced in England as a way to ensure that the King's justice would be dispersed throughout the land. Known as *justices of the assize*, these commissioners had original jurisdiction to hear a case from beginning to end with the authority to render whatever decision was appropriate.[23] It is only when *Deme* Justice and medieval assizes are juxtaposed, that one can appreciate how progressive was the Greek approach to local justice. It should also be kept in mind that the Greek "assizes" predated the medieval assizes by centuries! Furthermore, the Greek judges employed what is modernly referred to as "Med-Arb." The Greek "assizors" were empowered to render binding decisions; however, such decisions were to be handed down only after efforts to secure a compromise between the parties had failed.[24] Modern med-arb, indeed—*Plus ca change, plus c'est la meme chose.*

Athenian courts, like courts in most modern day jurisdictions, ran behind schedule due to a litigious populace.[25] In order to lessen the workload of the courts, two systems of arbitration developed: one for public arbitration and one for private arbitration. Necessity required that

Athens develop a rather extensive arbitration system, since for civil cases, juries numbered two hundred and one persons (five hundred and one for criminal cases).[26] Consequently, it was in the judicial system's best interest that civil disputes be decided in ways other than through the court system.

Private arbitration was contingent on the free will of the parties to arbitrate and not take their dispute to court. Only freemen (at that time, one seventh of the Athenian population) had access to the arbitral process. Freewomen and children had no such access.[27]

The law governing private arbitration, enacted in 403/2 BC, was stated by Demosthenes in his Oration against Meidias:

> If any parties are in dispute concerning private contracts and wish to choose any arbitrators, it shall be lawful for them to choose whomever they so wish by mutual agreement, they shall abide by his decisions and shall not transfer the same charges from him to another court, but the judgments of the arbitrators shall be final."[28]

Distinctively, the law provided that:

1. The parties have full rein to select an arbitrator of their choosing.
2. The parties agree to abide by the arbitrator's decision.
3. The parties agree not to transfer the matter to another court.
4. A written agreement was not required.

It is instructive to contrast the above "Greek Arbitration Act" with the U.S. Federal Arbitration Act that reads, in part,

> A written provision in any maritime transaction or a contract evidencing a transaction involving commerce to settle by arbitration, a controversy thereafter arising out of such contract or transaction, or the refusal to perform the whole or any part thereof, or an agreement in writing to submit to arbitration an existing controversy arising out of such a contract, transaction, or refusal, shall be valid, irrevocable, and enforceable, save upon such grounds as exist at law or in equity for the revocation of any contract.[29]

If the writing requirement and the savings clause from the U.S. law are put aside, one can, from a policy standpoint, see remarkable similarities between the two laws. Both support the arbitral process—each law comes down on the side of party autonomy, and each law espouses the finality of the arbitral process. And, even though the policies are temporally separated by millennia, the links in the arbitral chain are evident.

Greek arbitration was conducted in, essentially, the same fashion as arbitration today. The arbitrators were sworn in and pledged to do their duty; both plaintiff/claimant and defendant/respondent were sworn as well; witnesses were deposed or testified under oath; depositions became part of the arbitration's archival record; cross examination of witnesses took place. Once the arbitrator decided, his award was issued in duplicate and deposited in public places. Accompanying the award was the fine established for failure to fulfill the obligations stated in the arbitrator's award.[30]

Today's equivalent of civil arbitration was conducted by either members of the Board of Forty (the former *deme* judges) or the public arbitrator. It was the former *deme* judges (MacDowell refers to them as *tribal judges*—an excellent portrayal of their judicial role) who were responsible for the public arbitration of most private disputes (*dikai*).[31] These judges decided neither inheritance cases nor some mercantile cases and had summary judgment authority over disputes not exceeding ten drachmas. Some historians and economists have estimated that the drachma had a rough value of twenty five dollars estimated in 1990 dollars.[32]

If one wished to take a civil action, one sought arbitral relief from the four tribal judges within the *deme* in which the defendant resided. The four tribal judges could decide any dispute less than ten drachmas. If the issue in dispute was valued at over ten drachmas the dispute was, mandatorily, referred to the Arbitrators.[33] The four judges could wield their summary judgment "threat" in an effort to force the parties to relatively small disputes to settle their problem before being passed onto a hearing-in-chief.[34]

Aristotle writes in *The Constitution of Athens,*

> The Forty are also elected by lot, four from each tribe, before whom suitors bring all other cases. Formerly they were thirty in number, and they went on circuit through the demes to hear causes; but after the oligarchy of the Thirty they were increased to forty. They have full powers to decide cases in which the amount at issue does not exceed ten drachmas, but anything beyond that value they hand over to the Arbitrators.[35]

While the four tribal judges had responsibility for arbitration of matters that fell within their respective tribal purviews, the actual conduct of most arbitration proceedings was carried out by a public arbitrator who, at the proverbial last minute before the arbitration, was chosen by lot from a roster of men who had attained age sixty. Each party paid the arbitrator a small fee. In return, the arbitrator, at first, attempted to reconcile the parties, but, if unsuccessful, rendered a judgment solemnized by oath.[36]

This arbitrator, then, was an ordinary citizen deemed competent only by virtue of his age. Referring to an arbitrator to whom he was assigned, the great Demosthenes remarked, "I got Straton of Phaleron as arbitrator, a poor man, who took no interest in public affairs, but in other respects not bad, in fact very respectable."[37]

While one might scoff at the notion of using private citizens chosen at random to decide the weighty matters brought before him, Wyse writes, "The public arbitrators were one of the most interesting products of Athenian democracy."[38]

The poet Tyrtaeus described well the balancing act that took place within a public arbitration.

> The first to give their opinion are the overlords—answerable to the gods. . . . Then come the ordinary citizens, arguing backwards and forwards in turn about what is the right customary law, stating what is proper, doing what is right, so that they do not give the city any crooked counsel. It is the common people who are endowed with power and the final say.[39]

The arbitrator, on receiving the case from the four representatives of the Forty, first endeavored to bring the parties to an agreement. If this failed, he heard the evidence and gave a decision. If the decision were accepted, the case ended. Because of the mandatory nature of public arbitration for actions in excess of ten drachmas, the parties retained their right to a trial by jury. Not so for private arbitration, however, since both parties had agreed to accept the arbitral decision as final; thus placing the arbitration award on par with the judgment of a jury.[40]

If either of the two parties insisted on appealing to a law-court, the arbitrator placed in two caskets (one for each party) copies of all the depositions, oaths and challenges, and of all the laws quoted in the case. The caskets were sealed and along with the arbitrator's decision, were handed over to the four representatives of the Forty, who had originally referred the case. Documents that were not in evidence before the arbitrator could not be produced in court. The court consisted of either 201 or 401 jurors depending on the sum in question.[41]

Aristotle in *The Athenian Constitution* describes the process.

> The Arbitrators take up the case, and, if they cannot bring the parties to an agreement, they give a decision. If their decision satisfies both parties, and they abide by it, the case is at an end; but if either of the parties appeals to the law-courts, the Arbitrators enclose the evidence, the pleadings, and the laws quoted in the case in two urns, those of the plaintiff in the one, and those of the defendant in the other. These they seal up and, having attached to them the decision of the arbitrator, written out on a tablet, place them in the custody of the four justices whose function it is to introduce cases on behalf of the tribe of the defendant. These officers take them and bring up the case before the law-court, to a jury of two hundred and one members in cases up to the value of a thousand drachmas, or to one of four hundred and one in cases above that value. No laws or pleadings or evidence may be used except those which were adduced before the Arbitrator, and have been enclosed in the urns.[42]

Lawyers might very well agree that, at trial, testimonial evidence is preferable to documentary evidence. However, one does not appeal a trial court's judgment orally. The request for an appeal of a lower court's decision is made in writing and is based on the written record previously accumulated. Bonner writes, "In modern practice evidence is reduced to writing mainly for the purposes of appeal. In Athens also, appeals were based almost entirely on the affidavits presented at the arbitration. It is quite plausible, therefore, to suppose that the real motive for requiring affidavits was to ensure that the appeal should be taken substantially on the evidence as originally presented."[43] How remarkable that the modern structure for appellate pleadings may have found its roots in Greek arbitration—creating further evidence of the arbitral chain.

Once in the court room, eloquence and presence were not lost on the Athenians. It became obvious to 'court watchers' that an arbitrator or jury could be persuaded by an advocate through the advocate's power of persuasion. Hence, it became commonplace for a party to a dispute to hire a *rhetor* or orator to present the case for his 'client.' As more and more *rhetors* were used, *exagatai* or interpreters of the law were attached to the courts to 'assist' in the interpretation of the law.[44] Diogenes, perhaps complimentarily or perhaps snidely, remarked that Bias, a wise man of Prene. was an eloquent pleader who always reserved his talents for the "just side."[45]

Prof. Jebb relates the story of Euphiletos whose name had been struck from the rolls of his *deme* on the ground that he was illegitimate. His case went to arbitration where, even in light of the testimonial evidence given by his parents and friends, no redress was awarded to Euphiletos. It was only after he appealed to an ordinary court did he receive comfort in that the court held that the name of Euphiletos had been removed as the result of a conspiracy.[46] Perhaps, Euphiletos should have heeded Diogenes' words and engaged Bias of Prene for his arbitration.

## Analysis

The arbitral chain does not begin with the Greeks. One starts at this point in legal arbitral history because the Greek arbitral system was so well defined and there is substantial source material available by which to understand how the Hellenic arbitral process was carried out. As might have already been evident, most of the research that has been relied upon deals with arbitration in Athens. It is not at all unreasonable to assume that arbitration was conducted under similar circumstances in other Greek city-states.

Arbitral scholars can only marvel at the innovations brought about by the Athenians' institutions of public and private arbitration. Summarizing his views on Athenian arbitration, Niebuhr wrote that arbitration was a medicine intended to heal a disease of the body politic whose efficacy depended on its application—not its bare existence—and though failing at times, arbitration often was a remedy with immediate and lasting results.[47]

To stay with Niebuhr's words, the immediate and lasting results of Greek arbitration were substantial. Greek arbitral law, in no small measure, became the primary link in the arbitral chain by virtue of the Greeks' legal and communal commitment to the process. And while it is understandable that lawyers and scholars might become fascinated with the 'trial practice' elements of Greek arbitration , in fact, Greek arbitration was more; it was a prime mover that also resolved family and communal disputes. In fact, Manley-Tannis suggests that it was the success of private arbitration among the *oikos* (the extended family) that paved the way for adoption of a public arbitration process and, importantly, served as an ameliorative agent against the harshness of Athenian courts.[48] We will see later how important communal arbitration was within pre-Maoist Chinese society.

Leaving discussions on communal arbitration for later analysis, we turn to the procedural requirements that were part of Greek arbitration and note how much Greek 'Civ Pro' is part of civil and trial procedures in courts throughout the modern legal world. As is the case modernly, witnesses were sworn and testimonial evidence was presented to the arbitrator orally or in the form of written affidavits acknowledged by witnesses in court. In doing so, a "record" of original evidence was established in the event an appeal was granted to review an arbitrator's award[49]—one more link in the arbitral chain.

The commitment to and the emphasis on Med-Arb to resolve disputes in both public and private Greek arbitration is viewed as so salutary that it is seen time and time again when disputes between modern commercial parties come to pass. Again, we are not suggesting that the Greeks were the first or only society wherein Med-Arb was a major route taken by third party neutrals to resolve disputes. Rather, it is the profundity of commitment and the propagation of the Med-Arb process that causes the researcher to come back to the Greeks and rate them so high in the legal historiography of dispute resolution.

Recall that under the Greek system, the *deme* judges could use of the threat of a summary judgment to "compel" resolution rather than arbitrate disputes of relatively small amounts. Modernly, the recourse to a motion for arbitral summary judgment may or may not be available to the parties in dispute, the availability of such power being a function of whether or not the arbitrator has such power under either a national law or the rules of the arbitral institution under which the arbitration is being conducted. Contemporary arbitrators, even when given the authority, are far less inclined than were the Greeks to use summary judgment as a dispositive method of dispute resolution. Arbitrators are concerned that a pre-hearing attack by a disputant will result in a court's overturning their ruling and ordering the arbitrator to hear evidence.[50] It is just legally safer and easier for an arbitrator to have a hearing and deny summary judgment, and thus take, in Frost's words, the road less traveled.

Beyond process and procedure, the concept of equity became an institutionalized hallmark in Greek law. Aristotle's notion of *epiekia* became for future Jurists, according to Konvitz, the *locus classicus* of the notion of equity.[51]

Aristotle maintained that there were times where one should not look to the letter of the law rather one should look to

> the moral purpose; not to the part, but to the whole; not to what man is, but to what he has been, always or generally . . . to prefer arbitration to the law court, for the arbitrator keeps equity in view, whereas the dicast looks only to the law, and the reason why arbitrators were appointed was that equity might prevail.[52]

Equity was not in any sense a mere philosophical abstraction; rather equity became an essential part of Greek justice and administration. Hunter elaborates, "Arbitrators, in other words, based their awards on the norms and beliefs of the society around them, expressing what laymen thought what was right or wrong, normal or abnormal."[53] She goes on, "[an] arbitrator's decisions were not based on law but equity, their aim being to effect reconciliation and harmony without recourse to litigation."[54]

Typically, modern arbitrators do not have this remedial approach readily available to them and are permitted the opportunity of deciding on the basis of equity, or *ex aequo et bono*, only when the parties before them affirmatively grant such authority.

But equity, in both litigation and arbitration, endures as part of the world of legal remedies and stands as evidence of Aristotle's enduring impact on the common law, the civil law, and the private law of nations of today. We see next, as this chapter progresses, how relevant portions of Greek arbitration were adapted by the Romans and how the arbitral chain was fashioned by two great arbitral systems.

## Roman Arbitration

In a play reminiscent of Menander's tale, Plautus, in *The Fisherman's Rope*, composed a yarn about a fisherman, Gripius, and Trachalio, a servant. Each is arguing with the other over the ownership of a wicker basket that Gripius found in the sea. In order to resolve their dispute, Gripius suggests that Daemones, a neighbor, be selected as arbitrator. Unknown to Gripius, the person that he suggested is no other than Trachalio's master. In an attempt to assure Daemones' selection, Trachalio attempts to deflect any suspicion and says to Gripius, "Although you are driving me before an arbitrator whom I don't know, if he shall administer justice, although he is unknown, he is as good as known to me; if he doesn't, though known, he is the same as though entirely unknown.[55]

As we saw in Menander's *The Arbitrator*, the use of arbitration was known to Roman common-folk who, if one can draw likely conclusions, appear to be comfortable with the system and its use, notwithstanding, as we shall see, the hurdles one encountered when one wished to pursue arbitral dispute resolution. Indeed as much as arbitration was organic to the Greek legal system, it was ingrained in the Roman system as well. The first records of arbitration in Rome involved claims between the so-called "League of Cities" in the Roman territories of the Italian peninsula. Domke writes of one record that dates to a 446 BC arbitration between the Aricians and the Ardeans over a land dispute.[56]

By the end of the second century, Rome lay at the center of global trading. As its legal relations became more complex and its population increased, so did the need for an organized body of law developed by the national authority.

The development of Roman private law was, in no small measure, shaped by those who, modernly, would be referred to as Jurists—legal writers who, through the wisdom and influence of their writings, provided the impetus for development of the principles and rules of private law.[57] While a statute might represent the skeleton of the law, Buckland admiringly wrote of the flesh applied to the bone by Roman Jurists and, relying on Cicero, identified Jurists as "legal consultants on all walks of life."[58] One of the most quoted of the Jurists remains the great Gaius whose *"Omne autem ius quo utimur vel ad personas pertinet vel ad res vel ad actiones"* has been drilled into the minds of civil as well as international law students for years.

Jurists were called upon to give their opinion on any number of complex legal issues and to develop *responsa* as guides for judges or *judex* in their deliberations. Toward the end of the Roman republic, the institution of *judex* was abandoned and replaced by the Jurists or Jurisconsults to whom were given the right to make binding juridical decisions. thereby placing a trial in the hands of one person and fundamentally altering "the characteristics of the legal profession and the nature of its influence on Roman law."[59]

*Ius* (or *jus*) *civile* was the total body of Roman traditional law within which was embodied a reliance on customary norms (*mores maiorum*). Ultimately, the *ius civile* was expanded into the *ius gentium* that came to be the Roman common law covering legal matters that arose between

Romans and non-Romans alike. Some of the customary norms were regarded as manmade derivatives.[60] Others (*fas*), however, derived their binding force as a result of their reputed divine origin.[61]

*Lex* signified man-made law—the law of the Roman popular assemblies.[62] For example, unlawfulness fell under the normative principles of *ius*, a moral proscription for one who had committed an unlawful act. The act was simply *contra ius*. Conversely, an unlawful act under *lex* was legislatively proscribed and the contravention of the *lex* resulted in a strict application of the letter of the law.[63]

Even under the *ius gentium*, Roman law was applied differently for citizens and foreigners. The *ius civile* was used to denote those legal rights to which only Roman citizens were entitled; while *the ius peregrinus* applied to matters between foreigners who were free but not citizens of Rome. The *ius civitatis* distinguished between two categories of law: public law (*publica iura*) and private law (*privita iura*).[64]

Judicial proceedings (*iudicia*), likewise, fell into similar silos of categorization: *iudicia publica* and *iudicia privata*. It was under the umbrella of *iudicia privata* that arbitration fell.[65] In Rome, as in Greece, "the arbitrator acted by virtue of contract between the parties, and his authority to decide the case came from the contract between them and himself."[66]

The administration of the Roman judicial system was in the hands of the *Praetor*, a position similar in context to a minister of justice. The *Praetor* (later there were multiple *Praetors*) was invested with one of the most critical of judicial powers: the development of the forms and formalities of legal proceedings.[67] In addition to his administrative duties, there were certain cases which the *Praetor* was bound to decide himself, *i.e.*, matters dealing with the following offenses: oppression of the provincials by governors (*repetundarum*), bribery (*ambitus*), embezzlement (*peculatus*), treason (*majestatis*), murder (*de sicariis et veneficis*), and probably forgery (*falsi*).[68]

Below the *Praetors* were the *Magistrati* who, in civil cases, possessed a substantial amount of discretion over matters referred to them. *Magistrati*, for the most part, conducted preliminary examinations to determine whether or not there was sufficient substance to the claim before them to warrant sending the matter on for trial. They were quite distinct from those who decided questions of fact.[69] Most of the civil actions brought before the *Magistrati* were sent either to a judge or an arbiter—a *Judex* to whom the *Magistratus* gave instructions according to the Roman legal formulary. The formulary was intended to advise the *Judex* that if the plaintiff's case carried the day, what remedy he was to apply under the highly formalized system of Roman proceedings.[70]

Nichols provides an example of a formulary under which the *Judex* would have operated: "Let *X* be the *Judex*. If it appears the defendant ought to pay 10,000 sesterces to the plaintiff, let the *Judex* condemn the defendant to pay 10,000 sesterces to the plaintiff. If it does not so appear, let the *Judex* absolve him."[71]

A word regarding terminology is in order. Stephenson writes that the use of the terms *judex* and *arbiter* are interchangeable. "There seems to be no difference in the function of these two judges, unless it be that the latter was given greater latitude in reaching his decision." Roebuck, while recognizing a taxonomical distinction, is comfortable that any distinction is minor since the Romans themselves were unconscious in their writings of any particular difference.[72]

The *Judex* was not a magistrate but an ordinary citizen converted by the *Magistratus* to a judicial officer, a public arbitrator if you will, for a particular case. After rendering his decision, the tenure of the *Judex* ceased and he returned to being a private citizen. While the *Magistratus* was created and selected by the state, the *Judex* was a nominee of the *Magistratus* who, during his tenure, adjudicated, and spoke the law *(ius dicit)*.[73]

In the absence of an agreement to arbitrate and before obtaining a hearing on his case, the plaintiff would attempt to obtain from the *Magistratus* an *actio* or a predetermination as to the plaintiff's notion of an appropriate legal remedy.[74] Such hearings before the *Magistratus* were known as *jus* and took place *in judice*.

Before, the *Judex*, the proceeding was referred to as *judicium* and took place *in judicio*. It was a reflection of Roman genius to maintain a separation, a differentiation in fact, between legal procedure and legal proceedings so that a clear, logical, and practical private law system would be permitted to develop.[75]

The *Judex*, when appointed, was bound to discharge the functions of the office, unless he had some valid excuse not to do so. In any given case, the litigant parties agreed upon a *judex* or accepted him whom the magistrates had proposed. A party had the power of rejecting a proposed *judex*. In cases where one of the litigant parties was a *peregrinus* (a foreigner), a *peregrinus* might be *judex*. Whether *peregrinus* or not, the *judex* was sworn to discharge his duty faithfully.[76]

Aubert describes two examples of issues that came before a *Judex*:

- Two parties validly entered into a contract. A disagreement arose and one party unilaterally withdrew. After obtaining the formulaic remedy from the *Magistratus*, the task of the appointed *Judex* was to decide the contract's validity (*actio empti* or *venditi*). The remedy having been based on the nature of the contract, the *Judex's* role was simply to decide either for the plaintiff or defendant.[77]
- A businessman, *Julius Prudens*, had two slaves, *Hyginus and Hermes*, who took out a loan from the moneylender, *Sulpicius Cinnamus*. The loan was not repaid. The *Magistratus* ordered *Prudens* to deliver the slaves to the *Judex* for determination of the principal-agent relationship.[78]

Procedurally, the matter would have first been briefly stated to the *Judex* by the *oratores* of each party. Witnesses would have been produced on both sides and examined orally; the witnesses on one side would have been cross-examined by the other. Written documents, such as instruments and books of account, would have been entered into evidence; and, if necessary, the deposition of an absent witness would have been read, if it had been confirmed by an oath.[79]

There were no strict rules of evidence at the arbitration and, within the boundaries established by the *Magistratus*, the *Judex* had substantial leeway as to how the proceedings were to be conducted. Since the *Judex* was not a Jurist, he would have, if he saw necessary, consulted with Jurists on matters of law with which he was not familiar.[80] If the matter was one of some difficulty, the hearing might be adjourned as often as was necessary and if the *Judex* could not come to a satisfactory conclusion, he might declare this upon oath and so release himself from the difficulty. This was done by the form of words "*non liquere*" (It is not clear).[81]

After all the evidence was given, the *Judex* rendered his decision. The award would have been pronounced orally, and was sometimes memorialized through a writing on a tablet. The decision was binding only as between the parties. Since Roman law did not have within it the notion of precedent, the award had no wider significance.[82]

The Roman juridical system was laden with the restrictions and constraints imposed by the Roman formularies. *How things got done*—was important within the Roman legal system and in the private arbitral world, as well.

There is substantial evidence, according to Roebuck, that the earliest form of Roman arbitration was conducted by a *bonus vir* (lit. a good man) entrusted by the parties to resolve their dispute.[83] Menander's Smikrines and Plautus' Daemones, whom we met earlier, were *boni viri*. Everything about the process was *ad hoc* and conformed to the will of the parties. The *bonus vir* process was so pervasive in early Roman dispute resolution that the chronicles simply carry the abbreviation ABV for *arbitrium boni viri*. The general conduct of the *bonus vir* process was so highly admired that it justifiably influenced later Roman arbitration. Horace wrote, "Who is the *bonus vir*? The one who serves the senate's decrees, the statutes and the laws. Many a mighty suit is settled by his arbitration. His surety confirms matters and his testimony determines cases."[84] Given Horace's imprimatur, we can understand why private ABV endured alongside the public arbitration conducted by the judex/arbiter. Not satisfied with the system they had constructed, Romans placed along side these two arbitral processes still another—the arbitration *ex compromisso*.

Not all contracts in Rome were *per se* valid. Contractual consent, as we know it, was insufficient. In order for a contractual promise to be actionable, it needed first to be grounded in a basis recognized by law (the *causa civilis*). As Buckland wrote, "an agreement is not a contract unless the law, for some reason, erects it into one."[85] An agreement to arbitrate a *future* dispute was not a contract recognized in law. Any decision rendered under such an arbitration agreement was not binding and no damages were available if a party failed to honor an award.

To circumvent this obstacle, the system of arbitration *ex compromisso* was devised whereby a double promise (the *compromissium*) was added to an arbitral contract requiring one party to pay the other a fixed sum (the *poena*) if he did not submit to the arbitration or if the terms of an arbitral award were not honored. If for some reason a matter regarding the arbitration was subsequently litigated, the issue would not be decided on the legality or merits of the arbitration, but only upon whether the *compromissium* was adhered to.[86] An example to illustrate appears in the *Digest of Justinian*, a compendium of the works of Roman Jurists that were commentaries on Rome's civil law, the *Corpus Juris Civilis*.

> A boundary dispute had arisen between Castellianus and Seius. An arbiter was chosen to determine it by his arbitration. He declared his award in the presence of the parties and fixed the limits. The question was whether, if Castellianus did not obey the arbiter, the penalty provided by the compromissium was incurred. My answer was that the penalty was incurred if the arbiter was not obeyed in what had been promises in the presence of both parties.[87]

There is yet another twist on Roman arbitration. While a "stand alone" arbitration agreement was not recognized at law as a valid contract, if a proviso to arbitrate was part of a consensual contract, then the agreement to arbitrate was considered binding as the principle of good faith on the parties came into play and an *arbitrum boni viri* ensued.[88]

Examples of subject matter that might be the basis for an arbitration clause within a contract include a sales price for real or personal property or the amount due a partner in a partnership. David writes that the award of an arbitrator in such cases became part of the contract. And, since the decision of an arbitrator was subordinated to a condition of good faith, the award could be contested only on the basis that it was manifestly unjust and contrary to good faith.[89]

To summarize, absent an arbitration agreement, civil disputants sought relief under a public, bifurcated, arbitral system whereby the parties first obtained a magisterial formulary and then appeared before the *Judex*. Or, the parties could arbitrate *ex compromisso*. Or, under a stand-alone arbitration agreement, a controversy could be arbitrated but the award had no effect in law absent a compromissory clause. But, if part of a valid consensual contract, a dispute could be arbitrated with the award binding on the parties. The binding effect, however, came about not based on the *imperium* of the arbiter for he had no power to command; rather it came about as a result of the parties having agreed that the award would be binding on them.

Again, we turn to *Justinian's Digest* for an illustration of the arbitral process through Roman eyes.

> You entered into a partnership with me, on condition that Nerva our mutual friend should fix the partnership shares. Nerva fixed them at a third for you, two thirds for me. You ask whether that would be valid under the law of partnership, or whether we should nonetheless be partners in equal shares. But I think you would have done better to have asked whether we should be partners in the shares he had fixed or I those which a *bonus vir* would have fixed.

For arbiters are of two kinds: one kind we obey, whether their award is fair or not, which is when one goes to arbitration *ex compromisso*. The other is of the kind where the arbitrator is appointed to act as a *bonus vir*, even if the individual to arbitrate is appointed by name.[90]

Throughout this chapter, the male "he" or "him" has been used since Roman law classified women as physically and mentally incapable of arbitrating. Yet, Roebuck describes an archaeological find of a bone on which is the name, Sophe, an arbitrator, whose epithet was that of a dancer and who may have arbitrated disputes between dancers in her show.[91] Roebuck also relates a story by Plutarch wherein Celtic women performed so well as arbitrators that when the Celts formed an alliance with the Carthaginians, it was agreed that should any dispute be lodged against the Celts by the Carthaginians, Celtic women were to arbitrate the matter.[92]

## Analysis

Recall Aristotle's paean to arbitration, "And it is equitable to prefer arbitration to the law court, for the arbitrator keeps equity in view. . . ." Cicero's encomium is no less enthusiastic, "We come before the court with the expectation that we shall either win or lose the case; but we submit to an arbitrator on the understanding that we shall end up neither with nothing nor as much as we asked for."[93]

Both Aristotle and Cicero expressed one of the significant features of the arbitral process of their day, *i.e.*, the ability of the winning party, through arbitration, to potentially gain, minimally, something rather than nothing; whereas, in the courts, it was all or nothing at all. Whether it be the *epiekia* of the Greeks or the *aequitas* of the Romans, there was the notion that the arbitral process would render a fair award—perhaps not totally to one's liking—but a fair award, an equitable award.

If Rome gave the world nothing or no one other than Gaius that, in and of itself, would have been sufficient to demonstrate to successive legal generations the greatness of Roman legal astucity. However, Roman law gave its legal progeny more than Gaius. Roman law gave the world a basis on which a civil law system would be developed within which was embraced an arbitration system emphasizing the amicable resolution of disputes that "has had an important influence on civil procedure in continental Europe and can still be found in contemporary court practice, particularly in Austria, Germany, and Switzerland."[94]

Unlike the Romans, the Greeks did not have a legal system that divided legal actions into civil or criminal silos. In the Greek system, actions were either public or private. The Romans forged arbitral links with the Greeks by building upon the flexible civil procedure system that characterized Greek arbitration. If a scale capable of determining legal flexibility existed, the rigidity of the Roman formulary would, likely, be found at the outer end of the range. An excellent example is provided by Wolff who, relying on Gaius, wrote of a claim that had been non-suited because the claimant described the wrong committed as the cutting of his vines. The Roman Twelve Tablets only provided relief for damage done to trees! Say trees and the claim proceeds; say vines and the claim is dismissed.[95]

In time, Roman civil procedure was modified: witnesses who once appeared at hearing if they chose to do so could be officially summoned; rules of evidence appeared; hearsay evidence was excluded. And, as Buckland wrote, "[T]he main material in civil suits was documentary evidence, a practice borrowed from the Greeks, and rendered possible in commercial transactions, again a borrowing from the Greeks, commercial transactions were almost entirely written."[96] Not only were the procedural aspects of Roman dispute resolution adapting to the times but the nature of the judicial hearing as well. By the Age of Justinian (AD 527-565), the bifurcation of formulary and dispute resolution gave way to the competence of a single party hearing a case before him from start to finish.[97]

Notwithstanding the rigidity of the Roman system, Roman law, like Greek law, recognized the extra-judicial nature of arbitration whereby both civil and private matters could be resolved without resort to the court system. Mousourakis suggests that it was the Roman recognition of the private arbitral system that gave rise in later years to the development of ecclesiastical courts over private disputes.[98]

The rigidity of the Roman formulary was, in some way, counterbalanced by the extraordinary power of the *Praetor* to insert the notion of equity into his decrees. The individual Judex and arbitrator gave these pronouncements due decretal notice and deference. Indeed, Buckland suggests that the Praetor was equity's "chief source" and declared praetorian equity somewhat analogous to that of the Court of Chancery.[99] Whether under the state-sponsored civil process or the state-condoned arbitral process, praetorian ingenuity cannot be overemphasized. Prof. William Hunter credits the *Praetor* as having granted new rights and remedies when those at the extant civil law seemed insufficient and thus created new rights and new law.[100]

The Roman arbitral process rested on a foundation similar to that upon which the Greek arbitral process rested. However, the Romans forged and linked the arbitral chain and extended it well beyond the Roman Empire, thanks to their genius for administration. Hunter refers to the Roman genius as being essentially practical: "to the speculative or theoretical side of Jurisprudence it made no contribution . . . it was constrained to import from Greece elementary notions in respects to the foundations of law."[101] Buckland maintains that Roman law was far more skillfully elaborated upon than the Attic law (though never contending that the Romans were any cleverer than the Greeks).[102]

We see in Roman private law a continuation or a linkage—an arbitral linkage—of many of the elements so admired in Greek private law: the notion of equity, an adherence to civil procedure, testimonial evidence, and the use of arbitration to settle commercial disputes. After all, as Sir Henry Maine has postulated, "except for the blind forces of nature, nothing moves on this earth that is not Greek in its origin." Buckland, in his own way, supports Maine's panegyric of Greek influence on the Roman law by referring to early Roman law as "Graeco-Roman . . . filled with ideas derived from or held in common with the Greek tribes." And, going on, that "the Jurists [were] soaked in Greek philosophy."[103]

No wonder that Roman expeditions had been sent to Greece to study Attic law since the later half of the Roman republic. Foreign trade intercourse was substantial; especially with the Greek colonies established on the southern shores of Italy and Sicily.[104] The language of Roman merchants was Greek and it was either the first or second language of the Rome's *cognoscenti*. Mousourakis writes of Gaius' drawing attention, in his commentary on the law of the Twelve Tablets, to certain provisions within the Tablets that he viewed as of Greek origin.[105] Buckland cautions, however, that the Hellenistic influence should be put into perspective. The foreign influences that gradually crept into Roman society were not "directly expressions of Greek philosophy; [rather] they were the practices of trading classes in hellenised regions, with whom there was contact. There were borrowings not of ideas for the Jurist, but of ways of doing business, not of philosophy, but of a way of trade."[106]

This "way of trade," when the *Corpus Juris Civilis* was published, existed through the genius of Roman private law. While, initially, alien traders were barred from participation in Roman law, commercial trade demanded otherwise. For foreign traders to conduct a commercial transaction with a Roman and not have that transaction seen as having a basis in law required a rethinking of the commercial law as it affected both foreigners and Romans alike. Initially done by treaty with the states from which trade originated, the treaties set into place a reciprocal system whereby Roman commercial traders enjoyed the same rights in, say Carthage and, equally, Carthaginian commercial traders enjoyed the same rights in Rome. The *jus commercii* was especially carved out and specifically applied to commercial circumstances that required what was then quite novel thinking. In time, foreign trade, was, "raised to the rank of an independent power confronting the *jus civile* in Rome itself with distinct legal habits and distinct juristic acts (informal acts) of its own."[107] The unique utilization of the *jus commercii* permitted Roman private law to avoid the strictures of the Roman civil law by securing legal recognition for what Sohm called "the formless transaction"[108] or what we might modernly refer to as a consensual contract whether written or unwritten. In this way, dispute resolution arising out of commercial bargains that relied only on the good will of the buyer and seller laid the groundwork for and arbitrally linked with the *Lex Mercatoria*.

# Notes

1. MENANDER, *The Arbitration*, in MENANDER, THE PLAYS AND FRAGMENTS 86-91 (M. Balme trans., Oxford U. Press 2002).
2. Earl Wolaver, *The Historical Background of Commercial Arbitration*, 83 U. Pa. L. Rev. 132, 132 (1934).
3. FRANCIS KELLOR, AMERICAN ARBITRATION 3 (Harper and Bros. 1948).
4. R. Benham & A. Barton, *Alternative Dispute Resolution: Ancient Models Provide Modern Inspiration*, 12 Ga. St. U. L. Rev. 623, 625 (1996).
5. Benham & Barton at 625.
6. Martin Domke, *1 Domke on Com. Arb.* § *2:1* (August 2004).
7. MARCUS TOD, INTERNATIONAL ARBITRATION AMONGST THE GREEKS 170 (Oxford U. Press 1913).
8. Edward Harris, *Law and Economy in Classical Athens*, http://www.stoa.org/projects/demos/article_law_economy?page=all&greek Encoding=UnicodeC (visited August 31, 2006).
9. ALBERT HYMA, ANCIENT HISTORY 65 (Barnes and Noble 1940).
10. 2 WILL DURANT, THE STORY OF CIVILIZATION 262 (Simon and Schuster 1939).

11. DOUGLAS MACDOWELL, THE LAW IN CLASSICAL ATHENS 204, (Cornell University Press, 1978).

12. Derek Roebuck, *'Best to Reconcile': Mediation and Arbitration in the Ancient Greek World,* vol. 66, no 4, The Journal of the Institute of Arbitrators, 275 (1 November 2000).

13. Cited in Constantine Katsoris, *Punitive Damages in Securities Arbitration: The Tower of Babel Revisited,* 18 Fordham URB L.J. 573, 577 (1991).

14. R. Nelson, *Adapting ADR to Different Cultures,* http://www.gowlings.com/resources/publications.asp?pubid=776 (visited Sept. 1, 2006).

15. DURANT, at 257-263.

16. Paragraph gleaned from H.T. King & M. LeForestier, *Arbitration in Ancient Greece,* 49 SEP DISP. RESOL. J. 38, 39-40 (1994).

17. In this context, a *dike* is essentially a lawsuit. See *A Glossary of Athenian Legal Terms* at http://www.stoa.org/projects/demos/article_law_glossary?page=all&greekEncoding=UnicodeC (visited August 30, 2006).

18. V. Bers & A. Lanni, *An Introduction to the Athenian Legal System,* at 10, in A. Lanni, ed., Athenian Law in its Democratic Context (Center for Hellenic on-line Discussion Series), http://www.stoa.org/projects/demos/intro_legal_system.pdf (visited August 30, 2006).

19. R. BONNER, LAWYERS AND LITIGANTS IN ANCIENT ATHENS 39-40 (Benjamin Blum 1969).

20. Paragraph gleaned from MACDOWELL, at 206-7.

21. ARISTOTLE, THE ATHENIAN CONSTITUTION, part 16, http://classics.mit.edu/Aristotle/athenian_const.1.1.html (visited Sept. 3, 2006).

22. www.herodutuswebsite.co.uk/essays/clisthen.htm (visited August 30, 2006).

23. J.H. BAKER, AN INTRODUCTION TO ENGLISH LEGAL HISTORY 20-22 (Butterworth's 2002).

24. BONNER, at 39.

25. DURANT, at 260-1.

26. BONNER, at 36-7.

27. DURANT, at 260-1.

28. Cited by Kaja Harter-Uibopuu, *Ancient Greek Approaches Toward Alternative Dispute Resolution,* 10 WILLAMETTE J. INT'L L. & DISP. RESOL. 47, 53 (2002).

29. *U.S. Federal Arbitration Act,* 9 U.S.C. § 1, 2.

30. Martin Domke, *1 Domke on Com. Arb.* § *2:2* (August 2004).

31. BONNER, at 40.

32. http://www.answers.com/topic/greek-drachma (visited Sept. 5, 2006).

33. Harter-Uibopuu, at 56.

34. Harter-Uibopuu, at 57.

35. ARISTOTLE, CONSTITUTION Part 53.

36. DURANT, at 260-1.

37. MacDowell, at 208-9.
38. Bonner, at 40 cited simply as "Wyse in Whibley, *Companion to Greek Studies*, p. 386."
39. Cited by Roebuck, at 277.
40. MacDowell, at 209-10.
41. http://www.1911encyclopedia.org/Greek_Law (visited Sept. 5, 2006).
42. Aristotle, Part 53.
43. Robert Bonner, *The Institution of Athenian Arbitrators*, Vol. 11, No. 2, Classical Philology, 191 (1916).
44. MacDowell, at 209-210.
45. *Id.*
46. Sir Richard Jebb, The Attic Orators from Antiphon to Isaeos 361 (Macmillan 1876), www. Perseus.tufts.edu (visited January 19, 2005).
47. Marcus Niebuhr, International Arbitration Amongst the Greeks 188 (Clarendon Press 1913).
48. R. Manley-Tannis, *Greek Arbitration: Homer to Classical Athens*, (May, 1998)(unpublished thesis submitted to the Queen's University, Canada).
49. Niebuhr, at 188.
50. Jay Grenig, *Alternative Dispute Resolution*, 1 Alt. Disp. Resol. § 8:3 (3d ed).
51. Aristotle, Rhetoric, Book I, Chapter 13, cited in Milton Konvitz, Equity in Law and Ethics, http://etext.lib.virginia.edu/cgi-local/DHI/dhi.cgi?id=dv2-17 (visited August 3, 2006).
52. *Id.*
53. Virginia Hunter, Policing Athens: Social Control in the Attic Lawsuits 62 (Princeton U. Press 1994)
54. Hunter, at 24.
55. Plautus, Rudens or The Fisherman's Rope Act 4.3, http://www.perseus.tufts.edu/cgi-bin/ptext?doc=Perseus%3Atext%3A1999.02.0108 (visited Sept. 4, 2006.)
56. Domke, at § 2.2.
57. Peter Stein, Roman Law in European History 19 (Cambridge U. Press 2002).
58. W.W. Buckland, A Manual of Roman Private Law 15 (Cambridge U. Press 1957).
59. T. Graeville, *Background of Modern ADR*, 8A Mich Pl. & Pr. § 62A:3 (2ed).
60. Hans Wolff, Roman Law 61-62 (U. of Oklahoma Press 1951).
61. George Mousarakis, The Historical and Institutional Context of Roman Law 16-17 (Ashgate 2003).
62. Mousarakis, at 19-21.
63. *Id.*
64. Mousarakis, at 22-3.

65. MOUSARAKIS, at 127.
66. Domke, quote cited simply as "Englemann, *A History of Continental Civil Procedure,* 259."
67. WILLIAM SMITH, A DICTIONARY OF GREEK AND ROMAN ANTIQUITIES (John Murray London 1875), http://penelope.uchicago.edu/Thayer/E/Roman/Texts/secondary/SMIGRA*/Praetor.html (visited January 20, 2005).
68. *Id.*
69. WOLFF, at 72-3.
70. B. NICHOLS, INTRODUCTION TO ROMAN LAW 24-25 (Clarendon Press 1962).
71. *Id.*
72. A. STEPHENSON, A HISTORY OF ROMAN LAW 143 (Little Brown 1912). D. ROEBUCK, ROMAN ARBITRATION 15-16 (Holo Books Arbitration Press 2004). See also MOUSARAKIS at 128 who uses the term *arbiter* if the person were appointed by the Praetor or were a subject-matter expert.
73. STEPHENSON, at 142-44.
74. JEAN-JACQUES AUBERT, BUSINESS MANAGERS IN ROME 47, (E. J. Brill 1994).
75. STEPHENSON, 142-4.
76. MOUSARAKIS, 133-6.
77. AUBERT, at 47.
78. *Id.,* at 58.
79. MOUSARAKIS, at 133-134.
80. WOLFF, at 25.
81. WILLIAM SMITH, A DICTIONARY OF GREEK AND ROMAN ANTIQUITIES (John Murray London 1875), http://penelope.uchicago.edu/Thayer/E/Roman/Texts/secondary/SMIGRA*/Praetor.html (visited January 20, 2005).
82. WOLFF, at 25.
83. D. ROEBUCK, at 46.
84. *Id.,* at 64 citing *Epistles* 1.16.40.
85. W.W. BUCKLAND & A. MCNAIR, ROMAN LAW AND COMMON LAW 195 (1952 Cambridge U. Press).
86. R. DAVID, ARBITRATION IN INTERNATIONAL TRADE 84-5 (1985 Kluwer).
87. ROEBUCK, at 109 citing *Digest* 4.8.44.
88. DAVID, at 84-6
89. *Id.*
90. ROEBUCK, at 55 citing *Digest* 17.2.76.
91. D. ROEBUCK, A MISCELLANY OF DISPUTES 59-61 (Holo Books Arbitration Press 2000).
92. *Id.*, at 57-8
93. CICERO, PRO QUINTO ROSCIO COMOEDO, IV 6-11, cited by Nelson.
94. Christian Bühring-Uhle, *Traditional Mediation vs. Modern Mediation*, Stockholm Arbitration Newsletter, 1/2001.
95. WOLFF, at 63-4.
96. BUCKLAND & MCNAIR, at 403.

97. *Id.*, at 403-4.
98. MOUSARAKIS, at 375.
99. W.W. BUCKLAND, SOURCES OF EQUITY 5-6 (U. of London Press 1911).
100. W. HUNTER, HISTORY OF ROMAN LAW 12-3 (Sweet & Maxwell 1955).
101. *Id.*, at 2
102. BUCKLAND, (SOURCES OF EQUITY) at 133.
103. *Id.,* at 134-5.
104. W.W. BUCKLAND, THE MAIN INSTITUTIONS OF ROMAN PRIVATE LAW 20-21 (Cambridge U. Press 1931
105. MOUSARAKIS, at 118.
106. BUCKLAND, (MAIN INSTITUTIONS) at 23.
107. R. SOHM, THE INSTITUTES; A TEXTBOOK OF THE HISTORY AND SYSTEM OF ROMAN PRIVATE LAW 67 J. Ledlie, trans. (Oxford, Clarendon Press 1907).
108. SOHM, at 68.

# Chapter Three

# The *Lex Mercatoria*

Chapter Two confirmed that first the Greek and then the Roman arbitral systems were forged as the beginning links of an arbitral chain. We now turn from the Greeks and the Romans to the workings of the Law Merchant, an arbitral era with which the 'working lawyer' might not be familiar. This is understandable since the legal academy has given little attention to this vital legal period. However, the era of the Law Merchant, also known as the *Lex Mercatoria*, was as crucial a period for the development of modern civil and arbitral law as any before or since. Indeed, Kerr has written, "The Law Merchant furnishes the legal science its most romantic branch."[1] Through less "romantic" eyes than those of Prof. Kerr, we will in this chapter demonstrate the enduring effect of the Law Merchant and, in subsequent chapters, determine the role it played, if any, in the growth of Western arbitral processes.

The Law Merchant, according to Tudsberry, has always been associated with the *jus gentium* of the Roman jurists.[2] Recall in Chapter Two, the scope of Roman civil law was broadened from the *jus civile* to the *jus gentium*, thereby including the *pergrinus*, the foreigner, and bringing the weight of law to transnational transactions. The *Pax Romana* had given the trading world[3] peace for centuries; however, subsequent war and invasion saw the decline of the Roman Empire. Flourishing 'international' trade gave way to an introspective, domestic commercial system with little influence beyond its boundaries. Nearly everything produced on the manors of Europe, either by family or serfs, was exclusively for local use.

Economic doldrums might have put the *jus gentium* into practical disuse; however, it was not forgotten, thanks in large part to the legal academy of the day. Realizing its persistence and sustainability, Juenger, as he always has, wrote brilliantly of the rebirth of the *jus gentium* during the Middle Ages and credited it with being an impetus for the creation of mercantile institutions and instruments.[4] Carter went further; positing that the *jus gentium* was, in fact, the agent that bound the courts of the Chancery with the merchantmen of the day, and likening the Chancellor to the *praetor* since each rendered decisions *ex aequo et bono* and consistent with the *mores* of the day. "One might go further," Carter wrote, "and surmise that the law merchant was in fact largely based on the Roman law."[5] As we develop the Law Merchant's arbitral components, we will see that the words of Juenger, Carter, and Tudsberry all confirm—to use the words of this writing—an arbitral chain.

Historically, the domination of trade has often been regarded serially with one trading power, over time, giving way to the might of another trading power in whole or in part. Donahue concurs, writing that the Phoenicians gave way to the Greeks, the Greeks to the Romans, the Romans to the Arabs, and the Arabs to the Crusaders.[6] As merchants did business with each other throughout their trading regimes, it was natural that customs and usages developed that were peculiar to their commercial transactions and varied from country to country, or indeed region to region. It is, of course, a bit of chicken and egg to determine which came first: trade or the law. On one hand, we know that the *Lex Rhodia* had a great impact on Roman law. Conversely, it was the *Consolate del Mare*, the Laws of the Hansa Towns, and the Laws of Olereon that gave impetus to the international commercial trade of their constituents.

England was a bit of an anomaly, however. Given its insularity and, hence its isolation from the 'Continent,' there developed in England a system of international commercial dispute settlement, the virtues of which resonate in today's commercial arbitral settings. Arbitration in England, Harriss contends, was both a principal device and a social constraint created to avoid the "chronic lawlessness and the corruption of the legal system."[7] Arbitration occurred at all levels of English society: the gentry might have used Bishops; Lords arbitrated the disputes of their retainers; and the clergy were favored as mediators. However, arbitration and the law each served different functions. The law, writes Harriss, "was concerned with title and correct procedure rather than justice and social peace; arbitration offered an alternative and supplementary mode of dispute settlement, adjusted to social realities."[8] In the initial development of English law, both arbitration and the Law Merchant, because of their focus on social realities and not on formalities, constituted no part of the common law. Their decisions were neither binding nor viewed with approbation by the common law courts.

We should, however, first instantiate the unique characteristics that defined the merchant and his mercantile world. Within the Europe of the Middle Ages, there existed a variety of legal systems that took cognizance of peoples on personal rather than on territorial criteria. A Frank would live and be judged according to Frankish law, a Bavarian according to Bavarian law, a cleric according to ecclesiastical law, and peasant according to the law of the manor, etc.[9]

Personal attributes extended to the attributes of status, as well. A noble had a legal status different from that of a serf, a native different from a foreigner, and a man from a woman. Merchants, however, were different. The term *merchant* lost its attribute of status and simply became denotive. Merchants were seen as middlemen, wholesalers who engaged in regional and international trade. They were the men who traded outside the jurisdiction of their native land and/or did business with foreigners who lived under different laws.[10] They were also men from whom integrity and honor were expected.

In 1771, Wyndham Beawes, a lawyer and Majesty's Counsel, explained the standards that the commercial world, over the years, had come to expect of merchantmen. A merchant, Beawes wrote, need not

> be very learned . . . [but] ought on all occasions to have a strict Regard to truth, and avoid Fraud and Deceit as corroding Cankers to his Reputation and Fortune; for, however cunningly the Mask is wore, Chance may, or Time certainly will, discover the Cheat, and render the Wearer exposed to the Contempt and Insults of those he has imposed on. . . .[11]

Notwithstanding the efforts of this merchant class, and every merchant class since, to ply their goods wherever their trade took them, political events caused commerce to become regionalized. Commercial reciprocity was limited to nations of the same religious creeds.[12] Between the fall of the Western Roman Empire in the fifth century and the subsequent upswing of trade after the Crusades, merchants had to cope with what Mangels described as "vexatious conditions."[13] In time, however, merchant vexation gave way to merchant vessels as the era after the Crusades "ushered in a trade renaissance that lasted for six centuries."[14] Europe, through the efforts and energies of its merchant class, experienced an economic rebound as the markets of the East once again became accessible to commercial merchants. Heightened trade activity was coupled with a concurrent rise of cities and towns to contribute additional vigor to Europe's economic surge.[15]

Trade was conducted both by land and on the sea. As maritime trade expanded across the Baltic and Mediterranean Seas, various compilations of customary rules and usages governing the community of merchants evolved. In the mid-fourteenth century the *Consulado del Mar*, based on the ancient laws, statutes, and compilations of Italian cities, came to be accepted as the governing law in the commercial maritime centers around the Mediterranean.[16] Prof. Chase informs us that records furnish evidence that a fundamental motive of the *Consulado* was to secure the expeditious, economical, and equitable adjudication of disputes concerning maritime and mercantile contracts. The councilors of Majorca revealed in the *Consulado* their determination to circumvent the legalism and obstructions encountered in the ordinary courts "in order to do away with the expenses of lawsuits and the strife of judicial proceedings among merchants and navigators."[17]

Overland trade required a similar body of law. Consequently, a developing European trading community set in motion a new system of law that, in time, came to govern its commercial activities. The law, as Baron describes it, was "a special law for the merchant class that first grew in Italian cities and then spread to France, Spain, and the rest of Europe including England."[18] Merchants who traded across national boundaries transported and propagated the most favorable trading practices and customs of the various foreign markets within which they did business. And as the transnationality of trade expanded, the ability of the law and the courts to deal with this blossoming, unique set of commercial principles became strained.

While the universities of the day continued to teach the Roman law of sales, loans, and other types of civil obligations as well as the *ius gentium* (the law of nations), Roman law was seen as useful but rather dated when faced with the realities of a new trading system.[19] The growth of commerce demanded the development of a special *lex mercatoria* to regulate the transnational affairs of the markets and fairs as well as commercial maritime customs.[20]

Pirenne's description of the life of the merchantmen illustrates the transnationality as well as the hardships endured by the medieval Willy Loman.

Their members, armed with bows and swords, surrounded the packhorses and the wagons loaded with sacks, bales, cases, and casks. . . . the men were going as far as the mines of Goslar to get supplies of copper, the merchants of Cologne, Huy, Flanders and Rouen frequented the port of London, and numbers of Italians were already to be seen at the Ypres fair. Except in winter, the enterprising merchant was continually on the road, and it was with good reason that he bore in England the picturesque name of "dusty foot" (*pedes pulverosi, piepowders)*.[21]

The commercial requirements of the merchantmen led to a branch of law that at that time and perhaps even today, was the most inclusive of custom. Malynes wrote,

The said customary law of merchants hath a peculiar prerogative above all customs, for that the same is observed in all places, whereas the customes of one place doe not extend in other places, and sometimes they are observed and sometimes they are neglected. But the Customes of Merchants concerning trafficke and commerce are permanent and constant and when they are not truly observed in some places by errour or misprision . . . such Customs lose their names and they are called Usurpation which is the cause that many Customs are established for Lawes by him or them that have power to make Lawes."[22]

Contributing to this 'new law,' was the overall attitude of continental and English sovereigns who adopted a *laissez-faire* attitude toward the new merchant class in view of the increased tax revenues generated by them and the access to foreign goods that the merchants had obtained. The merchants were permitted to regulate their own affairs so long as they did not impinge upon local matters.[23]

Informal tribunals run by merchants sprang up to serve the common interests of medieval trade guildsmen. Initially guilds were founded for benevolent and caritative reasons; however, in time guilds developed into a major economic force within the towns in which they operated. So influential were some guilds that they were vested with complete control and monopoly over the manufacture and sale of certain goods by town governments via monopolistic trade charters. "We may notice the institution known as the Gild Merchant which seemingly was an association for the purpose amongst others of mutual arbitration. Members of the same gild were bound to bring their disputes before the gilds before litigating the matter elsewhere."[24] Kadens elaborates that guilds were designed to protect the membership from "biased courts and rapacious lords."[25] But guild influence was not necessarily limited to its peculiar bailiwick. In Florence, for example, the jurisdiction of guild courts was broadened to include any plea by its members against non-members so long as the complaint arose out of a guild transaction. The complaint need not have arisen from the guild hearing the case; it was sufficient, jurisdictionally, that the complaint related to the business of *any* guild in Florence.[26] Blackley writes, "The proof of this domination . . . can be seen in the twelfth-century appearance of the *Consules mercatorum*, the heads of the merchant guilds, who eventually were given control over the state judicial machinery, at least as far as it related to commercial matters."[27]

In addition to the system of guilds, merchant fairs had been established in England by the Romans, particularly along the borders.[28] And while the fairs were important for their formative value, it was the Magna Carta that gave English trade its first real impetus. Among the other rights enumerated within the Magna Carta were the commercial guarantees that, "All merchants shall have safety and security in coming into England and in staying and traveling through England, as well as by land as by water, to buy and sell without any unjust exactions, according to ancient and right customs. . . ."[29]

With the Magna Carta as their foundation, new institutions for trade blossomed in England including the Fair and the Staple Town, each of which became safe and reliable places to trade. The incipient law in these venues differed from that of the Continent whose commercial law had been developed within rich, powerful, self-governing and independent cities. There were no similar cities in England; hence, small towns and fairs relied on lordly charters for their development. Ultimately, however, in both England and on the Continent, commercial town centers developed alongside the fairs establishing both as integral parts in the machinery of Middle Age commerce.[30] The Statute of Staple illustrates the royal weight put behind these commercial fora.

> Edward, by the grace of God king of England and France and lord of Ireland, to all our sheriffs, mayors, bailiffs, ministers, and other faithful men . . . by the counsel and common assent of the said prelates, dukes, earls, barons, knights, and commons aforesaid, we have ordained and established the measures herein under written, to wit:—

First, that the staples of wool, leather, wool-fells and lead grown or produced within our kingdom and lands aforesaid shall be perpetually held in the following places: namely, for England at Newcastle-upon-Tyne, York, Lincoln, Norwich, Westminster, Canterbury, Chichester, Winchester, Exeter, and Bristol; for Wales at Carmarthen; and for Ireland at Dublin, Waterford, Cork, and Drogheda, and nowhere else. . . .[31]

These scattered locations were linked by generally accepted rules and customs that would govern their commercial activity. The amalgam of the rules and customs of the fairs combined with the rules of the sea became known, even in its day, as the Lex Mercatoria or the Law Merchant.[32] In fact, the Royal Statute of Staple expressly provided that "all merchants coming to the staple shall be ruled by the law merchant, of all things touching the staple, and not by the common law of the land, not by usage of cities, boroughs or other towns."[33]

Beside setting out specific places for the sale of commodities such as wool, the Royal Statute created Staple Courts in which the custom and usage of the Law Merchant was to be applied so as to "give courage to merchant strangers to come with their wares and merchandise into the realm." To insulate the Staple court from any incursion by the common law court, the Royal Statute declared, "In case our bench or common bench . . . come to the places where the said staples be [they shall not] have any cognizance there of that thing, which pertaineth to the cognizance of the mayor and ministers of the staple."[34] The Staple Town then became a respite for the merchantmen wherein they could find physical safety in a locale that operated continuously; in which they could find permanent residence; and in which they would incur lower commercial costs. The merchants "planted the Law Merchant enduringly on English soil. In the Staple Towns, the Law Merchant was a permanent resident of England."[35] Private law was given jurisdiction over commercial matters by none other than the King of England.

While academic literature focuses predominately on the English Law Merchant, the busiest fairs, in fact, were those of Champagne and Brie at which some seven major fairs per year were conducted. English and Flemish wool were brought to Champagne by the Florentines who had dyed the wool and sold it at the fair. From France came wine (some things never change); pots from Belgium; gold from the East; and jewels from Syria and Italy.

A French writer summarized the impact of the fairs from other than an English perspective.

> The influence of the fairs on our public law . . . is undeniable . . . the term fair is the equivalent of the term 'peace' . . . Thanks to the progress of the peace of the fairs . . . the communications of foreigner with foreigner become more certain; international relations multiply. . . . Little by little the last vestiges of primitive hostility disappear. . . . In the midst of the diversity of local law, the law of the great fairs everywhere remains the same in its essential features. This law is universal almost by the same right as the Canon Law. The jurisdiction of the fairs command obedience in all parts. And thus emerges the conception of the law merchant, outside and above civil statutes and local commercial usages.[36]

Once a fair was concluded, the merchants moved on but the fair bankers stayed behind having created bills of exchange, credit unions, and mechanisms for foreign exchange—each a permanent service available to the merchants upon their return to the fair.[37] And, indeed, what a contribution to the world of commerce were these instruments. While the common law created and relied on 'good title' as evidence of one's property rights, itinerant merchants could not inspect, demand, or inquire as to the proof of title of the goods they bought and sold. Recall the assumption of Lawyer Beawes above, that the merchant was a person who would not or could not engage in fraudulent dealing lest their reputation grievously suffer. On the assumption that the merchant would be dealing in good faith, those servicing the merchantmen developed bills of exchange through which goods were transferred without title searches and upon which a merchant could sue in his own name. This transaction stood in contrast to the common law,

> Whereas at Common Law no man's writing can be pleaded against him as his act unless the same be sealed and delivered in a suit between merchants, Bills of Lading and Bills of Exchange, but being tickets without seals, letter of advice, and credence, policies of assurance, assignations of debt, all of which are of no force at the Common Law are of good credit and force by the Law Merchant.[38]

Malynes found the Bill of Exchange even more praiseworthy, "The nature of a Bill of Exchange is so noble and excelling all other dealings between merchants that the proceedings therein are extraordinary and singular, and not subject to any prescription of law. . . ."[39] The Bill of Exchange and other negotiable instruments that were developed and perpetuated throughout the Law Merchant's world became so ingrained in the commercial dealings between merchants that their 'legality' was subsequently incorporated by the common law. Dispute resolution without the common law formalities of good title, consideration, and seal was, indeed, legally transformational.

Disputes over transactions at the Fair required a resolution device that was in tune with the requirements of the merchant class. Fair arbitrations filled the bill. The fairs were pro-business in their orientation and disputes were resolved by arbitrators out of the merchant class itself. The arbitrations, like the Law Merchant, were outside the judicial system of any nation, and amounted to self-regulation by the merchant class.[40] Merchants were, according to Bewes, particularly regarded before the laws of England such that "the common and Statute Laws of this Kingdom leave the Causes of Merchants in many cases to their particular laws."[41] Bewes not only described the domestic application of the Law Merchant but went on to explain its transnationality, as well.

> In former times it was conceived that those laws that were prohibitory against foreign goods did not bind the Merchant Stranger; but it has now been a long time since ruled otherwise. . . . in the Leagues that are now established between Nation and Nation . . . the English in France or any other Country in Amity are subject to the laws of that Country where they reside, so must the People of France, or any other kingdom, be subject to the Laws of England, when resident here."[42]

The transnational nature of the Law Merchant was especially beneficent for the foreign merchant who, if aggrieved, had been restricted to recovering civilly in whatever had been determined to be the appropriate court. The foreign merchant embarking for England no longer had to travel with oath takers to aid the merchant in sustaining his proof, if a suit at common law was required. And, even though the merchant's entourage might attest to the merchant's honesty, the merchant faced hostile judges with a penchant for supporting local citizens rather than an itinerant they might never again encounter.[43] In today's terms, we refer to this proclivity by domestic courts as local protectionism. It existed then and it exists now, as will be shown when we come to the chapters regarding Chinese arbitration.

As for how disputes between merchants came to be resolved, Malynes' commentary, *Consuedo, vel Lex Mercatoria*, provides the backdrop for dispute settlement of the day. After attempts at negotiation failed, the parties turned to, "Arbitrement, when both parties do make choice of honest men to end their causes, which is voluntary in their own power . . . and these men . . . give judgments by Awards, according to equity and good conscience observing the Custome of Merchants . . . with brevity and expedition."[44]

How easily Malynes forged the arbitral links of the Greeks and the Romans with the Law Merchant. Party autonomy, equity, speed, and brevity were all attributes of the Greek and Roman arbitral systems that now become the bases for dispute resolution between the merchants of the day.

Arbitrations at Fairs were designed to exercise jurisdiction over commercial disputes between merchants. The courts were manned by merchants with the mandate to render quick and informal justice. Carter observes, "The courts were popular judgment being given by those who knew the customs whether they were *prudhommes* at Oleron or Barcelona or *mercatores et marinarii* sitting on the Bristol quay or merchants in a Court of Piepoudre."[45] Arbitrations came to be referred to as *Piepoudre* or "Pie Powder" courts since, given the speed with which hearings were conducted, participants still had dust from the fairground on their feet (*pieds poudres*).[46]

Since speed in resolution of disputes was a necessary ingredient to the success of the fair courts, the civil procedure of the common law courts was truncated in order to accommodate the merchant. For example, the time for answering a summons by a defendant in a common law court was fifteen days. Bracton contrasts the Law Merchant, "Likewise, on account of persons who ought to have speedy justice, such as merchants, to whom speedy justice is administered in courts of pepoudrous . . . the time of summons is reduced."[47] So important was the requirement of speedy resolution that some panels were established to resolve disputes between the ebb and flow of the two tides, that is, in twenty-four hours from petition to award.[48] A dispute in the piepowder court of Colchester illustrates.

> The plaintiff sued for the recovery of a debt at 8 a.m. and the defendant was summoned to appear at 9 o'clock. He did not come at that hour and the serjeant was ordered to distrain him at 10 o'clock at

which hour he made default. Similar defaults were made against him at 11 and 12 o'clock. At a latter session judgment was given in favor of the plaintiff and appraisers were ordered to value the defendant's goods which had been attached. They made their report at 4 o'clock and the goods were delivered to the plaintiff.[49]

Swift justice was not only dispensed at the English fairs but the same principle was adhered to in the Champagne fairs, as well. The Champagne Guards spoke of "*bon droit et hastifs us des foires.*"[50] Speedy resolution was possible since the merchant was "*in loco proprio* as the fish in water, where he understandeth himself by the custom of merchants, according to which merchants' questions and controversies are determined."[51] Prof. Thayer elaborates, "The men with dusty feet who plied their trades from Champagne to St. Ives, from Wye to Nuremberg, had little concern with legal differences. Their disputes were settled with the same method and dispatch in the pie powder courts of England as in the fair courts of the continent. The voices of the consuls of the sea in Genoa and Barcelona found a ready echo in the maritime tribunals of Bristol and of Ipswich where the court sat on the beach and dispensed justice to passing mariners between the tides."[52] Not only were the judgments settled consistently and speedily, they were settled with finality. In the words of Lawyer Beawes, "The Chancery will not give relief against the Award of the Arbitrators, except it be for Corruption and where their Award is not strictly binding by the Rules of Law. . . ."[53]

Merchant panels were permitted to expeditiously decide disputes between commercial parties unencumbered by the procedural rigidity of the extant law. Cordes describes one of the earliest recordings of merchant arbitration. The law book *Fleta*, dating to the 1290s, explained the complexities of the writ of debt and the rigid distribution of proof between plaintiff and defendant. Exceptions were made, however, *in favorem mercatorum*. Plaintiff merchants were, by "royal grace" exempted from the law's evidentiary rigidity. Under certain circumstances, disputes between merchants could be resolved based on proof brought forward according to the law of the merchant, as opposed to the regulations in continental law. (". . . *quod parti affirmative secundum legem mercatorim erit probacio.*")[54]

This speed and informality stood in sharp contrast to the prevailing state of the law in England at the time. Sir John Fortescue described the English courts as being presided over by judges who worked three hours and once "haven taken their refreshments spend the rest of the day in the study of laws, reading the Holy Scripture, and other innocent amusements at their pleasure."[55] Sir Henry Spellman was less generous suggesting that judges, because of their appetite for the grape were given to drunkenness and did not sit for more than three hours "lest repletion should bring upon them drowsiness and oppression of spirits.[56] Contrast the lethargic common law courts with, for example, the fair at Champagne which met three times a day!

What we might modernly refer to as civil procedure was laboriously slow within the common law courts. Because the writ was the prime instigator for a common law action, expeditious judgments were not expected. Judgments were determined, in the first instance, on a strict interpretation of the then prevailing law and whether or not the law was in conformity with the original writ of the plaintiff. And given the formality of the writ system (recall the Roman formulary), the cost of the suit was heightened since lawyers were employed to craft actions and responses for the common law courts.

The merchant courts, on the other hand, because of their simplicity of form required no lawyers. Indeed, common law lawyers of the day were more like the Roman jurisconsulats who studied and focused on the legalities of their action rather than acting as advocates in court. "The lawyers . . . should be employed to settle points of law and not argue matters of fact, and to put a good face on a bad case." [57] This cumbersome, lengthy, expensive procedure within the Royal courts turned out to be one of the most important catalytic agents that gave cause to the rise of the Court of Chancery on one hand and increased the favor of the Law Merchant on the other.[58]

There can certainly be honest differences of opinion over which of those principles of the Law Merchant most defined its contribution to the world of non-judicial dispute resolution. This author falls down on the side of the Law Merchant's reliance on the principles of equity. The merchant courts were neither the first nor the last to render judgments based upon principles of equity. It might be recalled that the Greeks and Romans, especially the Romans, considered equity an abiding principle of dispute resolution. "Equity means to the Romans, fairness, right feeling, the regards for substantial as opposed to formal, and technical justice, the kind of conduct which would approve itself to a man of honor and conscience."[59]

But the Law Merchant went a step further. In England, it borrowed the principles of equity out of the competing judicial systems of the common law (The Chancery), the Admiralty (to some extent), and canon law courts. It then placed its trust in the hands of merchant arbitrators who were not lawyers to judge according to what was right and just. In one of legal history's more remarkable forms of private justice, peers were called upon to render judgment when disputes between other peers occurred.

Perhaps the most famous court of equity to have ever graced the legal stage was the English High Court of Chancery. The similarities between the Law Merchant and the Chancery portray the support one provided the other and the reliance on equity that was beginning to permeate the common law legal system. Both the Chancery and the Law Merchant were swift in their proceedings. Both looked to intent rather than form; in the Chancery, for example, the requirement of seal had been dispensed with. Both the Chancery and the Law Merchant accepted the notion of contractual assignment, with the Law Merchant taking this notion to a higher plane by permitting the "negotiability" of such instruments as Bills of Exchange. Neither the Chancery nor the Law Merchant considered time as of the essence in a contract; and in both venues the bona fide purchaser was protected.[60] Sanborn's comments reflect the author's view. "There is nothing more characteristic of the medieval law of commerce than its spirit of equity. . . . This principle of substantial equity runs all through the *lex mercatoria* in every place and in every period."[61] Indeed, the Roman principle of *ex aqueo et bono* pervaded the mercantile world from Bergano to the English Admiralty to the statutes of Marseilles, "*Pour juger et decider sommairement tous procès et différends entre marchands, sans s'atteindre aux subtilités des lois et ordonnances.*"[62] The Consuls of Bologna decreed that merchant judges should decide *secundum quod aequum crediderint* (following what they believe is fair) and in Venice, the arbitrator was to look first at custom and failing that he was directed to use *secundam bonam conscientiam* (follow good conscience).[63]

The Law Merchant's concept of equity stood in stark comparison to the early common law that relied more on *outcome* than proof of facts. Tragically, common law outcomes were often determined by the perjury of compurgation, or by ordeal or wager of law. Prof. Baker characterized this 'judicial' process as judgment preceding truth, "once it was adjudged that one of the parties should swear or perform a test there was no further decision to make except whether he had passed it."[64] When juxtaposed with the machinations that took place in the courts of the realm, the attractiveness of the merchant law's timely and decisive decisions is obvious.

By way of review, the Law Merchant was transnational in its scope, its principal source for the resolution of commercial disputes, mercantile custom. The process of dispute resolution was often superintended by the merchants themselves rather than by professional judges. The Law Merchant's dispute resolution procedure was summary, speedy and informal. The overriding arbitral principle was Equity—*bona fides* in the medieval sense of fairness.[65]

It was noted in Chapter Two that the Roman law's imprimatur of a private arbitral system provided the foundation for the subsequent development of ecclesiastical courts. Arguably, it was the binding effect of equity by which Roman arbitration, private ecclesiastical courts, and the merchant courts became linked and, subsequently, caused the infusion of equity into mercantile arbitral decisions.[66] On that point, Kerr would concur. Before the merchant law, canonical equity rather than the Roman formality was more commonly influential. Roman Law was cumbersome and dilatory. From the tenets of canonical equity, good faith and mutual confidence found roots in the Law Merchant, thus, Law Merchant procedure more closely resembled those of canonical rather than Roman courts.[67]

While this chapter is not intended to provide a full blown analysis of the legal *gestalt* of the Law Merchant, the contributions made by this body of law to subsequent legal and arbitral eras were so substantial that their import might be lost unless those contributions were separately— though briefly—enumerated so that the Law Merchant's lush legal landscape can be viewed and admired. In addition to the notions of speed, equity, summary proceedings, and negotiable instruments, other features of the Law Merchant contrasted it with the common law and hence expanded the horizons of the law.

- Notarial attestation on documents was subordinated to the 'good faith' dealings between merchants.
- Oral evidence could contradict written evidence in a fair court.
- Merchant journals could be introduced as evidence.
- Property in the *res* passed to the purchaser without delivery.

- Unlike Roman law, partners were agents of the partnership and could bind a partnership even when a partner was acting alone.
- Parol partnerships were sufficient.
- The limited partnership was introduced.
- The law of agency permitted an agent to bind his master and a third party if the agent were acting on the master's behalf.
- There was no prescriptive acquisition of property between merchants.[68]

Admittedly, some of the contributions listed above were not exclusively derived from English and Continental customs and usage. Agency, for example, can be found in Islamic law well predating the Law Merchant, as can the prohibition against the prescriptive acquisition of property. Nonetheless, the list is sufficiently impressive. The *Lex Mercatoria* was not, however, without its shortcomings.

Perhaps the first deficiency of the Law Merchant is the question of whether the Law Merchant was, in fact, law. The fact that this question is a) raised and b) is a matter of some debate, in and of itself demonstrates an inherent deficiency.

As we will see, the Law Merchant has been variously viewed by scholars as a form of customary international law, or by positivists as on par with legislatively enacted law; and it has been characterized as no law at all.

Viewing the Law Merchant in an aspirational context and basing its legality on custom, Malynes wrote, "I have Intilted the Book [on the Law Merchant] according to the ancient name of Lex Mercatoria and not Ius Mercatorum because it is customary law approved by the Authority of all Kingdoms and Commonwealths, and not a Law established by the Soveraignty of any Prince."[69] In the same vein one hundred years or so later, Lord Mansfield held that the Law Merchant "is not the law of a particular country, but the general law of nations."[70] The Law Merchant has also been described as a sort of "rebirth of the old *jus gentium* of the Mediterranean"[71] and "a kind of *Jus Gentium*."[72]

On the other hand, Carter was far more a positivist, an Austinian perhaps, when it came to the Law Merchant declaring,

> [W]e can arrive at an opinion . . . that there was a definite body of mercantile law, slightly affected perhaps by local variations, which

was recognized in this country [England] and in the ports of Europe . . . supported by royal authority. It really was law and it really was International."[73]

Carter evidences his view by pointing to a Chancery case wherein a foreigner had his goods stolen at Southampton. The Chancellor held that the foreigner should be permitted to sue in England according to the law of nature that is the merchant law. The Law Merchant, the Chancellor averred, was universal law throughout the world.

> *C'est suit est pris un merchant alien que est venu par safe conduit ici; et il n'est tenus de suer seloniques le ley del terre a tarier le trial de xii homes et autres solempnites del ley de terre, mes doit suer icy et sera determine solonques le ley de Nature en le Chancery, viz. est ley Marchant que est ley universal par tout le monde.*[74]

Burdick would concur with Carter, writing that the law of the merchants was a true body of law "as distinct from the law administered by the common law courts, as was the civil or the canon law. It was part of the unwritten law of the realm. . . ."[75]

Ewart, however, specifically and personally responded to Burdick's claims with his own characterization of the Law Merchant, "As against this I contend that there was nothing but a heterogeneous lot of loose undigested customs which it is impossible to dignify with the name of a body of law and [relying on Mansfield] its rules are not traceable to any foreign or extraneous body of laws."[76]

Does it really matter whether the Law Merchant was, in fact, law? In a rather understated fashion, Thayer hit the proverbial nail on the head, "The ordinary undertakings of merchants became binding because they were intended to be binding."[77] To the merchant at St. Ives or Champagne, it mattered only that his dispute be quickly and fairly resolved. For the disputants, it was irrelevant whether the *jus gentium* was undergoing a rebirth or whether the Chancery viewed his cause as actionable under the laws of nature. What mattered is what mattered. Prof. Baker, like Prof. Thayer, gets to the core of the essence of the Law Merchant when he described it as

> much a corpus of mercantile practice or commercial law. . . . an expeditious procedure especially adapted for the needs of men who could not tarry for the common law. It was essentially negative. Like the

justice of the Chancery, it offered an exemption from or a short circuit through the delays of due process as embodied in the forms of action and jury system of the two benches (Baker is referring to the King's Bench and the Court of Common Pleas).[78]

Whether the Law Merchant was or was not law does not deprive us of the heritage it passed on to the modern arbitral world. In fact, as we shall see later, the Law Merchant may be undergoing a renaissance of sorts.

While it later became incorporated into continental civil codes and into the common law, the medieval Law Merchant was crafted for and limited its access to a special class of persons: the merchants. It was not a common law applicable to all. If it was to work, better its scope be narrow. "The first step in creating a successful Law Merchant is to have some limitations on membership in the club. The greater the homogeneity in knowledge and capacity, the easier it is for any substantive rules to work."[79]

Within the context of the day, such specialization would have raised few eyebrows. After all, there were the Royal courts which dispensed the King's justice but were available only to those who could afford a writ; there was, of course, the Chancery in London, which, while dispensing equity, was remote to most; the Admiralty judged matters concerning the high sea and merchants; the Star Chamber had its property expertise; and ecclesiastical courts dealt with God's business. The merchant law was different from the purported common law in that it was limited to a discreet populace and was narrow in its scope. In the earliest English treatise on the *Lex Mercatoria* translated from the Latin, the separation and restrictive nature of the common law and the merchant law were framed. "The law merchant is understood to come out of the market . . . from which such laws arise. . . ." and within those markets the common law was not sought "unless the owners and parties pleading prefer to withdraw and prosecute pleas in said places by appeals to the common law. . . ."[80] The default for a commercial dispute appears to be arbitration under the merchant law. The parties might pursue common law litigation only if they agreed to do so.

To some extent, whether the Law Merchant was law or not is relevant for the determination as to whether decisions rendered under the Law Merchant were arrived at via adjudication or arbitration. Arbitration is a better view since decisions under the Law Merchant were typically applicable only to the instant case. The award, once rendered, was neither relied upon nor looked to as a guide for deciding a similar dispute, should one arise. In fact, awards of the day while in writing and timely gave the parties no reasoning behind the award. Beawes explains why: "Arbitrators should give their Award without entering into Particulars, or assigning their Reasons for it, as this might expose them to a Chancery suit from a dissatisfied Party."[81]

No matter, usage and custom were the forces that drove the arbitration, not what one fair judge had decided the previous day, month, or year. Fair decisions, unlike arbitration decisions outside the fair, were typically rendered orally. There was no written record of the proceeding of the fair court lending credence to the notion that fair law was arbitral "law" and not part of the common or continental law wherein proceedings were memorialized and came to be relied upon by royal courts as guides to their future decision making.

If litigated, the merchant law, even though practiced on common law territory, was viewed by the common law courts as foreign law. Prof. Thayer confirms, "It seems in a way almost solecistic to speak of comparative law in connection with the law merchant. . . ."[82] The law merchant, said Lord Mansfield, "is not the law of a particular country, but the general law of nations: *'Non erit alia lex Romae alia Athenis; alia nunc alia posthac; sed et apud omnes gentes et omni tempore una eademque Lex obtinebit'*—Neither Rome nor Athens had any other law, neither today nor previously; but in all countries and at all times the same rule would did [sic] apply."[83] Hence, should a commercial case find its way into a common law court, a choice of law question inevitably came before the presiding judge. Recall the incident above related by Carter regarding the foreign merchant whose goods were stolen. Beawes, likewise, described the incident. From the perspective of a choice of law question, the incident is worth revisiting. The merchant stranger first made suit before the King's Privy Council for bales of silk that had been feloniously taken from him. Initially moved that the matter should be decided under the common law, "it was answered by the Lord Chancellor that as this Suit was brought by a Merchant, he was not bound to sue according to the Law of the Land."[84] The details of the dispute are mundane but what is interesting is the fact that *three* courts were involved in a choice of law question: Privy Council, Chancery, and a law merchant tribunal to which the Chancellor ultimately gave leave for suit.

The merchant arbitrators had no enforcement mechanism available to them outside the four walls of their jurisdiction. The voluntary and participatory nature of the Law Merchant process contributed to its acceptability and, resultantly, its self-enforcement. Should a merchant fail to accept a decision made at a fair or staple court, what was tantamount to economic capital punishment was meted out: ostracism.[85] The reputation that Beawes described as so valued would be tarnished, typically, beyond repair.

Earlier in this chapter, we wrote of the executory process whereby a dispute was adjudicated in a fair court and settlement made within the day. However, there were occasions when not all ran to form, as when the losing party chose not cooperate. In those circumstances, the Mayor of the fair town selected a posse of twelve or more men to carry out the judgment.

> And if perchance then [one] finds resistance of hand or body, at once the hue and cry is raised over such resistor or resistors, and they are attached by their bodies and are kept safely in the prison of the King if it be his market or in the prison of the lord if it be another's.[86]

In today's terms, imagine Silicon Valley Company *A* securing a judgment against Silicon Valley Company *B* who does not *immediately* satisfy the arbitral judgment. Company *A* proceeds to obtain the assistance of the Mayor of San Jose who, along with a coterie of Deputy Sheriffs, invades Company *B's* premises and if the CEO of the Company gives the Sheriffs any problem, the CEO is hauled off to the Santa Clara County jail. While the winning party might find delight and glee in arbitral justice's swift sword, the losing party would find no solace in the prison's equivalent to the arbitral sword: a plastic eating knife.

Lest one think that the Law Merchant has faded into the recent legal past, one need only look to the substantial expansion in the use of international commercial arbitration over the past decades. Admittedly, there are controversies surrounding the existence of a modern day *Lex Mercatoria*. A persuasive argument can be made that transnational norms possess no legal force in the absence of contractual incorporation, national statutes or international conventions.[87]

On the other hand, national legislation legitimizing and supporting the power and autonomy of the arbitral 'court' has seen a recrudescence in most of the modern commercial world. In what would have been unheard of decades ago, arbitration tribunals now regularly limit state sovereignty in matters commercial.[88] Prof. Milenkovic-Kerkovic[89] has ascribed the following elements to the modern *Lex Mercatoria* highly reminiscent of the attributes we discovered in our exploration of the medieval *Lex Mercatoria*:

1. Transnationality
2. Standard form of contracts
3. Trade Usage as a source of law
4. Arbitration
5. Codification

In those circumstances wherein the parties choose not to have their dispute arbitrated under a national law, the standards by which an arbitrator might decide the case before her include the custom and trade usage of the commercial world in which the parties are engaged or on an unspecified predeterminant that the arbitrator thinks is fair and just. Powell suggests, "As the boundaries of the common law set fast, leaving outside them many significant areas and causes of dispute, positive stimulus was given to the elaboration of existing equitable resorts in order to fill the gaps and these in turn take on an institutional form of their own (as with the equitable court of chancery)."[90] Lando would, undoubtedly, concur finding arbitrators in Continental Europe increasingly applying a sort of law merchant to those international disputes to fill in the lacunae created by mandatory national law.[91]

A recast Law Merchant has also found its way into modern, formal regimes. For example, Article 28 (1) of the UNCITRAL model law permits the parties to choose "the rules of law," by which the arbitral tribunal will make its decision, clearly implying that a form of Law Merchant is available to the arbitrator for her use. The Austrian Supreme Court, the English Arbitration Act, and the English Court of Appeal have each, in its own fashion, given support for the use of the Law Merchant in an arbitration proceeding.[92] The modern Law Merchant was further impressed with legitimacy. The *UNIDROIT Principles of International Commercial Contracts 2004* maintained that the mercantile principles may be applied "when the parties have agreed that their contract be governed by general principles of law, the lex mercatoria or the like."

How an award rendered under Law Merchant principles would or could be enforced is still a matter of some debate among arbitral scholars. Enforceability, however, might be a secondary consideration for those parties who select the Law Merchant as the regime under which to have their disputes settled. Avoidance of the legal uniqueness or peculiarities of a national law(s) might be primary. Or the parties, by using the Law Merchant, might be seeking to avoid certain substantive and procedural hurdles as, for example, common law precedent or civil law formalities. Time will tell. In time, of course, the staple courts and fair courts died out and merchants had to rely on national courts. The merchant courts then came full circle—initially crafted to navigate around the common law courts, the merchants ultimately had to steer their complaints back to the courts they had so assiduously averted.[93] The transition was eased through the genius of the great Scottish barrister and Lord Chief Justice of England, Lord Mansfield, whose intellectual prowess and perseverance led to the successful incorporation of merchant law into the then existing commercial and common laws.[94] How this was done and how the arbitral chain was developed even further will be left for the next chapter.

## Analysis

The arbitral chain progressively extended from the Greeks to the Romans to the Law Merchants. The arbitral chain forged in these three eras contributed arbitral features that have been carried into the today's modern, progressive, commercial arbitration world.

The attributes of Greek arbitral concepts, the discipline of Roman arbitral formality and finality, and the Law Merchant's speed of resolution have become expectations of modern day arbitration. It seems a bit unfortunate how little is known by modern arbitral practitioners that the speedy hearing they have come to expect can be traced to Law Merchant arbitrations that began in the commercial settings of medieval fair grounds for merchantmen briefly in port.

The emphasis on good faith, equity, and practicality as the essential attributes of the Greek, Roman, and Law Merchant arbitral worlds represent archetypal characteristics sought after in the practice of modern day arbitration. Unfortunately, as arbitrations take on more of the common law model of legal pugilism, the emphasis on the Law Merchant's good faith, speed and practicality may be severely compromised.

Unlike the Roman reliance on process and writ, the reliances of the Law Merchant were custom and practice in the *relevant* trade out of which the dispute arose. This commercial expertise gave the parties great relief since in Law Merchant arbitrations, the disputants were before merchant-judges operating under arbitral standards reserved exclusively for them. In addition, reliance on custom and usage meant that the expensive and complex civil procedures engaged in by the Royal courts were unnecessary, hence eliminated, for merchant disputes. Reflecting the Law Merchant's legacy, modern arbitral disputants may select as much or as little procedural rigidity as they choose by which to settle their dispute.

One can easily connect the dots from medieval merchantmen to modern arbitral participants who would both contend that arbitrations work best when a person familiar with the commercial workings of a trade or industry arbitrates a dispute between members of the same commercial class and the decision of the expert arbitrator once rendered is final, save for any misconduct on the part of the arbitrator.

The intent behind Greek and Roman law was the peaceful resolution of commercial disputes. The Law Merchant took this concept one step further. The *Lex Mercatoria's* purpose was not only dispute resolution but also the promotion of honorable commerce. In that endeavor, the merchantmen of the day created or advanced commercial instruments that are still in use today, yet whose genealogy is neither considered nor honored. To its credit, the *Lex Mercatoria* often made good sense in terms of its origin and purpose, and often makes good sense in today's terms as well.

Would that this writer possessed the eloquence of Prof. Goodyear when he summed up the Law Merchant. Rather than a synthesis of his words, we expose them fully.

> Today motor buses and lorries thread their devious but steady way over the trade routes of the Moslems and Sicilians; huge ocean liners cut the main where once Phoenician galleys glided; the Hanseatic League and the castles of sturdy Rhenish knights no longer rule the world's markets; international fairs are but a memory and a tradition; while the guilds and their methods remain only a fountainhead for the inquiring student of history; and yet despite all these mutations there survives the law merchant—a monument to the mind of man for generations. Like the beautiful coral, it grows and appears ever new and fresh,

drawing its life from the surging tides of life about it and supported by the substantial precedents of the generations that gave it birth.[95]

# Notes

1. C. Kerr, *The Origin and Development of the Law Merchant*, 15 VA. L. REV. 350, 350 (1928-1929).
2. F.C.T. Tudsberry, *Law Merchant and the Common Law*, 34 L.Q. REV. 392, 394 (1918).
3. See generally, ROGER FISHER AND WILLIAM URY, GETTING TO YES: NEGOTIATING AGREEMENT WITHOUT GIVING IN, (Bruce Patton ed., Penguin Books 2 ed. 1991) and Michelle Maiese, *Negotiation, available* at www.beyond intractability.org/essay/negotiation/ visited on July 19, 2006.
4. F. Juenger, *The Lex Mercatoria and Private International Law*, 60 La. L. REV. 1133, 1134-5 (2000).
5. A.T. Carter, *The Early History of the Law Merchant in England*, 17 L.Q. REV. 232, 240 (1901).
6. C. Donahue, *Medieval and Early Modern Lex Mercatoria*, 5 CHI. J. INT'L L. 21, 21 (2004).
7. G. Harriss, *Political Society and the Growth of Government in Late Medieval England*, 138 PAST AND PRESENT, *1*, 28-57 (1993)
8. *Id.*, (Harriss).
9. A. Mangels, *Are the Roots of the Modern 'Lex Mercatoria' Really Medieval?* 65(3) SOUTHERN ECONOMIC JOURNAL, 427-450 (1999).
10. E. Kadens, *The Empirical and Theoretical Underpinnings of the Law Merchant*, 5 CHI. J. INT'L L. 39, 44-47 (2004).
11. W. BEAWES, LEX MERCATORIA REDIVIVA OR THE MERCHANT'S DIRECTORY, at 31 (London: J. Rivington 1771). The quotes from this source contain Beawes' original spelling and punctuation. The medial "s" was not used since the usual substituted character is the symbol for integral " + " which this writer chose not to use.
12. Kerr, at 352.
13. Mangels, at 47-50.
14. Kerr, at 353.
15. H. Berman & C. Kaufman, *The Universality of International Commercial Law*, 19 HARV. INT'L L.J. 224, 225 (1978).
16. *Id.* at 225.
17. A. Chase, *Notes on Lawyers and Commerce*, 29 NOVA L. REV. 201, 205 (2005).

18. G. Baron, *Do the UNIDROIT Principles of International Commercial Contracts form a new lex mercatoria?* http://www.cisg.law.pace.edu/cisg/biblio/baron.html#b1 (visited October 2, 2006).

19. T. Milenkovic-Kerkovic, *Origin, Development and Main Features of the New Lex Mercatoria*, facta.junis.ni.ac.yu/facta/eao/eao97/eao97-10.pdf (visited February 1, 2005).

20. Milenkovic-Kerkovic, at 89.

21. H. Pirenne, *Economic and Social History of Medieval Europe* 93, 94 cited in W. Jones, *Merchants, The Law Merchant, and Recent Missouri Sales Cases*, 1956 WASH. U. L.Q. 397 (1956).

22. G. Malynes, *Lex Mercatoria*, p. 3, ed. 1636 cited in F.C.T. Tudsberry, *Law Merchant and the Common Law*, 34 L.Q. REV. 392, 394 (1918).

23. B. Cremades & S. Plehn, *The New Lex Merxatoria and The Harmonization of The Laws of International Commercial Transactions*, 2 B.U. INT'L L.J. 317, 318 (1984).

24. Quote cited by Wolaver at 134 simply as English Legal Institutions (1899) 268.

25. Kadens, at 51.

26. F. SANBORN, ORIGINS OF THE EARLY ENGLISH MARITIME AND COMMERCIAL LAW, 147 (W.S. Hein 2002).

27. F.D. Blackley, *The English Law Merchant*, 1 ALTA. L. REV. 263, 264 (1955-1961).

28. Kerr, at 359.

29. *Magna Carta or The Great Charter of King John Granted June 15th, A.D. 1215, In the Seventeenth Year of His Reign* cited by Kerr at 359.

30. Sanborn, at 326.

31. *Ordinance and Statute of the Staple* (1353) available at http://www.constitution.org/sech/sech_062.txt.

32. F. Burdick, *What is the Law Merchant*, 2 COLUM. L. REV. 470, 478-82 (1902); Kerr, at 356-61.

33. Burdick, at 473.

34. *Id.*

35. R. Stewart, *Arbitration and Insurance Without the Common Law*, Volume 11, No. 3 ARIAS-U.S. QUARTERLY, 10-11, (Third Quarter 2004).

36. M. Huvelin, cited in W.A. BEWES, THE ROMANCE OF THE LAW MERCHANT, at 137-8, (Sweet & Maxwell 1923).

37. M. McCloskey, *Medieval Merchants and Artisans*, www.florilegum.org (visited on October 1, 2006).

38. Carter, at 242 cites this comment to Sir John Davis' *Concerning Impositions* without further attribution.

39. *Id.,* at 242 citing Malynes *Lex Mercatoria* at 74.

40. Burdick, at 472-5.

41. BEWES, at 35.

42. *Id.*
43. Kadens, at 46-7.
44. G. Malynes, *Consuedo vel, Lex Mercatoria*, cited in L. Fortier, *International E-Commerce Dispute Resolution*, 19 ALTERNATIVES TO HIGH COST LITIG. 23, 25 (2001).
45. Carter, at 232, 236.
46. Burdick, at 471 points out the confusion over the etymology of this term. Blackstone accepted the usual etymology whereas Coke held that the term came from the French *pied puldreaux* which in Old French denotes *a pedlar* (one who peddles, a low tradesman).
47. Bracton, *De Legibus Angilicae* l.v.f. 334 a cited by Burdick at 470.
48. John Mo, *International Commercial Law*, sec. [1.9] (LexisNexus, 1st ed. 1997).
49. C. Gross, *Selected Cases Concerning The Law Merchant* (S.S) I .xxv-xxvi cited in F.D. Blackley, *The English Law Merchant*, 1 ALTA. L. REV. 263, 266 (1955-1961).
50. SANBORN, at 193.
51. Burdick, at 474.
52. Philip Thayer, *Comparative Law and The Law Merchant*, 6 Brook. L. REV. 139, 141 (1936-7).
53. BEAWES, at 307.
54. Albrecht Cordes, *The Search for a Medieval Lex Mercatoria*, Ox. U. COMPARATIVE L. FORUM 5 available at ouclf.iuscomp.org (visited January 31, 2006).
55. Burdick, at 472 citing Fortescue without citation.
56. H. SPELLMAN, SPELLMAN'S ORIGINAL TERMS, (1614) Sec. V. Chap. 1 cited by Burdick at 472.
57. SANBORN, at 196-7.
58. Excerpted from the writer's English Legal History class notes—Oxford University (2004).
59. BRYCE'S STUDIES IN HIST. AND JUR. at 581 cited as such in J. Ewart, *What is the Law Merchant?* 3 COL. L. REV. 135, 149 (1903).
60. Anonymous, 2 LAW COUCH 2 at 3 (1921-1922).
61. SANBORN, at 195.
62. *Id.*
63. Leon Trakman, *The Evolution of the Law Merchant*, 12 J. MAR. L. & COM. 1, 10 (1980-1981)
64. J. H. BAKER, AN INTRODUCTION TO ENGLISH LEGAL HISTORY, 4-6, (Butterworth's 2002).
65. Milenkovic-Kerkovic, at 89.
66. Paul Sayre, *Development of Commercial Arbitration Law*, 37 Yale L.J. 595, 597 (1927-8).
67. Kerr, at 353.

68. W. Bewes, THE ROMANCE OF THE LAW MERCHANT, 19-25 (Sweet & Maxwell 1923).

69. Malynes, *Consuetdo*, cited by L. Trakman, *From the Medieval Law Merchant to E-Merchant Law*, 53 U. TORONTO L.J. 265, 271 (2003).

70. *Luke v. Lyde*, 2 Burr. 883, 887 (K.B. 1759) cited in Philip Thayer, *Comparative Law and The Law Merchant*, 6 BROOK. L. REV. 139, 139 (1936-7)

71. F. Juenger, *The Lex Mercatoria and Private International Law*, 60 LA. L. REV. 1133, 1134 (2000)

72. *The Law Merchant*, 2 Law Coach 2 (1921-22). Article published without attribution.

73. A.T. Carter, *The Early History of the Law Merchant in England* 17 L.Q. REV 232, 240 (1901)

74. *The Carrier's Case*, Y.B. 13 Edw. IV (1473) at 9 cited by Carter at 240.

75. F. Burdick, *at* 470, 478.

76. J. Ewart, *What is the Law Merchant?*, 3 COLUM. L. REV. 135, 138 (1903).

77. P. Thayer, *Comparative Law and the Law Merchant*, 6 BROOK. L. REV. 135, 148 (1937-1937).

78. J. Baker, *Law Merchant and the Common Law Before 1700*, 38 CAMBRIDGE L.J. 295, 301 (1979)

79. R. Epstein, *Reflections on the Historical Origins and Economic Structure of the Law Merchant*, 5 CHI. J. INT'L L. 1, 17 (2005-5).

80. *The Little Red book of Bristol* Chapter 2 cited in P. Teetor, *England's Earliest Treatise on the Law Merchant*, 6 AM. J. LEGAL HIST. 178, 181-2 (1962)

81. BEAWES, at 308.

82. Thayer, at 139.

83. Cordes, at p.2.

84. BEAWES, at 35.

85. J. BARRETT, A HISTORY OF ALTERNATE DISPUTE RESOLUTION 16 (Jossey-Bass 2004).

86. *Little Red Book* available in Teetor at 196.

87. W. Tetley, *Mixed Jurisdictions: Common Law vs. Civil Law*, available at http://www.unidroit.org/english/publications/review/articles/1999-3.htm (visited October 2, 2006).

88. O. Lando, *The Law Applicable to the Merits of the Dispute*, in P. SARCEVIC, ESSAYS ON INTERNATIONAL COMMERCIAL ARBITRATION, ¶ III A. (Springer 1989).

89. Tamara Milenkovic-Kerkovic, *Origin, Development and Main features of the New Lex Mercatoria*, Vol.1, No 5, FACTA UNIVERSITATIS, 87-91 (1997).

90. Edward Powell, *Settlement of Disputes by Arbitration in Fifteenth-Century England* 40 LAW AND HISTORY REVIEW, Vol. 2, No. 1 (Spring, 1984).

91. Lando, ¶ III A and B.

92. O. Lando, *Some Features of the Law of Contract in the Third Millennium*, *available at* www.frontpage.cbs.dk/law/commission_on_european_contract_law/literature/lando01.htm (visited October 10, 2006).
93. Burdick, at 479.
94. *id.*
95. Jacob Goodyear, *The Romance of the Law Merchant,* 34 Dick. L. Rev 218, 225 (October 1929 to June 1930).

# Chapter Four

# The Arbitral Chain and the Common Law

In previous chapters, we examined the linkage connecting Greek, Roman, and Law Merchant arbitration. We now explore whether the linkage established extended into the arbitration of post-medieval England and, subsequently, arbitration within the United States.

Notwithstanding the widespread adoption of commercial arbitration during the era of the Law Merchant, England began to retreat from that arbitral acceptance in the late Middle Ages. Perhaps the arbitral chain was to be broken in view of the pronounced decline in the effectiveness of commercial arbitration, especially in Great Britain and, later, within the United States. "A watershed year in the history of arbitration was 1504, when a statute was passed prohibiting the guilds from barring suits at law. This statute initiated a trend that was only later reversed by the *English Arbitration Act* of 1889."[1] The once vaunted autonomy of private arbitration tribunals was eroding and, as a result, the tribunals became increasingly subject to the jurisdiction and oversight of national courts. But why? Given the success of commercial arbitration during the era of the Law Merchant, why did arbitration regress in its usage and see its regression come about at the hands of England's courts?

It was a highly competitive time for English courts during the period when the common law was developing. The courts contended with each other over jurisdictional matters and, generally, for their 'place in the world.'[2] Royal Law courts consisting of the King's Bench, the Court of Common Pleas, and the Exchequer, coexisted with ecclesiastical courts, manor courts, and the conciliar courts (Chancery, Star Chamber, Admiralty)—and, of course, the fair and staple courts of the Law Merchant. The King's Bench was especially aggressive in seeking legal business since cases meant fees from which the justices derived much of their income.[3] While merchants had the freedom to seek redress through various avenues, as their fairs became less and less available, they tended to migrate toward the royal courts, finding them well capable of resolving merchant disputes. An added benefit to the merchants was the realization that as they utilized the royal courts, a commercial law "database" within those courts was being built up, as well.

Competition among the various courts, ultimately, meant choosing sides. And so, the common law courts came to support Parliament over Royal Courts by championing Parliament as THE *uber* common law court. Cleverly, the reasoning of the common law courts went along these lines: for Parliament to be superior, it required something over which to be superior and Parliament's superiority was to be realized by what was, in reality, the willing yet chary subordination of the common law courts.[4] We shall see later in this chapter, in *Vynior's Case*,[5] a reflection of this newly formed alliance between Parliament and the national courts.

Concurrent with the jostling taking place between the various courts, the judiciary's heightened involvement and oversight over the commercial arbitral process recrudesced as national courts came, more and more, to regard the *Lex Mercatoria* as a threat to judicial prerogatives.[6] So, through the kluge of legal commercial equality, the privileged status afforded to merchants during the medieval era virtually ended as merchant courts became more and more integrated into the national court system. Trakman illustrates.

> By restricting the dynamic use of trade custom in various ways, the English common law courts precluded resort to the pliable framework of the Law Merchant. Either they refused to admit custom into the legal system in any form whatever, or custom was required to satisfy onerous tests of admissibility before it was received into English law. . . . custom had to comply with the rules of positive law. It had to be truly "ancient" in its origins in order to be admitted in law, and it had to be consistently practiced, notwithstanding the changing environment of business itself . . . In this way, the Law Merchant became rigid as post-medieval English judges sought to integrate the Law Merchant into the established confines of a centralized common law.[7]

This development occurred rather gradually in England in view of the continuing popularity among merchants of self-regulated dispute resolution. The popularity of merchant arbitration during the Tudor reign (1485-1603) is illustrated, "[T]he Privy Council, a major forum for commercial matters, solved its merchant cases by reference to merchant arbitrators."[8] In fact, a variety of English courts continued to refer commercial disputes to arbitrators or, alternatively, often had commercial cases heard before juries composed of merchants.

Even so, the innovations developed by the Law Merchant were blended into the national court system without retaining any of the Law Merchant's distinctiveness. The Law Merchant was, over time, judicially morphed.[9] Adding proverbial fuel into the proverbial fire, Lord Mansfield declared, in *Pillans v. van Mierop* that the rules of the Law Merchant were questions of law to be decided by the courts rather than questions of custom to be proved by the parties. Mansfield declared, "The law of merchants and the law of the land, is the same: a witness cannot be admitted, to prove the law of merchants. We must consider it as a point of law."[10]

Further complicating the matters of the day was the need to enforce arbitration awards since commercial relationships had became more distant, impersonal and complex. The ability of commercial parties to fashion agreements to arbitrate future disputes as a way of easing commerce found less and less favor in the English courts. "The English courts were of little assistance. The English courts, while giving full effect to agreements to submit controversies to arbitration after they had ripened into arbitrators' awards, would . . . do little or nothing to prevent or make irksome the breach of such agreements when they were still executory."[11] The 'poster child' demonstrating the English courts' antipathy toward the validity of arbitration agreements containing an agreement by the parties to arbitrate future disputes is *Vynior's Case*.[12]

Plaintiff Vynior sought, via an action in debt, against defendant Wilde to obtain judgment on a one hundred pound bond plus twenty pounds in damages. It was rather commonplace at the time for a penalty bond to be posted by an obligor who, if he failed to perform, defaulted his bond to the party for whom the bond was provided. Recall in Chapter Two the discussion of the Roman practice of arbitration *ex compromisso* whereby one party was required to post a bond (a *poena*) that would be subject to default if the obligor failed to arbitrate. In no small measure, this is similar to the bond requirement posted by defendant Wilde in *Vynior's Case*.

Defendant Wilde, it was alleged, refused to arbitrate a dispute between Vynior and Wilde under an agreement calling for a named arbitrator who would, "rule, order, adjudge, arbitrate, and finally determine all Matters, Suits, Controversies, Debates, Griefs, and Contentions heretofore moved and stirred, and now depending between the said Parties."[13] Wilde demurred and Lord Coke found for Vynior. Wilde was liable on his bond.

But Lord Coke quite inexplicably went on, in *obiter dictum*, to pontificate his thesis regarding the revocability of an arbitration agreement, a pronouncement that lived on long after the good Lord himself. Coke wrote, "[A]lthough William Wilde, the defendant, was bound in bond to stand to, abide, observe, etc. the rule, etc. of arbitration, etc., yet he might countermand it, for one cannot by his act make such authority, power, or warrant not countermandable which is by the law or of its own nature countermandable."[14]

Since it was the parties who conferred authority on the arbitrators, the reasoning of the courts went, the authority conferred could, subsequently, become authority withdrawn. Why the thinking of *Vynior* persisted is not entirely clear when viewed through the lens of public policy. But it did and was expanded in *Hide v. Petit*, a late seventeenth century case wherein even a court referrral to arbitration was held to be revocable.[15] Professor von Mehren suggests simply that, "the argument became that public policy required judicial settlement of disputes."[16] More likely, the predicate put forth in *Vynior* gave the English courts shelter by which to solidify their position of superiority over the arbitral process.

Sayre is less conspiratorial suggesting there might have been a consideration of agency principles that braced the thinking in *Vynior*.[17] In the context of putting power into the hands of an arbitrator/third party to act on behalf of the disputants, Prof. Sayre's suggestion is a scholarly insight of note. On *Vynior*, Professor von Mehren concludes, "Whether as a departure from the agency-based argument of *Vynior* or as a result of judicial self-protection, the reasoning of courts for specifically refusing to enforce arbitration clauses in the eighteenth century turned increasingly on the issue of judicial authority."[18]

In *Vynior*, Lord Coke found that even though the executory arbitration clause was revocable, Wilde was required to pay on his bond since the bond had been made and delivered under seal. In all likelihood, Wilde's loss to Vynior gave impetus to the enactment of the *English Statute of Fines and Penalties*[19] that limited the recovery of damages to those actual damages suffered for breach of an arbitration agreement and not the entire penalty. But since such damages were often of nominal value, the revocation of an arbitration agreement came with virtually no penalty to the revoking party. Additionally, the exact amount of damages one incurred due to the revocation of an arbitration agreement was difficult to calculate, hence, difficult to prove.

Granted, there was an effort to ameliorate the lack of enforcement of executory arbitration agreements. Parliament enacted a statute in 1698[20] permitting courts to homologate the parties' submission to arbitration, thereby providing finality to an arbitral award through a court judgment on the award "providing that, if an agreement to arbitrate so provided, it could be made a 'rule of court' (i.e., a court order), in which event it became irrevocable, and one who revoked it would be subject to punishment for contempt of court; but the submission was revocable until such a rule of court had been obtained. This statute, limited in scope, was narrowly construed and was of little help."[21]

The state of the law during this period was nicely summed up by Quain J. of the Canadian High Court in 1875:

> Now with regard to the revocation: Prior to the Act of Wm. 4, it was well established that whenever parties have agreed to refer there is also the right to revoke before the award is made. That is shewn as early as Vynior's Case. . . . The common law enabled either party before the award to revoke the submission at his will and pleasure. The first attempt to restrict this power was by 9 & 10 Wm. 3, c. 15, but that was by attachment, which was a very imperfect remedy. . . . Then came the Act of 3 & 4 Wm. 4, c. 42, s. 39, which enacts that where there is a submission to arbitration by an agreement which is to be made a rule of Court, there shall be no power of revocation without leave of the Court. That is the way the law stood at the time of the passing of the Common Law Procedure Act, 1854.[22]

That Parliamentary limitations came to stand side by side with expressions of judicial antipathy toward arbitration is well demonstrated by the Royal Court in *Kill v. Hollister*.[23] There the King's Bench held that executory arbitration agreements were unenforceable based on the "ouster of jurisdiction" doctrine. The court maintained that executory arbitration agreements were not to be enforced since "the parties cannot oust this court." and, such agreements, the court went on, deprived either disputant of his right to litigate rather than arbitrate.[24] "Thus, the earliest judicial defenders of the revocability doctrine spoke of the courts' interests, suggesting that the common law judges of England saw arbitration as an undesirable threat to their control of dispute resolution."[25]

Later legislation did little to help the matter (depending, of course, on what side of the issue one stood). In 1833, an attempt was made to reinforce the 1680 statute by maintaining that any arbitration award that had been made a rule of the court "in any action now brought or which shall be brought by or in pursuance of any submission to reference containing an agreement that such submission shall be made a rule of any of His Majesty's Courts of Record, shall not be revocable by any party to such references without leave of court."[26] Whether it be through reference, rule making, or leaves of the court, the English judiciary was determined to control "how and why" an executory arbitration award was to be implemented—or not.

With the doctrine of revocability rather firmly entrenched in the judicial psyche, it appeared that arbitration was to get a much needed boost when in a House of Lords case, *Scott v. Avery*, Lord Campbell wrote,

> What pretence can there be for saying that there is anything contrary to public policy in allowing parties to contract, that they shall not be liable to any action until their liability has been ascertained by a domestic and private tribunal, upon which they themselves agree? Can the public be injured by it? It seems to me that it would be a most inexpedient encroachment upon the liberty of the subject if he were not allowed to enter into such a contract.... Is there anything contrary to public policy in saying that the company shall not be harassed by actions, the costs of which might be ruinous, but that any dispute that arises shall be referred to a domestic tribunal, which may speedily and economically determine the dispute? I can see not the slightest ill consequences that can flow from such an agreement, and I see great advantage that may arise from it. Public policy, therefore, seems to me to require that effect should be given to the contract.[27]

Lord Campbell was moving the arbitral ship a bit into the wind by holding that if the parties agreed that a dispute was to be settled through arbitration, such agreement served as a condition precedent to a cause of action even if the arbitral matter was for all elements of liability under the entire contract. Contracts containing executory arbitration agreements were binding, but should a dispute arise, a contract containing an executory arbitration agreement could also be revoked. Benson points to the sagacity of the Scots[28] who characterized such thinking as irrational and absurd.[29]

As for the suggestion that courts were being ousted, Campbell wrote that, "It probably originated in the contests of the different courts in ancient times for extent of jurisdiction, all of them being opposed to anything that would altogether deprive every one of them of jurisdiction."[30] Later that year Lord Campbell again wrote on the issue of revocability and characterized English courts as having somehow developed "a horror of arbitration." However, he went on, "I never could imagine for what reason parties should not be permitted to bind themselves to settle their disputes in any manner on which they agreed."[31] In spite of Lord Campbell's attitude, Prof. David characterized the feeling of the early common law judges as viewing "arbitration as a dangerous device, a threat to the privilege of the courts and the law, which ought not to be accommodated or encouraged in any way. Parties ought not to be allowed to oust the jurisdiction of the courts."[32] While the *Vynior's Case* had been repudiated over time, *Kill v. Hollister* was still good law well into the twentieth century. As for *Scott v. Avery*, Wolaver believed that it "represents one of the various views of the English law of arbitration and is scarcely entitled to the exalted place it holds."[33] Perhaps not exalted, but after years of restrictions on the independence of arbitration, *Scott* was at least a breath of much needed fresh air—a modern day energy bar.

An additional and substantial boost to arbitration was provided by the English Arbitration Act of 1889.[34] Section 1 of the Act broadly declared, "A submission, unless a contrary intention is expressed therein, shall be irrevocable except by leave of the Court or a judge, and shall have the same effect in all respects as if it had been made an order of the court."

The Act, furthermore, bifurcated the issues of law and matters of fact. Matters of fact could be left to the judgment of an arbitrator. Judgments regarding issues of law, however, were reserved for the courts. Von Mehren viewed the intent of Parliament, "Parliament had now legislatively sanctioned the proposition that the courts could not be ousted from their jurisdiction over matters of law."[35] The Act found judicial reinforcement in *Hamlyn & Co. v. Talisker Distillery*[36] in which an arbitration clause, it was held, did "deprive the Court of jurisdiction to inquire into and decide the merits of the case [however, it also] leaves the

Court free to entertain the suit, and to pronounce a decree in conformity with the award of the arbitrator."

The notion that courts and only courts should decide matters of law was not a particularly unique thesis. As far back as the Romans, arbitration was regarded as a matter of contract and the arbitrator's role was, under the contract, to determine who was or was not to be the successful disputant. "The award of an arbitrator was not a judgment; the duty of an arbitrator was not to say what the solution was at law; rather he was expected to settle the dispute equitably."[37]

But lest one conclude that arbitration had little chance in the courts, there are striking examples of the arbitral process having been given substantially more leeway by the English judiciary than the judiciary gave itself. For example, in the 1791 case of *Knox v. Symmonds,*[38] an English court held that

> [T]he arbitrator has a greater latitude than the court in order to do complete justice between the parties; that he may relieve against a right which bears hard upon one party, but which, having been acquired legally and without fraud, could not be resisted in a court of justice. The chancellor gives as an example of the latter statement an earlier case before him, in which specific performance was sought of an agreement to take a public house, which turned out to be a very improvident bargain for the defendant, who had entered into it incautiously, yet, as there was no fraud, the relief asked for could not be refused by the court, although a compromise was recommended and was effected, it being noted that if the case had been before an arbitrator, he might have let the defendant off upon his paying a sum less than the plaintiff insisted on, and that the award could never have been set aside on that account.

In *Tehno-Impex*, Lord Denning referenced *Page v. Newman*, a mid-nineteenth century case and, in consideration of *Page*, gave arbitrators somewhat more freedom than that possessed by the courts writing,

> [In] Page v. Newman (1829) 9 B. & C. 378 Lord Tenterden C.J. held that interest was not recoverable on the principal sum unless it appeared on the face of the instrument that interest was intended or was to be implied from the usage of the trade. . . . *At the same time the courts decided that this "rule of practice" did not apply to arbitrators.*[39] [emphasis added]

In the above opinion, Lord Denning referenced the *In re Badger*, a case decided just ten years before *Page v. Newman*. The *Badger* case centered around interest on an unliquidated claim. In that case, the judge, Lord Abbott, maintained,

> If an arbitrator acts contrary to a general rule of law, it is undoubtedly the duty of the court to set aside his determination. But there is a material distinction between those rules which are founded on the immutable principles of justice from which neither the court nor an arbitrator can be allowed to depart, and those which depend on the practice of the court.[40]

The notion of "immutable principles of justice" rang well in the Chancery for it followed *Badger's* lead in *Harcourt v. Ransbottom* declaring that revocation of an arbitration agreement even if "good at law" could be bad "in equity."[41]

From the above, one may rightfully adduce that arbitration in England was, at times, a respected vehicle for commercial dispute resolution. At other times, however, the English courts viewed arbitration as a prickly intrusion into their domain. On the continent, no such duality existed, however. Rather, David writes, "law was, basically, made up of rules of substance, and that procedure was important only to ensure the application of such rules. Inferior courts and arbitrators were expected, for the sake of true justice, to apply the substantive rules of the law."[42]

What was true in England however, was that the arbitral chain, having been linked through previous commercial, eras had fallen into a legal abyss. Courts, not tribunals; courts, not parties; courts, not custom; and courts, not equity were the intonations of the judicial litany under whose chants commercial dispute resolution was, for the most part, conducted.

Even so, and despite its post-*Lex Mercatoria* history of judicial antipathy, commercial arbitration was and is widely used in Great Britain in transactions involving international trade. Since the late nineteenth century, commercial arbitrations under the sponsorship of organizations such as the Liverpool Cotton Exchange, the London Corn Trade Association, and the Coffee Trade Association have taken place. According to Jones, "almost all mercantile cases, even those which eventually came to the courts, went through arbitration."[43] Therefore, even in the face of a judiciary wary of the arbitral process, the arbitral chain was not irreparably broken; however, the judiciary did represent a weak link. It was not until 1996 that the links forming the arbitral chain were forged once again.

The Arbitration Act of 1950,[44] originally derived from the Arbitration Act of 1889, permitted the English courts to continue to wield significant judicial control over arbitration, especially in the arena of enforcement of arbitral awards.[45] The Arbitration Act of 1979[46] repealed a number of common law powers of the English judiciary to meddle in the enforcement of arbitral awards. But not until the passage of the 1996 Arbitration Act did England's approach to commercial arbitration take a dramatic turnaround.[47] In the *Lesotho* case, an English court characterized the 1996 Act.

> The Act has however given English arbitration law an entirely new face, a new policy, and new foundations. The English judicial authorities . . . have been replaced by the statute as the principal source of law. The influence of foreign and international methods and concepts is apparent in the text and structure of the Act, and has been openly acknowledged as such. Finally, the Act embodies a new balancing of the relationships between parties, advocates, arbitrators and courts which is not only designed to achieve a policy proclaimed within Parliament and outside, but may also have changed their juristic nature.[48]

One of the more notable practitioners who, like all practitioners, must live in and slog through the arbitral trenches, agrees with the *Lesotho* court's depiction of the 1996 Act. On the tenth anniversary of the Act, Barrister Veeder Q.C. provided the following retrospective (in part).

> [A]n English arbitration practitioner from the early part of the 19th century would recognize much. There are still a large number of lay-arbitrators; there is a high degree of professionalism in the specialist fields of arbitration; many arbitral institutions find their home in London, including purpose-built arbitral facilities; there is a multi-culturalism among both international parties and their legal representatives; there is a procedural flexibility allowing an arbitration to conform to the particular requirements of the parties, the arbitration tribunal and the dispute itself; international arbitrators in London form a cosmopolitan elite; and there is an increasing transparency to the English arbitral process. English arbitration remains private but it is not rigidly confidential if the interests of justice require openness. And, above all, there is an aversion to the deliberate aggravation of a commercial dispute, with a corresponding tendency to seek an acceptable settlement

as soon and as cheaply as possible, with the old maxim that the best arbitration is usually no arbitration.[49]

Finally, after decades of suffering judicial disapprobation for a variety of reasons, most of them self-centered, the arbitral chain of the Greeks, the Romans and the *Lex* Mercatoria was once again forged by virtue of the 1996 Arbitration Act. Arbitration became and will, no doubt, continue to be secure in England.

## The American Experience

Given the historical and commercial ties between the United States and England, it is not surprising that the arbitral chain crossed the Atlantic with colonial American jurists mirroring their common law cousins' thoughts regarding arbitration. The English attitude toward arbitration was adopted by most nineteenth century courts in the United States. Even the Bar objected to arbitration. An 1881 editorial in the Central Law Journal illustrates. "The significant feature of the establishment of the system of arbitration by such bodies as merchants, is not the danger that it will by virtue of its excellence absorb any appreciable portion of the current litigation of the community; but the fact that so crude and imperfect a method of settling disputes is tolerated and receives any patronage at all."[50]

Was the arbitral chain, which had been put through so much judicial strain in England, in danger of a similar fate by the American courts? One would think not in view of the Supreme Court's 1854 holding in *Burchell*.

> Arbitrators are judges chosen by the parties to decide the matters submitted to them, finally and without appeal. As a mode of settling disputes, it should receive every encouragement from courts of equity. If the award is within the submission, and contains the honest decision of the arbitrators, after a full and fair hearing of the parties, a court of equity will not set it aside for error, either in law or fact. A contrary course would be a substitution of the judgment of the chancellor in place of the judges chosen by the parties, and would make an award the commencement, not the end, of litigation.[51]

In spite of the endorsement in *Burchell*, U.S. judicial antipathy reflected the antipathy of England. U.S. courts, like the English courts, drew a distinction between arbitration awards rendered, as in *Burchell*, and executory agreements. The *angst* with executory agreements was, as in England, founded on two premises.[52]

> First, the "agency" theory holding that an arbitrator was merely a dual agent of the parties and, as such, either party could revoke his authority at any time. Second, the "ouster of jurisdiction" theory reinforced the public policy position espoused by the judiciary that a private agreement could not bar a court from deciding a dispute otherwise within its jurisdiction. As had happened in England, U.S. courts exhibited English-like antagonism but, despite the antagonism, commercial arbitration continued to take place. In the 1600s, for example, Connecticut courts advocated the use of arbitration as a means to settle disputes; in the 1700s the New York Chamber of Commerce laid down arbitration procedures for its members.[53]

By the early twentieth century, nearly every trade or profession had developed its own machinery for arbitration and commercial contracts within certain industries routinely began to include arbitration clauses.[54] But as Judge Cardozo wrote in the *Meacham* case,

> [T]he arbitral cause, while embraced commercially, did not find a similar reception by the judiciary. . . . If jurisdiction is to be ousted by contract, we must submit to the failure of justice that may result from these and like causes. It is true that some judges have expressed the belief that parties ought to be free to contract about such matters as they please. In this state, the law has long been settled to the contrary. The jurisdiction of our courts is established by law, and it is not to be diminished, any more than it is to be increased, by the convention of the parties.[55]

Relying less on agency principles and more on the "ouster" principle, U.S. courts continued to hold that "An executory agreement to arbitrate would not be given specific performance or furnish the basis of a stay of proceedings on the original cause of action. Nor would it be given effect as a plea in bar, except in limited instances. . . ."[56] In the early twentieth century, Judge Hough, who according to Professor Cohen was "one of our ablest Federal Judges,"[57] described the state of arbitration at the time. Judge Hough observed,

Whatever form of statement the rule takes, the foregoing citations show that it always amounts to the same thing, viz., the courts will scarcely permit any other body of men to even partially perform judicial work, and will never permit the absorption of all the business growing out of disputes over a contract by any body of arbitrators, unless compelled to such action by statute.[58]

Even though he, personally, could not rationalize the treatment of executory arbitral agreements, Judge Hough, on the basis of *stare decisis,* held that the ouster rule would be considered void, at least in a federal forum. "I think the decisions cited show beyond question that the Supreme Court has laid down the rule that such a complete ouster of jurisdiction as is shown . . . is void in a federal forum. . . . Inferior courts may fail to find convincing reasons for it; but the rule must be obeyed, and these motions be severally denied."[59]

Why arbitration was so judicially handicapped is difficult to fathom. "Why," asks Emerson, " [should] a people so bent on freedom, self-discipline, and self-regulation . . have ignored arbitration, which so embodies these qualities."[60] It would take, of course, an entire socio-legal treatise to adequately suggest an answer. But, this writer prefers the mandate of Occam's Razor: to explain a phenomenon with as few explanations as possible. It seems logical and cogent that potential users in the colonial and post-colonial legal eras simply knew little of the arbitral process and litigation was simply the automatic, perhaps even knee-jerk, default. Prof. Emerson would seem to concur: "Since in trade and commerce the margin of profit was then sufficient to allow for a very considerable waste, the attribute of economy was not an attraction to arbitration. In industrial relations, parity of power between employers and employees had not yet reached the point of encouraging arbitration."[61]

Further handicapping private commercial arbitration were those international experiences as when the world's nations attempted to put public disputes before international arbitral bodies. Regrettably, those attempts at public arbitration had not gone well, at all. The Conferences of 1899 and 1907 established the Permanent Court of Arbitration at The Hague. World War I was not averted. After World War I, the League of Nations was formed as was the Permanent Court of International Justice. Both organizations did little to avert World War II.[62]

Shortly after Judge Cardozo's concurrence in *Meacham*, New York passed an arbitration statute, unique for its time, that legislated executory arbitration agreements enforceable.[63] This was, obviously, a big step forward in arbitral legal history since it not only marked the first time that such an arbitration clause was enforceable, but the law came out of a legislature representing one of the world's major commercial centers. There appears to be little question that the New York statute provided a stimulus to the subsequent passage of federal legislation.

Arguably, the three major events in the United States that molded the arbitral chain, reinforced it, and ultimately discontinued the "judicial as well as the professional hostility by lawyers to arbitration [that] continued well until after the Great War of 1914 . . ."[64] were:

1. The Federal Arbitration Act of 1925
2. The federal courts' support for the Act
3. The accession of the United States to the New York Convention.

A word first on the FAA and the U.S. courts.

In 1925, the Federal Arbitration Act (FAA)[65] was enacted to reverse the longtime judicial hostility to executory arbitration agreements that had existed at English common law and had been adopted by American courts.[66] Henceforth, arbitration agreements were to be on the same footing as other contracts.[67]

The FAA consists of three chapters. The first chapter deals with arbitration of domestic agreements and awards affecting either interstate or foreign commerce. Chapter Two contains the implementing legislation of the New York Convention; and Chapter Three is the implementing legislation for the Inter-American Arbitration Convention.[68]

The FAA did not follow one of the key arbitral practices of England. Whereas in England, English arbitrators submitted their awards to the courts for a final adjudication on matters of law, the FAA did not provide that errors of law were grounds for setting aside an arbitration award. Simply, if the procedures followed by a U.S. arbitrator were correct, the award would be enforced. In England, however, both procedure and substantive were subject to review by the courts.[69] The FAA required that in the case of both pre-dispute and post-dispute arbitration, ". . . an agreement in writing to submit to arbitration an existing controversy arising out of such a contract, transaction, or refusal, shall be valid, irrevocable, and enforceable, save upon such grounds as exist at law or in equity for the revocation of any contract."[70]

The intent of the statute was validated by the U.S. Supreme Court in *Prima Paint* wherein Justice Fortas wrote,

> In so concluding, we not only honor the plain meaning of the statute but also the unmistakably clear congressional purpose that the arbitration procedure, when selected by the parties to a contract, be speedy and not subject to delay and obstruction in the courts. . . . As the 'saving clause' in s 2 indicates, the purpose of Congress in 1925 was to make arbitration agreements as enforceable as other contracts, but not more so.[71]

Arbitration agreements, henceforth, were to be regarded by the courts as instruments on par with any other contractual relationships that had been entered into.

Rarely can a scholarly document pass muster without a citation to the ever-quotable Chief Judge Posner of the 7th Circuit. This writing is no exception. In support of arbitration and in his own inimitable way, Judge Posner wrote, "Indeed, short of authorizing trial by battle or ordeal or, more doubtfully, by a panel of three monkeys, parties can stipulate to whatever procedures they want to govern the arbitration of their disputes; parties are as free to specify idiosyncratic terms of arbitration as they are to specify any other terms in their contract."[72]

All fine and well in federal fora. However, the question of whether the FAA applied in U.S. state courts also required address. Even though Section 2 of the Federal Arbitration Act clearly provided that both pre-dispute and post-dispute arbitration agreements within its scope were enforceable, the Supreme Court was, nonetheless, asked to review the issue of federal preemption in *Southland Corp. v. Keating*. The Court held that section 2 of the FAA, in fact, applied in state court and pre-empted conflicting state laws. "In creating a substantive rule applicable in state as well as federal courts, Congress intended to foreclose state legislative attempts to undercut the enforceability of arbitration agreements."[73] However, *Southland* dealt, for the most part, with the resolution of a conflict between state and federal law.

In *Volt*, the Court elaborated on the issue of federal preemption, holding, "The FAA contains no express pre-emptive provision, nor does it reflect a congressional intent to occupy the entire field of arbitration."[74] The court then proceeded to uphold a stay of arbitration pending resolution of related litigation. So, in addition to the FAA, and to the extent there was no attempt to preempt federal authority, states were also free to play in the arbitral sandbox. In their attempt to play, a number of states adopted what was the state version of the FAA: the Uniform Arbitration Act.[75]

The federal courts have maintained that because of the effect of arbitration on interstate commerce, Congress possessed a wide swath of authority when it came to arbitral legislation. The *Allied-Bruce* case well reflects this support since, in *Allied-Bruce*, the scope of the FAA itself was at issue. The Court took a rather generous view of Congress' power and upheld the preemption of an Alabama statute that precluded specific performance of a pre-dispute arbitration. Even though the parties did not intend to engage in an interstate commercial transaction, the written arbitration provision in the termite prevention contract evidenced a transaction "involving commerce." "Involving commerce," the Court reasoned, was the functional equivalent of "affecting commerce" which normally signals Congress' intent to exercise its commerce power to the full.[76] Perhaps a better case might have been chosen for the Court to be as supportive of the scope of the FAA as it was. The reasoning, based on the facts, is a bit tortured. Nonetheless, federal courts could, as a matter of routine, overturn attempts by states to interpose their arbitral notions through state preemption laws.[77]

In matters other than scope and preemption, the U.S. federal courts have been rather uniformly and consistently supportive of commercial arbitration. The following examples reinforce this view.

- Arbitration is a contractual relationship between the parties and, consequently, can take the shape and form the parties desire; *Mastrobuono v. Shearson Lehman Hutton*, Inc., 514 U.S. 52, 57 (1995).
- An arbitrator has the authority to rule *ex aequo et bono*; *Advanced Micro Devices Inc., v. Intel Corp.*, 885 P.2d 994, 1001 (Cal. 1994) (en banc).
- In handling evidence an arbitrator need not follow all the niceties observed by the federal courts. He need only grant the parties a fundamentally fair hearing; *Bell Aerospace Co., Division of Textron, Inc. v. Local 516* . . . 500 F. 2d, 921, 923 (1974).

But lest one get the impression that all started arbitrally well for all matters commercial in the United States, the Court's decision in *Wilko v.*

*Swan* should abuse that conclusion. The Court was faced with the issue of whether or not to uphold an arbitration agreement between a securities broker and a customer. The buyer/customer sought relief from the Court to pursue his suit in a federal court as provided by the Securities Act; the broker wished the arbitration agreement enforced. On one hand, the Court, in *Wilko*, was generous in its view regarding the authority of arbitrators, "In unrestricted submissions, interpretations of law by arbitrators, in contrast to manifest disregard thereof, are not subject, in federal courts, to judicial review for error in interpretation."[78] On the other hand, the Court held for the customer/buyer writing that, "Recognizing the advantages that prior agreements for arbitration may provide for the solution of commercial controversies, we decide that the intention of Congress concerning the sale of securities is better carried out by holding invalid such an agreement for arbitration of issues arising under the Act."[79] Arbitration was fine for most commercial disputes, the Court held, but in view of Congressional intent, disputes over the sale of securities were carved out from the arbitral norm.

*Wilko* took some body blows in the cases of *Mitsubishi Motors*[80] and *Shearson* v. *McMahon*,[81] but not until *Rodriques de Quijas* did *Wilko* go down for the ten-count. Having decided in *Wilko* that issues under the Securities Act were not arbitrable, the Supreme Court reversed itself and held that a dispute agreement to arbitrate claims under the Securities Act of 1933 was, in fact, enforceable. "Our conclusion is reinforced by our assessment that resort to the arbitration process does not inherently undermine any of the substantive rights afforded to petitioners under the Securities Act."[82]

While certainly not all-inclusive, the above cases reflect the progress made in the U.S. courts regarding their receptivity of the arbitral process. The U.S. federal courts have gone out of their way to enforce the decisions of privately contracted adjudication systems putting these systems on the same level playing field as public adjudicative systems. Indeed, as Professor Feerick elaborates, "The Court has facilitated the growth of arbitration, resolved doubts over arbitrability in favor of arbitration, compelled arbitration of statutory claims, insisted that arbitration agreements be treated on an equal basis with other contracts, and allowed for complementary and supportive state legislation."[83]

We turn now to the New York Convention, to which the United States acceded in 1970, and implemented its provisions with the enactment of Chapter 2 of the FAA.

The scope of the Convention provides that,

> This Convention shall apply to the recognition and enforcement of arbitral awards made in the territory of a State other than the State where the recognition and enforcement of such awards are sought, and arising out of differences between persons, whether physical or legal. It shall also apply to arbitral awards not considered as domestic awards in the State where their recognition and enforcement are sought.[84]

Reflecting on the New York Convention and the aim behind U.S. accession, Justice Potter Stewart of the U.S. Supreme Court wrote,

> The goal of the Convention, and the principal purpose underlying American adoption and implementation of it, was to encourage the recognition and enforcement of commercial arbitration agreements in international contracts and to unify the standards by which agreements to arbitrate are observed and arbitral awards are enforced in the signatory countries.[85]

To some, the wording of the Convention was troubling. When faced with an enforcement decision between allegedly foreign awards, how was the court to decide what, indeed, was to be considered a domestic award and, conversely, what a foreign award?

In a formative case involving an arbitral award made in New York State wherein both parties were foreign corporations, Circuit Judge Cardamone maintained,

> We adopt the view that awards "not considered as domestic" denotes awards which are subject to the Convention not because made abroad, but because made within the legal framework of another country, e.g., pronounced in accordance with foreign law or involving parties domiciled or having their principal place of business outside the enforcing jurisdiction.[86]

But, why, considering the importance of the document was the notion of foreign and domestic so vague. After reviewing what in the United States we would refer to as legislative history and on the continent as the *travaux preparatoires*, Judge Cardamone scored a bull's eye: "Omitting the definition [of domestic and foreign awards] made it easier for those states championing the territorial concept to ratify the Convention while at the same time making the Convention more palatable in those states which espoused the view that the nationality of the award was to be determined by the law governing the arbitral procedure."[87] Unfortunately, and notwithstanding Judge Cardamone's astuteness, the question of the definition of domestic and foreign awards still persists.

The Convention permitted states to accede to the Convention with two reservations:

1. a reciprocity reservation limiting recognition and enforcement of awards to those made in a country that had also acceded to the Convention and
2. a commercial reservation limiting recognition and enforcement to matters considered commercial based on the national law in the *lex fori* .[88]

The United States ratified the Convention with both reservations[89] and federal courts, subsequently, have narrowly construed each reservation.[90]

As to the reciprocity reservation, in *Fertilizer Corp. of India v. IDI Management, Inc.* the court held that the mere fact that a foreign state (India) had acceded to and was a signatory of the Convention was, in and of itself, sufficient to satisfy the reciprocity requirement of the Convention. "It is undisputed that India is a signatory to the Convention; therefore, the reciprocity of the first sentence in question is satisfied."[91]

And as for the commercial reservation, a federal district court, in a dispute between two foreign companies, denied the contention of one of the disputants who argued for a narrow construction of the commerce reservation. The court held that the interpretation of "commerce" was not a limiting factor in the FAA's applicability and went on, "To hold that subject matter jurisdiction is lacking where the parties involved are all foreign entities would certainly undermine the goal of encouraging the recognition and enforcement of arbitration agreements in international contracts."[92]

U.S. courts have, for the most part, reflected Justice Stewart's views in *Scherk*, and have followed his lead as in *Bergesen* which held, "Nonetheless, the [N.Y. Convention] treaty language should be interpreted broadly to effectuate its recognition and enforcement purposes."[93] Furthermore, consistent with *Scherk*, foreign arbitration awards will, more often than not, be well received by U.S. courts. "Absent extraordinary circumstances, a confirming court is not to reconsider the arbitrator's findings."[94] In just once sentence, the court in *Rhone Mediterranee*, summed up the U.S. view, "The policy of the Convention is best served by an approach which leads to upholding agreements to arbitrate."[95]

Since parties typically contract to arbitrate disputes in order to avoid the divisiveness of litigation and, consequently, maintain amicable and confidential relationships with their commercial partners, successful claimants must be certain that an award can be adequately enforced. The clear pro-enforcement policy underlying U.S. enforcement of the New York Convention through the legislation and judicial decisions referred to should provide comfort to commercial contracting parties and ensure that arbitration continues to gain in popularity as a method of dispute resolution in the United States.

At the outset of this section, it was posited that there were three major developments that shaped arbitration in the United States: the passage of the FAA; decisions by the federal courts upholding the FAA; and the accession by the United States to the NY Convention. As we have seen, all three ingredients have contributed to the baking of a U.S. arbitral cake upon which domestic and foreign commercial parties can and will, for some time, feast to their hearts' content.

More important for this book is the demonstration of constant reinforcement of links of the arbitral chain. The English common law, from whence came U.S. law, ultimately found itself linked with the Law Merchant into which so much of the Greek and Roman influences had been absorbed. It is fascinating how each arbitral era took the arbitral law or practice that preceded it and in some significant way not only made it its own, but enhanced it as well. The Law Merchant incorporated the Greek and Roman notions of private justice, process, and procedure and brought an informal and speedy consummation to commercial disputes. Although initially troubled by executory agreements, the English common law, in fact incorporated the Law Merchant into English law thereby providing legislatively condoned and judicially sponsored recognition to arbitral awards. In recognition of its common law legacy, the United States took its inheritance and so built on it as to become, arguably, the most looked to nation for emulation of national laws dealing with arbitration. In their insightful essay on arbitration, Professors Haydock and Henderson have a section heading entitled "Arbitration is Here to Stay For Good."[96] And it is no doubt so.

With the completion of this arbitral journey we have finalized what is tantamount to Part I of this book. Our voyage from the Greeks to the

Romans, to the Law Merchant, to the Common Law and to U.S. law has revealed, through the eye of historical legal analysis, an arbitral chain forged over eras with generational modifications enhancing its utility and effectiveness. We do not suggest that the links of an arbitral chain were easily created and passed on. We saw, for example, the hostility of the English judiciary to arbitration that took decades to erase. We have, it is hoped, provided a backdrop against which to measure and evaluate arbitral dispute resolution over time.

Our analysis, thus far, has focused on the fashioning of an arbitral chain within the law of the "West." We now switch directions and go "East." Subsequent chapters will turn to arbitration in the People's Republic of China to determine whether an arbitral chain was established during the course of Chinese legal history or whether an arbitral chain was established through the linkage with another era—even a non-Chinese era.

# Notes

1. James Beckley, *Equity and Arbitration*, 949 PLI/Corp 31, 44 (1996).

2. For an excellent reading on this subject, see J. BAKER, AN INTRODUCTION TO ENGLISH LEGAL HISTORY, Chapters 1-3, (Butterworth's 2002).

3. B. Benson, *Law and Economics*, an unpublished paper, http://garnet.acns.fsu.edu/~bbenson/elgarl&e.doc (last visited Nov. 3, 2006).

4. *id.*

5. 8 Co. Rep. 80 (1609).

6. B. Cremades & S. Plehn, The New Lex Mercatoria . . . , 2 B.U. Int'l L.J. 317, 319-20 (1983-4).

7. L. Trakman, THE LAW MERCHANT: THE EVOLUTION OF COMMERCIAL LAW 27 (Rothman 1983).

8. Soia Mentschikoff, *Commercial Arbitration*, 61 COLUM. L. REV. 846, 854-5 (1961).

9. Cremades & Plehn, at 319-20.

10. *Pillans v. van Mierop,* 97 Eng. Rep. 1035 K.B.1765, cited in Charles Bane, *From Holt and Mansfield To Story To Llewellyn and Mentschikoff: The Progressive Development of Commercial Law,* 37 U. MIAMI L. REV. 351, 360 (1983).

11. A short but fascinating history of common law arbitration can be found in Judge Frank's opinion in *Kulukindus Shipping Co., S.A. v. Amtorg Trading Corp.*, 126 F.2d 978, 982-85 (1983). Above quotation at 982.

12. 8 Co. Rep. 80 (1609) discussed in R. von Mehren, *From Vynior's Case to Mitsubishi . . .* , 12 BROOK. J. INT'L L. 583, 585-6 (1986).
13. Cited in Von Mehren at 585.
14. Cited in T. Metzloff, *The Revocability of Contract Provisions Controlling Resolution of Future Disputes Between Parties,* 67-SPG LCPR 207, 209 (Winter/Spring 2004).
15. *Hide v. Petit,* 1 Ch. Cas. 185 (1670) cited in von Mehren at 585.
16. Von Mehren, at 586.
17. P. Sayre, *Development of Commercial Arbitration Law,* 37 YALE L.J. 595, 598 (1927-8).
18. Von Mehren, at 586.
19. *The English Statute of Fines and Penalties,* 8 & 9 Will. III. c. 11 §.8 (1687).
20. *An Act for determining differences by arbitration,* 9 & 10 Will. III. c. 15 (1698).
21. *Kulukindus,* at 982.
22. *Randell, Saunders & Co. (Limited) v. Thompson,* (1875-76) L.R. 1 Q.B.D. 748, 75-4 CA
23. *Kill v. Hollister,* 95 Eng. Rep. 532 (K.B. 1746)
24. Amy Schmitz, *Ending a Mudbowl: Defining Arbitration's Finality Through Functional Analysis,* 37 GA. L. REV. 123, n.80 (2002).
25. B. Benson, *Law and Economics,* an unpublished paper found at http://garnet.acns.fsu.edu/~bbenson/elgarl&e.doc
26. *An Act for the Further Amendment of the Law, and the Better Advancement of Justice,* 3 & 4 William IV. c. 15 (1833) cited in Sayre at 606.
27. *Scott v. Avery,* 5 H.L. Cas. 811 (1856) cited in *Caven v. Canadian Pacific Railway*; *1925 Carswell Alta 100, Judicial Committee of the Privy Council (1925).*
28. From whom, in the interest of full disclosure, this writer traces his heritage
29. B. Benson, *An Exploration of the Impact of Modern Arbitration Statutes on the Development of Arbitration in the United States,* 11 J.L. Econ. & Org. 479, n.12 (October, 1995).
30. *Scott v. Avery,* cited in E. Wolaver, *The Historical Background of Arbitration,* 83 U. Pa. L. Rev. 132, 141 (1934-5).
31. *Russell v. Pellegrini,* 6 E. & B. 1020, 1025 (K.B. 1856) cited in Wolaver at 142.
32. R. DAVID, ARBITRATION IN INTERNATIONAL TRADE, at 110. (Kluwer 1985).
33. Wolaver, at 143.
34. *Arbitration Act,* 52 and 53 Vict., ch. 49 (1889).
35. Von Mehren, at 587.
36. 21 Sess. Cas. L.R. (4th ser.) A.C. 202 (1894) cited in von Mehren at 587.

37. DAVID, at 111.
38. *Knox v. Symmonds,* (1791) 1 Ves. Jr. 369, 30 Eng. Reprint, 390 cited in 112 A.L.R. 873 (1938).
39. *Tehno-Impex v. Gebr. Van Weelde Scheepvaartkantoor B.V.*, [1981] 2 W.L.R. 821.
40. *In re Badger*, (1819) 106 ENG. REP. 517.
41. *Harcourt v. Ransbottom*, 1 Jac. & Walter 505, 512, 1820 cited in von Mehren at 586.
42. DAVID, at 111.
43. William Catron Jones, *History of Commercial Arbitration in England and the United States*, in INTERNATIONAL TRADE ARBITRATION, Martin Domke, ed., 132 (American Arbitration Association 1958).
44. *The Arbitration Act of 1950*, 14 & 15 Geo. 6 c. 27
45. Arthur von Mehren, 7 INTERNATIONAL ENCYCLOPEDIA OF COMPARATIVE LAW 1,at 52-56 (Tübingen : J.C.B. Mohr; Boston: M. Nijhoff 1982).
46. *The Arbitration Act of 1979.* 53 & 53 Vict. c. 49.
47. *Arbitration Act 1996*, 1996 Chapter 23. A copy of the Act can be found at www.hmso.gov.uk/acts/acts1996/1996023.htm. (last visited November 18, 2006).
48. *Lesotho Highlands Development Authority v. Impregilo Sp A and others*, [2005] UKHL 43 at para. 17.
49. V. V. Veeder, *The English Arbitration Act 1996: its 10th and Future Birthdays*, http://www.expertguides.com/default.asp?Page=10&GuideID=150&CountryID=117 (last visited Nov. 19, 2006).
50. Cited in S. Jones, *Historical Development of Commercial Arbitration in the United States,* 12 MINN. L. REV. at 240, 256 (1927-8).
51. *Burchell v. Marsh*, 58 U.S. 344, 349 (1854).
52. *Kulukindis,* at 984.
53. J. Feerick, *Why a Federal Arbitration Act*, p. 8, speech given to the New York Bar on October 25, 2004 and found at http://www.adr.org/si.asp?id=1731 (last visited Nov. 18, 2006). Professor Mann has written an interesting study of Connecticut arbitration in Bruce Mann, *The Formalization of Informal Law . . .* 59 N.Y.U. L. REV. 443 (1989).
54. Amy Schmitz, at 123, 135.
55. *Meacham v. Jamestown*, 211 N.Y. 346, 354 (1914).
56. *Meacham,* at 984.
57. J. COHEN, COMMERCIAL ARBITRATION AND THE LAW, at *ix*, (Appleton and Co. 1918).
58. *U.S. Asphalt Refining Co. v. Trinidad Lake Petroleum Co.,* 222 F. 1006, 1010-11 (D.C.N.Y. 1915).
59. *U.S. Asphalt,* at 1012.
60. F. Emerson, *History of Arbitration Practice and Law*, 19 CLEV. ST. L. REV. 155, 158 (1970).

61. Emerson, at 158.
62. Emerson, at 160-1.
63. *N.Y. Arbitration Law*, ch. 275, §§ 1-10 (Cahill 1923) (repealed 1937) cited in M. Harding, *The Clash Between Federal and State Arbitration Law* . . . , 77 NEB. L. REV. 397, 430 (1998).
64. Martin Domke, *1 Domke on Com. Arb.* § 2:5 (August 2004).
65. *Title 9, U.S. Code, Section 1-14*, was first enacted February 12, 1925 (43 Stat. 883), codified July 30, 1947 (61 Stat. 669), and amended September 3, 1954 (68 Stat. 1233). Chapter 2 was added July 31, 1970 (84 Stat. 692), two new Sections were passed by the Congress in October of 1988 and renumbered on December 1, 1990 (PLs669 and 702); Chapter 3 was added on August 15, 1990 (PL 101-369); and Section 10 was amended on November 15.
66. Domke, § 7:4 (August 2004).
67. H.R. Rep. No. 68-96, at 1 (1924) cited in Harding at n.256.
68. A discussion of which is beyond the scope of this book.
69. Soia Mentschikoff, *Commercial Arbitration*, 61 COLUM. L. REV. 846,856 (1961).
70. FAA, at Chap. 1, sec. 2.
71. *Prima Paint Co. v. Flood and Conklin Mfg. Co.*, 388 U.S. 395,404 (1967).
72. *Baravati v. Josepthal, Lyon & Ross, Inc.*, 28 F.3d 704, 709 (7th Cir. 1994).
73. *Southland Corp. v. Keating*, 465 U.S. 1, 16 (1984).
74. *Volt Information Services v. Board of Trustees of Leland Stanford* . . . 489 U.S. 468, 477 (1989).
75. *Uniform Arbitration Act* (adopted by the National Conference of Commissioners on Uniform State Laws in 1955, amended in 1956, and approved by the House of Delegates of the American Bar Association on August 25, 1955, and August 30, 1956). Since state arbitration did little to forge an arbitral link, any discussion of state arbitration is beyond the scope of this book. The text to the UAA can be found at http://www.adr.org/sp.asp?id=28104
76. *Allied-Bruce Terminix Companies, Inc. v. Dobson*, 513 U.S. 265, Westlaw KeyCites [2&3].
77. C. Drahozal, *Federal Arbitration Act Preemption*, 79 IND. L.J. 393, 394 (2004).
78. *Wilko v. Swan*, 346 U.S. 427, 436 (1953).
79. *Wilko*, at 438.
80. *Mitsubishi Motors Corp. v. Soler Chrysler Plymouth*, 473 U.S. 614, (1985).
81. *Shearson/American Exp., Inc. v. McMahon*, 482 U.S. 220 (1987).
82. *Rodriquez de Quijas v. Shearson/American Express*, 490 U.S. 477,486 (1989).

83. Feerick, at 15.
84. *The New York Convention,* Article I, (1).
85. *Scherk v. Alberto Culver Co.,* 417 U.S. 506, 520 at n.15 (1974).
86. *Bergesen v. Joseph Muller Corp.,* 710 F.2d 928, 932 (1983).
87. *Bergesen,* at 931.
88. *The New York Convention,* Article I, § 3.
89. Hans Harnik, *Recognition and Enforcement of Foreign Arbitral Awards,* 31 AM. J. COMP. L. 703, 705 (1983).
90. Elizabeth Weiss, *Enforcing Foreign Arbitration Awards, 53 DISP. RESOL. J. 71, 75 (1998).*
91. *Fertilizer Corp. of India v. IDI Management, Inc.,* 517 F.Supp. 948, 953 (S.D. Ohio 1981).
92. *Sumitomo Corp. v. Parakopi Compania Maritima, S.A.,* 477 F. Supp. 737, 740-1 (S.D.N.Y. 1979).
93. *Sigval Bergesen v. Joseph Muller Corp.,* 710 F. 2d, 928, 933 (C.A.N.Y. 1983).
94. *Europcar Italia, S.p.A. v. Maiellano Tours, Inc.,* 156 F.3d 310, 315, C.A.2 (N.Y.) 1998.
95. *Rhone Mediterranee Compagnia Francese Di Assicurazioni E Riassicurazoni v. Lauro,* 712 F.2d 50, 54, C.A.Virgin Islands, (1983).
96. *R. Haydock & J. Henderson*, Arbitration and Judicial Civil Justice . . . 2 *PEPP. DISP. RESOL. L.J. 141, 179 (2002).*

# Chapter Five

# Chinese History and the Arbitral Chain

## Does Chinese Legal History Reveal the Existence of An Arbitral Chain?

The terra cotta soldiers of Xian are among the most popular attractions in all of China. The figures "guard" the burial tomb of *Qin Shi Huangdi* who, it is alleged, buried 460 scholars alive in 214 B.C. The execution of the scholars was punishment when one of their lot fled to Japan. The fugitive was an alchemist who *Qin Shi Huangdi* had charged to develop a potion for longevity. In revenge, the Emperor had all the scholars of his ilk executed. Keeping in mind that a similar sentence might befall this legal alchemist, we, nonetheless, go undaunted and begin the second part of our journey to establish whether or not an arbitral chain was established in China. Why China?

In recent times, one can hardly pick up a newspaper without the economic importance of The People's Republic of China's being discussed, dissected, and deliberated. It might be China's consumptive demand for oil and the consequential upward pressure on oil prices; it might be the burgeoning trade deficit between the United States and the PRC; or a reminder of that dreadful repression that followed what has come to be known simply as: *Tiananmen*. Regardless of the issue(s), China occupies a prominent place in our newsgatherings, be it in print, video, or electronic.

As far back as 1993, the corporate bluebirds were chirping the praises of this land that seemingly possessed unique and abundant commercial opportunities. The Wall Street Journal warbled, "Step into the corporate boardroom these days and you can almost hear the hearts pounding. The topic of conversation is China—the next great business frontier, the land of boundless profit. The hype is extraordinary."[1] Over a decade later, the hype continues.

No wonder. China is a vast land encompassing some 9.6 million sq. km.; is home to approximately 1.3 billion people;[2] and is in the midst of an economic boom. In 2005, China's real GDP grew at an astounding 10.2 percent. This growth comes on top of previous growth rates of 10.1% in 2004 and 10 % in 2003.[3] At this writing, China's GDP growth is on track to exceed 10 percent in 2006.[4]

Fueling this economic boon had been the continuing inflow of foreign direct investment (FDI). The *FDI Confidence Index* reports that China was considered the world's most attractive FDI location, with India at number two and the United States in the number three position.[5] What makes China particularly unique, it seems, is the fact that China was the top FDI location for *first time* investors. That investors who have never committed capital overseas before should choose China, given the inherent cultural and linguistic difficulties, is remarkable, indeed.

In quantitative terms, during 2004, foreign direct investment poured into China at record levels: more than $153 billion dollars in new agreements, up by one-third over 2003.[6] In December, 2005, the Chinese Ministry of Commerce ceased reporting foreign direct investment numbers given the constant and substantial disparity between the *realized* foreign investment numbers and the *contracted* foreign investment numbers. Apparently, local governments were fattening their contracted FDI numbers in order to acquire central government incentives. The $153 billion mentioned above is contracted foreign investment. Realized FDI for the same period was $60 billion dollars. It was reported that after a leveling off in 2005, foreign direct investment increased by over 6 percent in the first quarter, 2006. The lower numbers in 2005, likely, reflect Beijing's effort to cool off the economy following periods of dazzling growth.

While China's economy is second in the world only to the United States (excluding an aggregated EU), it is still a relatively poor country with its 2006 national per capita income at $1740.[7] Farmers' income was substantially lower at RMB 3255 Yuan as of 2005.[8] However, these figures are somewhat deceiving. China is the world's largest cell phone user; the world's second largest PC market; the only car market with double-digit growth potential; and China represents a substantial market for health care products, venture capital, and upscale consumer goods.[9] The World Bank reports that Chinese consumption growth continued its robustness as reflected in retail sales increases of 13% in 3Q, 2006.[10] How a nation with such a relatively low per capita income is able to support an expanding consumptive economy is attributable to, at least, two causes: the higher income levels found in the coastal urban areas and the undervalued Chinese currency.

Notwithstanding the glowing economic statistics, Prof. Pat Chew and others take a less sanguine view of foreign investment in the PRC. Chew likens China to a chimera—the legendary female monster with disparate parts. Depending on the illusion of China an investor wishes to see, China willingly and skillfully complies. Seduced by the prospect of a market of over a billion consumers, business people, either wittingly or unwittingly, fail to focus on China's complex and precarious political environment. Tiananmen is rationalized as an aberration and China's declarations of commitment to the "rule of law" and a "socialist market economy" become the selected mantras upon which to hang one's commercial hat.

Professor Chew writes that a strategic investment in China should not be predicated on a chimera, or the tactical vagaries of creative imagination and opportunistic faith. Caution needs to be at the vanguard of strategic thinking. Chew warns that an uncritical reliance on the allegations of China's institutionalized protection against political risks, in fact, may develop into a business investment fraught with ambiguity and unpredictability.[11] The Carnegie Endowment's Pei is downright apocalyptic writing that China is a neo-Leninist state, blending "one party rule and state control of key sectors of the economy. . . . [It] practices elitism, draws its supports from technocrats, the military, and the police. . . . [Its] political system is more likely to experience decay than democracy."[12] Chew and Pei may be right; however, recent FDI statistics suggest that if investors have a concern with the future of the Chinese political entity, their concern is obscured within factories, software, and neon.

One thing is certain, as China's growth and direct investment continue, commercial disputes between Chinese and foreign business interests will occur and will require resolution. Understanding the "whys" of an arbitral system and its foundations is especially important in the international arena and, certainly, in the People's Republic of China, wherein one, if not both parties, may be faced with different cultural norms, with different native languages, and, perhaps, engaged in only a superficial relationship with one another. To illustrate these points, during my business career I observed that Western and Chinese businesspeople view contracts, for example, through different sets of lenses. A Western businessperson views a contract as an embodied series of agreements that are binding on the parties. A Chinese businessperson, however, often views a contract as a foundation upon which to build further relationships. The Chinese have an expression: *Tong chuang yi meng*; translated: same bed, different dreams. Western businesspeople who are "new kids on the international block" often express frustration when it comes to business dealings in Asia. They complain that after Asians sign a contract, only then do negotiations begin. If, however, the contract is viewed in the context of an organic relationship and not a series of static obligations then, even though the dreams are different, there should be no surprise that discussions continue well after "delivery" of an agreement.

It is not the intent of this and successive chapters to provide a tome on Chinese legal history. A retrospective is, however, consistent with the predicates we established in previous chapters. For those only interested in a 'how-to' manual of Chinese arbitration, there is a substantial amount of "handbook" material on the subject. But, there is a paucity of material on the history and spirit of Chinese arbitration. To get a better sense of the Chinese arbitral *gestalt,* I felt it necessary to visit the PRC and make inquiries of the practitioners within China's arbitral world. After all, Prof. Alford teaches that when one embarks on a comparative legal undertaking, one should "appreciate more fully the importance of description, particularly the type of textured, reflective examination. . . . Legal academics typically place little value upon descriptive work in legal scholarship."[13]

It is easy to find and read the Chinese arbitral rules of the road, just as one can look at a map and see two highways going to the same destination. Local guides or guidebooks might relate the relative benefits of each road. The Chinese have an aphorism, *Bai wen bu ru yi jian*: Hearing a hundred times is not as good as seeing once. Therefore, unless one drives each road, one might never see the unattractive byway of one and the scenic passageway of the other. In concert with Prof. Alford's guidance, I drove the arbitral paths in China by visiting with and talking to officials of China's arbitral commissions, foreign and domestic lawyers based in Beijing and Shanghai whose litigation practice included arbitration, as well as academics versed in private dispute resolution. Throughout the remaining chapters, references and attributions will be made to those Chinese sources. The sources will, however, be unnamed and remain unnamed. My commitment to their anonymity was the *quid pro quo* for their candor.

The fact is that the PRC is still a Communist Party dirigisme. Consequently, there was, among those individuals with whom I spoke, a concern over the potential for repercussions should they speak too frankly and, subsequently, be publicly identified. In fact, as I began my discussions with various Chinese lawyers from all stripes of Chinese society, the tone of our conversation was typically and expectedly formal and depthless on the subject of arbitration. Nary a *mauvais mot* was spoken. When, however, I simultaneously assured my host of his/her anonymity and put away my notepad, the tone and substance of the arbitral conversation changed palpably. There was a remarkable transformation in both attitude and in candor. I do not wish to suggest or intimate that I was, in some way, exposed to the psycho-legal *sanctum sanctorum* of China's arbitral mentality. But, it is indisputable, at least in this writer's mind, that through the generosity of my hosts' candor, I was afforded a great deal of insight as to the practical workings of Chinese arbitration that I would have never received simply from academic texts or from putting my hosts in front of a tape recorder.

Lest it be suggested that my hosts were engaged in needless paranoia about the content of their speech, below is a posting from the blog of the eminent Sinologist Prof. Donald Clarke of George Washington School of Law dated *December 7, 2006*

> *Blocked again*
> As of a few days ago, this blog is once again blocked in China (as are all blogs in the Law Professor Blogs network). Interestingly, I can still post to it from China. I'm not going to speculate about why the blocking has been imposed—I'm not going to start down the road of figuring out what *I've* done wrong. ("Why did we arrest you? Why don't you tell us why you think we arrested you?") It's those imposing the block who should have to explain themselves (but I'm not holding my breath).[14]

On June 24, 2006, I was dining with an acquaintance, now friend, who is a Chinese trained lawyer, the recipient of an LL.M. from a prestigious U.S. law school and a former CIETAC arbitrator, whom I shall name *Lee*. *Lee* intends to return to China after passing one of the U.S.

state bar exams. I was explaining to *Lee* the research upon which I had embarked. *Lee* sat back in his restaurant chair, smiled in an avuncular way that was far too knowing for his age (41) and said, "Art, you must remember that the history of China is the history of small groups. China has always been governed or greatly influenced by small groups. Focus on this and your research on arbitration will be more meaningful." We shall see if *Lee* was correct.

Throughout this chapter, it will be necessary to refer to the names of various Chinese dynasties. In order to get a sense of the timeframes of the various dynasties, an abbreviated chronological chart of the Chinese dynastic eras is provided below. The Chinese scholar, no doubt, will notice that there are "sub-dynasties" within the "major" dynastic headings that are not shown. That is true. The detailing of the sub-dynasties would not enhance the subject matter of this book and were, consequently, not included. The reader, consequently, has a simpler and better-focused reference.

### Timeline of Chinese Dynasties[15]

| | |
|---|---|
| Xia Dynasty | 2070-1600 B.C. |
| Shang Dynasty | 1600-1046 B.C. |
| Zhou Dynasty | 1111-249 B.C. |
| Qin Dynasty | 221-206 B.C. |
| Han Dynasty | 206 B.C.- 220 A.D. |
| Sui Dynasty | 581-618 |
| Tang Dynasty | 618-907 |
| Song Dynasty | 960-1127 |
| Yuan Dynasty | 1206-1368 |
| Ming Dynasty | 1368-1644 |
| Qing Dynasty | 1616-1911 |
| Republic of China | 1912-1949 |
| People's Republic of China | Founded October 1, 1949 |

There were, for the purposes of this book, two significant forces in China's arbitral legal history that compel analysis in order to determine if Chinese legal history reveals the existence of an arbitral chain:

1. The absence of commercial law in Chinese dynastic and post-dynastic regimes, and
2. The purported influence of Confucian philosophy on dispute resolution.

## Trade and Commercial Law

China's imperial rule survived for some 2000 years ending with the abdication of the Qing dynasty in 1912. Throughout this period, there was little notion of the rule of law, of a national government, or of individual rights. The written law of pre-modern China was "overwhelmingly penal in emphasis, that it was limited in scope to being primarily a legal codification of the ethical norms long dominant in Chinese society . . . Chinese traditional society, in short, was by no means a legally oriented society despite the fact that it produced a large and intellectually impressive body of codified law."[16] The preeminence of criminal law caused the subsumption of civil law into the penal codes. Simply stated, pre-modern Chinese law did not formally distinguish between the civil and the criminal. For example, in the Tang Code, should one occupy another's land without permission, the punishment set was a flogging of from 60 to 100 strokes depending on how many *mou* of land were occupied.[17] There was no provision for a civil action either to dispossess or to seek financial redress (rent, for example) for the unauthorized occupancy.

Entities such as a legislature, or a judiciary, as we tend to think of them, were non-existent. As Chow put it, "Whereas law derived its ultimate authority over human affairs from its supernatural origin under natural law in the United States, the emperor derived the same ultimate authority from Heaven under Imperial Chinese ideology . . . the emperor was above the law."[18] Throughout the imperial period, China was governed, "by the rule of man not by the rule of law."[19] Government might have been for, but it was not by the people. Persons other than a small ruling elite were encouraged to remain wherever they had been brought up, "there to carry out to the best of their ability the particular tasks that are theirs to do."[20] Later in this chapter we shall see the significance of the lack of mobility by the Chinese populace. It was not until

1949, when the Communist Party of China (CCP) came to ascendancy, that any systemic approach to legal form took shape.[21]

China has been criticized as a country with a history of laws but without a history of the "rule of law."[22] If the rule of law means anything, it means that a government, any government, is subordinate to the law and not superior to the law. This was neither the case in Imperial China nor the case in Maoist China, nor the case in the China of today. A quote of the U.S. Supreme Court in the *Youngstown Steel* case serves to illustrate the rule of law: "With all its defects, delays and inconveniences, men have discovered no technique for long preserving free government except that the Executive be under the law, and that the law be made by parliamentary deliberations. Such institutions may be destined to pass away. But it is the duty of the Court to be last, not first, to give them up."[23]

There was, in pre-modern China, no judiciary comparable to that found in the West. Dynastic officials possessed the power to both administrate and adjudicate, concurrently. Most "civil" disputes were heard in the first instance by a district magistrate: an official who was not legally trained and was, consequently, forced to rely on his legal staff or his own wits for advice and counsel. While legally trained, the magistrate's subordinates did not come to be known for their scholarship, rather their reputation blossomed in infamy thanks to their insolence, greed, corruption. They became known to the populace as "wolves" or "rats under the altar" who "saw money as flies saw blood." Bribes were paid since the legal clerks' tenure well outlasted that of the magistrate. And so, in the words of the time, bribery was a necessary cost that did not always assure results: "[Y]ou pour wine and put meat into the leather bag but the suit is still before the court."[24]

The magistrate, in addition to hearing cases as the judge, also served in the roles of the plaintiff's or district attorney, as well as the defense attorney. In addition, while performing his judicial role, the magistrate was also responsible for collecting taxes, keeping order, public works, etc. And, as if to add further complication to the life of the local magistrate, transfers out of an assignment came about every two years or so since the magistrate was precluded by law from being a native of the territory which he administered. From his office (*yamen*), the magistrate administered and adjudicated with little knowledge of the local customs or even the local dialect of those under his dominion.[25]

It should come as no surprise that absent a judiciary and the rigor of a legal education, no distinct legal profession emerged. Rather, there resulted, what Wang and Zhang refer to as, the "irrational practice of law" by which a trial was more akin to an inquisitorial process that might include physical torture.[26] Furthermore, when employed, court procedures were lengthy and expensive. Should a matter be appealed either to the provincial government or to the central government in Peking, the cases would receive review by appellate magistrates who had a reputation for being preoccupied, corrupt, and lazy.[27] The legal process, according to Prof. Cohen was "not one of the highest achievements of Chinese civilization but was, rather, a regrettable necessity."[28] Some pre-modern Chinese court watchers commented, "Of ten reasons by which a magistrate may decide a case, nine are unknown to the public [since the magistrates followed] their own unpredictable emotion."[29] As has often been the case throughout history, the misgivings of the ordinary folk have accurately reflected governmental attitudes. As to law in China, those perceptions found substance in the words of the *K'ang-hsi* Emperor,

> [L]awsuits would tend to increase to a frightful amount, if people were not afraid of the tribunals, and if they felt confident of always finding in them ready and perfect justice. As man is apt to delude himself concerning his own interests, contests would then be interminable and the half of the Empire would not suffice to settle the lawsuit of the other half. I desire, therefore, that those who have recourse to the tribunals should be treated without any pity, and in such a manner that they shall be disgusted with law, and tremble to appear before a magistrate."[30]

The "good" subjects found ways to get their disputes resolved extra-legally; as for the litigious among the populace, their Emperor decreed "let them be ruined by the law-courts."

Disregard for civil law in general, and for commercial matters in particular, is well illustrated by the contents of the Qing Code. Each dynasty, as if to authenticate its being, formulated a legal code that would supplement, replace, or modify the code of the preceding dynasty. One can think of this ritual as a sort of a regal spraying in order to establish a dynasty's legal territory. Brockman's research revealed that of the 436 statutes in the Qing Code only eight dealt with commercial law. The Code's attempt at regulation was limited in scope. Little of what would modernly be referred to as commercial law is mentioned and where mentioned is done in strictly penal terms. For example, manufacturers who produced substandard products would have been punished with 50 blows; a creditor who accepts a wife and child as security would have received 100 blows; usury was punished by blows in a quantity commensurate with the amount of usury charged.[31]

In order to seek legal redress, which quite often was simply the satisfaction of having one's legal opponent flogged, plaintiffs often had to travel substantial distances, since the county seat was rarely nearby the more populated villages. After arrival, putting up with the cost for a prolonged stay was a prohibitive expense for many. It becomes clearer why local or village adjudication became the preferable vehicle for dispute resolution. From a legal standpoint, there was nothing particularly cultural about local dispute resolution at all. Courts were distant; the journey and sojourn were expensive; satisfaction was limited to the infliction of punishment on one's co-disputant; and inept magistrates were surrounded by extortive law clerks.

In spite of the absence of a formal commercial law, Chinese commerce over the centuries was carried on and commercial disputes took place. Reflecting on China's history, Ahn wrote "many people seem to forget that contemporary China is not a creation, but a gradual evolution. . . . It is older than Greece . . . Chinese history of capitalism is much older than in the western world."[32] In a similar vein, Scogin, comparing the contemporaneous Han dynasty (226 BC- 220 AD) and the Roman legal system, noted that "markets, commercial transactions and contracts . . . were present in China earlier, and to a greater extent, than they were in the West."[33] Both Han dynastic and Roman legal systems ratified contracts through writings and witnesses. The physical format and the use of documents were, "remarkably consistent."[34]

It is not entirely certain when Chinese merchants began to trade with foreign merchants. We are, of course, familiar with the Silk Road that linked northwest China with the Middle East and Europe. Fairs (somewhat akin to the medieval merchant fairs) were established between inland Chinese merchants and merchants who lived along or near the Silk Road.[35] Commercial activity between Rome and China took place either through the Silk Road or in the *entrepôts* of maritime commerce. Many foreign traders including Turks and Southeast Asian merchants arrived in China by sea. Chinese porcelain, textiles, and craft goods were exported.[36] For centuries, China had a vigorous and extensive trade with a number of nations throughout the commercial world. Anand elaborates,

"In the *entrepôts* and trade centres, foreign traders engaged in peaceful business according to well-recognised customs protected by local laws."[37] Persians, and Arabs, Indians and Chinese all used the sea for trade and enjoyed its bounties in perfect peace. Yet, in spite of the contacts enjoyed by Chinese merchants, commercial law in China did not develop as it did in England and on the continent.

We shall see more of Confucian thought elsewhere in this book; suffice to say for the moment that Confucian society generally stratified people into four classes: at the top rung was the warrior-administrator; followed by the peasants (farmers); who, in turn were followed by the artists and artisans; with merchants at the bottom of the ladder. Merchants bore a heavy tax load. They could not wear silk or own land.[38] While merchants could move to an upper class, their allotted position in China afforded them no particular legal protection.

Prof. Howell has a different take, however. He posits that Confucian attitudes emphasized the need to acculturate the "barbarians" and that business transactions with the foreigners would have been acceptable means for accomplishing this feat.[39] Howell may be right. We shall see, as we go along, the Chinese ability, indeed their propensity, for blending various schools of thought that on their face seem in opposition to each other—here, Confucianism and commercialism. The Chinese tended not to jugulate conflicting ideas; rather they harmonized them into a morph more readily acceptable to diverse thinkers.

Foreign trade was an active part of commercial life during the Tang dynasty whose eponymous Code included rare instances of Chinese law dealing civilly with commercial trade. A provision of the code, for example, stated that disputes between foreigners of the same nationality should be determined by referring to the foreigners' customs and laws; disputes between foreigners of different nationalities should be resolved under the code.[40] Post-Tang, however, no subsequent body of commercial law was developed. In fact, commercial law became quite useless once the Ming dynasty banned overseas trade. Lakritz elaborates.

> The Ming Dynasty (A.D. 1368-1644) was not only sealed off from Western influences, but also from Chinese society. Trade meant movement and change, which threatened Imperial China's hermetically preserved status quo. Most foreign trade in the period was one-sided, and served particular political and limited economic purposes for China: first, it represented an "unimportant adjunct to the political act of sub-

mission on the part of foreigners;" and second, it fulfilled some basic Chinese needs for foreign-produced raw materials."[41]

While in England and on the Continent, foreign trade led to the settlement of commercial disputes through the private courts of law merchant and the staple fairs, no similar mechanism came into existence in China. In truth, Chinese commercial law had hardly any impact on international commercial law and vice versa, since, throughout dynastic China, it was agriculture, not trade, that was viewed as the prime mover behind all industries.

Agriculture was the essential industry of the state; commerce was not. Imperial rulers traditionally regarded agrarian societies as the proper basis for their empire. This view was shared almost unanimously by Chinese thinkers of all times and stripes.[42] Wang and Zhang, for example, refer to traditional Chinese law as being agrarian-autarchic that nested within a totalitarian regime. Private law does not evolve from such a society. Private law is a reflection of market exchanges among equal persons—a notion absent in dynastic China. "This phenomenon poses a striking contrast with Western legal tradition which is based to a great extent on private law such as the *jus civile* in ancient Roman law and the "law merchant" in European countries."[43] So, while trade and contact with foreigners took place, no commercial law developed in China; no trade-based dispute resolution system came into existence; and merchants received no particular recognition or protection similar to that received during the time of the law merchant.

Yet, reminiscent of the Law Merchant fairs, the Chinese conducted trade in government-organized marketplaces. The market in the Eastern Han capital of *Lo-yang* required an administrative force of thirty-six who supervised merchant registration, prices, and contractual relations.[44] There existed, on the market site, officials (*chih-jen*) whose duties included the harmonizing of sales and sales prices, as well as drafting contracts for parties to a sales agreement that occurred in the marketplaces.[45] But, there is little beyond these regulated markets, however, that might cause one to equate the Chinese system of commercial contractual enforcement with the merchant system of arbitration that developed in England.

In addition to the difficulty of finding arbitral links between eras in dynastic China, one encounters similar difficulties when mining for contemporary arbitral links between pre-modern Western and Chinese legal systems. Each legal regime came with its own set of contractual postulates. In the case of a Roman contract dispute, a Roman judge would recognize the contractual rights and responsibilities that were vested in every individual before him. A Chinese judge, on the other hand, would look to the behavioral and ethical norms involved such as *hsin*, the value of faithfulness or trustworthiness, when deciding matters before him. A breach of contract was not an issue to be decided on the law, but was conceptualized within the general notion of deceitfulness.[46] The remedy for the breach of a Chinese agreement was not found in the Roman law of contract but in the penal law, with a harsh and punitive punishment meted out to the deceiving party.[47] Writing of Western versus Chinese law, Ladany observed that, "The *praetor* in classical Roman law adjudicated the complaints of individuals. Law, one can say, came from below. In China, it came from above. . . . The Western system takes as its starting point the rights claimed by the individual. The Chinese system begins with the state as the guardian of rights and the punisher of transgressors."[48]

And yet, just ninety miles off the Chinese shore, Professor Brockman found evidence of a highly stylized system of contracts in Taiwan.

On the mainland, disputes of contract often never made it to the Chinese judiciary. Rather, within the informal, stable agrarian communities of China, contract enforcement was a function of community pressure whether exercised formally or informally. Such informal methods of dispute resolution fit a system of simple commerce between merchants who lived interdependently one with the other.[49]

Commerce in Taiwan, on the other hand, was complex and spread beyond the bounds of local environs. "A high level of impersonal commerce existed . . . made possible not by the use of the judicial system nor by dependence on informal social controls but rather on the development of contract forms and substantive contract rules which incorporated mechanisms of self-enforcement and self-execution directly into the contracts themselves."[50] Brockman detailed the most common self-enforcement mechanisms including penalty clauses, advance deposit payments, provisions for simultaneous performance, and third party guarantors. The contracts and their provisions for self-enforcement permitted dispute resolution independent of the formal legal system and the pressures of local organizations.[51] While this system worked well for the Taiwanese, the disputes that inevitably arose from contract interpretation should have served as building blocks upon which an arbitral system might have been constructed. None was, hence, the Taiwanese system did little to contribute to the arbitral history of China.

The system by which some Chinese merchants organized themselves invites review in the quest for arbitral links. Chinese merchants in the 17th century developed collective bodies—what we would refer to as guilds (*hanghui*). Shi points out that these guilds were more akin to a *Landsmannschaf-t* which, translated loosely, refers to organizations of people from the same ancestral town who come together in a territory other than their own. There were bankers' guilds, tea guilds, silk guilds, etc. that developed and maintained networks with other merchants, officials, and the local folk with the same town origins.[52] Guild membership consisted of only about thirty members and was rather passive with respect to decision-making. Guild issues were discussed; decisions were not. Senior members of the guild were deferred to. Should there be an external business issue affecting the guild, the matter was discussed between the firm involved and the guild's committee. Any decision reached was relayed to the membership as a *fait accompli*. Within the guild, should a dispute arise between guild members over money matters, the disputing members could bring their issue before the guild for arbitration.[53] The guilds were important as influences over the supply and transport networks of their members. However, as adjudicatory or regulatory systems, little has survived permitting scholarship as to their utility for dispute resolution. One can submit determinatively, however, that the Chinese guilds were of a form and nature different from those in Europe. Regrettably, the Chinese guilds left no arbitral legacy.

One additional matter that affects commercial law and dispute resolution is the presence of, and utility of ethics/equity and the law.[54] We noted in previous chapters that Roman law and, later, the Law Merchant gave rise and impetus to the legal principle of equity as a vehicle for dispute resolution. The English courts (except for the Chancery) were, fundamentally, positivist and based their rulings on legislated acts and legal precedent. The Chinese, likewise, went through a similar legal "hand wringing." At times, the *zeitgeist* was that the dynastic enterprise, to be successful, should be modeled on Confucian ethical considerations; at other times, the Legalists maintained that governance should not be held hostage to the whim of ethics but on law that was fixed and known. The syncretic amalgamation of both schools of thought ultimately prevailed in China. Even in today's PRC, "No one ever has an absolute legal right. All the circumstances, of which law is only one, are to be considered to determine the rights of the parties. It is best if morality and law are in harmony. But if they are in conflict, legal rules normally yield to justice. Law, being merely a code of conduct made by people, should not be and often is not followed, if it is in conflict with their sense of right, the feelings of the people upon which the concept of justice is founded."[55]

Thus far, it seems relatively clear that pre-modern Chinese legal history, as far as we have seen, yielded no arbitral links one era with the other. The ingredients for the arbitral cake were absent: commercial law; merchant law; judicial equity; a judiciary under which an arbitral tribunal could sit; a legislature to enact commercial law. Dynastic codes were revised with each succeeding dynasty and within those codes, matters commercial were treated as matters criminal. Perhaps, we can find arbitral links in the Confucian legacy.

# Confucian Influence on Chinese Dispute Resolution

It is arguable that the most, or certainly one of the most, influential dynasties on Chinese thought is the Zhou, for it was during that period that the School of Literati (*ru*) came in to being. The combined effect of Confucius , the codifier and interpreter of a system of relationships based on ethical behavior, and Mencius, the synthesizer and developer of applied Confucian thought, was to provide traditional Chinese society with a comprehensive framework on which to order virtually every aspect of life.[56] The Zhou period also saw the development of Taoism, the focus of which is the individual within the natural realm rather than the individual within society. The Taoist life goal is to adjust oneself to the rhythm of the natural (and the supernatural) world,—to follow the Way (tao) and by doing so, to live in harmony. In many ways the opposite of rigid Confucian moralism, Taoism was for many of its adherents a complement to their ordered daily lives. A scholar on duty as an official would usually follow Confucian teachings, but at leisure or in retirement might seek harmony with nature as a Taoist recluse.[57] Besides Confucianism and Taoism, the Zhou period's, Xun Zi embraced a theory of law one hundred and eighty degrees from that of the ethicists. Xun Xi argued that the most efficient government was one based on authoritarian control, rather than on amorphous ethical standards. These sentiments were, ultimately, to take hold in the Legalists' School of Law.[58]

The Legalists, who reached the zenith of their power during the Qin dynasty, espoused a school of thought that sought a social order to be achieved through *fa*, or the law. *Fa* in the minds of Professors Bodde and Morris is, "the most important word in the Chinese legal vocabulary."[59] In addition to representing the positivist, general notion of law, *fa* "is a model or standard imposed by superior authority to which the people must conform."[60] From a practical point of view, the Legalists averred that *fa* was a societal requisite necessary to protect the citizenry against the self-interests of his fellow man. The doctrine maintained that since man was incorrigibly selfish, the only way to preserve the social order was to impose discipline from above, and to require the strict enforcement of laws. The Legalists exalted the state above all, layering national prosperity and martial prowess above the welfare of the common people.[61]

The law, by which people were governed, the Legalists insisted, should be universally known and universally taught. The law should be "the authoritative principle for the people and . . . the basis of government."[62] Prof. Lakritz explains, "Law did not serve the individual directly, nor was it constructed by him. Nevertheless, the teleological function of *fa* was social harmony, the endpoint of good government in China."[63] Curiously, while the Legalists preached the efficacy of *fa*, civil litigation continued to be discouraged in China. "It is better to die of starvation than to become a thief; it is better to be vexed to death than to bring a lawsuit."[64] The Legalists' ascendancy to power during the Qin dynasty was short lived and when replaced by the Han Dynasty, Confucianism, once again, became the national orthodoxy.

During the Han Dynasty, the most practical elements of Confucianism and Legalism were shaped to form a sort of synthesis, marking the creation of a new form of governmental *ethos* that would remain foundationally intact as an instrument of governance until the late 19th century. There occurred, throughout this period, what has been described as "the Confucianization of law."[65] Confucians stressed the rationality of man and his ability to inculcate ethical norms or *lĩ*, which, in turn, shaped the individual into a socially acceptable human being. It is somewhat difficult to provide an *éclairissement* for the notion of *lĩ*. It stood, in one sense, for the correct performance of religious ritual. In another sense, *lĩ* embodied appropriate societal behavior that incorporated rules of relationships and hierarchy. And, in the broadest and, perhaps, most influential sense, *lĩ* were the designates for political and social institutions to foster harmonious living. "The *lĩ*, in short, constitute both the concrete institutions and the accepted modes of behavior in a civilized state."[66] *Lĭ*, it followed, encapsulated the standards by which a government should conduct itself; *fa*, on the other hand, was considered compulsive and the instrument of a tyrant. Yet, Confucian thinkers, Zweigert points out, "had to admit that under existing conditions state laws were needed for regulating human conduct, although they had less value and merit than the *lĭ*."[67]

For Confucian adherents, *lĭ* established one's status in the family, clan, and the state. Status was a function of age, sex, career, family position—all deemed to be part of the social order that was to be respected if social harmony were to be maintained. During the Han period, traditional social rites became law: the ruler guides the subject, the father guides the son, and the husband commands the wife."[68] Birth rites rather than birth rights defined *lĭ*.[69] Confucians had only a marginal regard for the law or its enforcement by courts even though actual provisions of the Confucian *lĭ* became part of the Chinese legal codes during Han times and thereafter continued over several centuries.[70]

Since the days of the Han, Confucianism has influenced dispute resolution in China.[71] Lakritz elaborates, "As applied, Confucianism was pragmatic and antifoundational. Institutions for conflict resolution reflected the values of compromise and community functionalism."[72] Imbued with these principles, Confucian officials did not adjudicate disputes by focusing on the right or wrong of the issue brought to them. Rather, their decisions reflected their attempts to keep society in harmony—legal rights gave way to other extrinsic considerations such as social human relationships. An aphorism of Confucius evidences this uniquely Chinese judicial approach: "As to hearing lawsuits, I am no different to an ordinary person; it is best to prevent all disputes."[73]

A dispute in the Ming Dynasty over land well illustrates the seriousness with which this principle was taken to heart. A certain plaintiff argued that his family had owned the land since time immemorial and produced documents to support his assertion. The plaintiff claimed that the defendant had wrongfully claimed the land and trespassed on it. The defendant insisted that he was the owner of the land and adduced documents to prove his title. Without even attempting to determine who the true owner was, the adjudicating official gave his decision,"The land is not very valuable. Yet the two parties never stopped disputing over it. Their conduct could only be a waste of time and money. It is no good at all. For the purpose of settling the dispute, the land should be forfeited."[74]

The official settled the dispute by transferring the land to the Mingzhi Academy rationalizing that there could be no dispute without the land. Clearly, the official was sending a message to others in the locale in order to discourage similar ill-founded disputes.

When forced to make judgments, Confucian judges might well opine: "Often people fight for their immediate interests. . . . But, what can they get from litigation? . . . Even if a man wins a case, the other party may revenge in the future. . . . [so] today's winning becomes tomorrow's big loss. . . ."[75] Big losses were to be avoided by conciliating, negotiating and mediation. Judges were respected, not for their ability to decide, but for their ability to educate the parties through a conciliatory or meditative process.

During the Han and, certainly by the time of the Tang Code of 618 A.D., Chinese Imperial leaders had intertwined the Confucian *li* with the Legalists' *fa* and used this hybrid to regulate, control, and harmonize society. Professors Bode and Morris characterized the Confucianism of the Han period as

> a highly eclectic thought system—one that borrowed extensively from its philosophical rivals. Because these rivals included Legalism, the eclipse of Legalism as a recognized school by no means meant the complete disappearance of Legalist ideas and practices. On the contrary, Legalism continued to influence the political and economic thinking of the Han and later times. . . .[76]

Professor Kim is even bolder characterizing Chinese laws as "the means to rule and dominate the people. . . . [the] authoritarian structures of laws [were]strengthened by the ethical authoritarianism of Confucian school of thought."[77] A Chinese lawyer, whom I shall name *Lawyer Seven,* since he/she was the seventh legal professional I met in China, described Confucian influence to me as one centering on the ruler and the ruled. The Confucian emphasis on filial devotion was transferred to the Emperor—the ultimate father figure. Confucianism was the preferred philosophy of the imperial few since it centered power in their grasp. Confucius, Seven told me, required that the rules be obeyed and, throughout China's history, it made no difference whose rules as long as they were the rules that the power elite wished to promulgate. "First, we had Confucius," *Seven* said, "then Marx and Engels who were foreigners, then Mao looked to Stalin, another foreigner, and now I'm not sure. . . ."

Harmonization in Confucian society fostered compromises, common interest and interdependence. Adherence to these values assured that the good of society rather than the good of the individual was considered paramount. And it is no wonder; people lived in small, stable, agrarian groups, generation after generation. People did not move nor could they move. Social "peace" required conciliation and meditative techniques by the intervention of, perhaps, a family head or the oldest of a kin group. As was argued to me by *Seven*, the issue was not Confucianism, it was the social necessity that everybody got along. "Can you imagine being the person in the village never invited to the birthday parties? Don't you have a saying in English that to get along you have to go along?" Neither *Seven* nor I wish to suggest that the Confucian ethic was irrelevant to the community. Rather, it is a better hypothesis that it was the blending of Confucianism with imperial and communal social mandates that caused mediation and conciliation to be heavily relied on. Unquestionably, the tradition of settling disputes by mediation has grown over the centuries and has become an integral part of Chinese dispute resolution. Modernly, Mao expounded that people's disputes should be settled by "discussion, criticism, persuasion, and education, not by coercive oppressive means."[78] All fine and good, if this book were attempting to establish a mediation chain. But, a tradition of communal, mediative necessity does nothing to reveal the existence of a Chinese arbitral chain.

Additionally, strict legal obligations were attached to familial relationships. It was the community or the kin that would protect the individual by protecting the family. Unlike Western law that reached into the private and economic rights of the individual, the family/group were the important units within the political and social spheres. Settling disputes, according to Professor Pei, "through a legalistic, adjudicatory system never became rooted in Chinese thinking." Pei continues, "Even today, most Chinese people still prefer settling a dispute through a flexible, informal, less confrontational process, such as consultation or mediation, by which parties can maintain an amicable 'relationship.'"[79] To take a dispute to the state courts meant social castigation by one's community. Recall, that in pre-modern China, there was virtually no difference between criminal and civil law. Virtually all law was criminal law in pre-modern China. As an example, when a commercial regulation was instituted, such as the Han dynasty's licensure system for foreign trade, the penalty for failing to get a trading license and, subsequently, trading with a foreigner, was death![80] "Law," even delict, was subject to and carried out through the criminal law. A lawsuit dealt with "crime" and was thus disgraceful. Litigation was a humiliating process. The lack of a civil code reinforced the tendency to resolve conflicts through other than official channels.[81] This attitude explains, in part, why, in more than two thousand years of Chinese history, China had no civil procedure code until 1910 when Shen Jiaben drafted the Provisional Qing Procedural Law.[82] And once recodified in 1991, Article 16 of the Civil Procedure Code still looked backward to pre-modern techniques to resolve modern problems.

> The people's conciliation committees shall be mass organizations to conduct conciliation of civil disputes under the guidance of the grassroots level people's governments and the basic level people's courts. The people's conciliation committee shall conduct conciliation for the parties according to the Law and on a voluntary basis. The parties concerned shall carry out the settlement agreement reached through conciliation; those who decline conciliation or those for whom conciliation has failed or those who have backed out of the settlement agreement may institute legal proceedings in a people's court.[83]

Confucianism as a major determinant of dispute resolution in China is too simply accepted at face value. Confucianism was important but it did *not* create or forge an arbitral link in Chinese legal history. Disputes were settled within locales rather than in courts because courts were often too distant and the journey to the court was prohibitively expensive, Mediative techniques were required for the health and social cohesion of the group and family that would be in place for generations. Imperial support for Confucianism meant that filial devotion was transferred to the Emperor's quiver as an additional arrow with which to rule.

It is not surprising then that against this backdrop, the intellectually adroit among the post-revolutionary theorists ensured their path to national dominance by relying on purported Confucian values: rural life became organized under communes; various Party reforms stressed decentralization of decision making, as well as a preference for and encouragement of extrajudicial dispute resolution through mediation and arbitration. A very delicate walk along the doctrinal path had to be walked by the CCP cadre, however. After all, revolutionary thought was disparaging of Republic and imperial law and practice. Mao emphatically rejected the inheritability of the old law as exploitive of the masses.[84] China's alleged long culture of mediation was replaced by Maoist claims that pre-revolutionary mediation was exploitive, whereas the system developed by Maoist revolutionaries in the remote, rural, liberated areas prior to the Communist assumption was reflective of a proletarian dispute resolution system in consonance with Maoist doctrine.[85]

For Mao, contradictions between the people were to be resolved benevolently through mediation and conciliation. By stressing mediation and conciliation, the early Maoist regime was able to accomplish what the dynastic rulers likewise accomplished: deemphasizing litigation, hence retarding the development of law. Cohen describes this process as the emasculation of the growth of law.[86] One need only look to the PRC's *Civil Procedure Law* as an illustration of the lingering effects of Mao's dictates. Articles Two, Sixteen, and Eighty-Five of that law direct today's officials to judge as Confucian officials did: by utilizing conciliation, by distinguishing right from wrong, by educating citizens to abide by the law, and in this way to maintain social and economic order.

The coinage that Confucianism was a major determinant of dispute resolution in China is far too casually accepted at face value. Perhaps, Prof. Peter Corne put it best, writing that while Confucian rites vanished with the Cultural Revolution, remnants of the old moral culture still exist. Manifestations of these remnants include kinship and quasi-kinship relationships that bind stronger than newly formed relationships with strangers. The result is preferential treatment for those things local. These Sino-kinship relationships become concretized through the pursuit of *quanxi*—those alliances, and connections which collectively bring about the desired influence on local officials. Lubman expands on this notion of judicial preference for matters local. "The use of *guanxi* (relationships) to influence outcomes is common enough to cause Chinese judges to refer to cases whose result was influenced by a relationship between judges and local officials or others as '*guanxi* cases' as if they were a separate type of case."[87] Thus, Corne suggests that to do business in the PRC requires an understanding of "the underlying common sense rules that motivate the outlook of the individual regulator to understand why legal implementation takes the form that it does in China." He goes on, "The source of the problem does not necessarily lie in the context of legal norms themselves—it lies in the internal world of the regulator,"[88] *i.e.*, the judge.

While we read much in the press about various reform movements and the influx of foreign investment, and, as a corollary, of foreign ideas, the fact remains, as Chow writes, "the Communist Party views itself as holding unchallenged authority. In modern China, the Communist Party is supreme."[89] This excerpt from the PRC Constitution illustrates the foundational support for Chinese Communist Party supremacy:

> Both the victory of China's new-democratic revolution and the successes of its socialist cause have been achieved by the Chinese people of all nationalities under the leadership of the Communist Party of China and the guidance of Marxism-Leninism and Mao Zedong Thought, and by upholding truth, correcting errors and overcoming numerous difficulties and hardships. China will stay in the primary stage of socialism for a long period of time. The basic task of the nation is to concentrate its efforts on socialist modernization by following the road of building socialism with Chinese characteristics.[90]

As if relying on the institutional standards established by their dynastic ancestors, the exercise of Communist Party dominance has been played out in the PRC through the fusing of governmental apparatuses and the *apparatchiki* who inhabit virtually every key post within the PRC.[91] The vertical, dynastical rule of law of Imperial China was replaced by a similar, vertical Maoist rule of law. Solipsistic in its *Weltanschauung*, the Maoist rule of law was bounded at its perimeters only by the Four Cardinal Principles enunciated by Deng Xiaoping: the socialist road, a proletarian dictatorship, the leadership of the CCP, and adherence to Marxist-Leninist-Maoist thought.[92]

Yet, there can be little disagreement that economic reform has favorably impacted the lives of many in the PRC. Entrepreneurship, the creation of wealth, and access to modern methods of communications have dissipated CCP control over its citizenry. We shall see later how the PRC has opened up its commercial law to foreign influences once considered heretical. However, genuine commitment to establishment of the rule of law would require the abandonment of PRC principles and CCP implementing policies.[93] It is yet to be seen whether the PRC will shed the straightjacket effects of Maoist restraints and adopt a more syncretic approach to future non-economic law reforms.

We failed to discover an arbitral link or chain connecting pre-modern arbitral generations. Laws changed as dynasties came and went. Civil law was predominately penal. Dispute resolution took place mainly within the confines of a static agrarian economy. Confucian ideals were distorted into instruments of power permitting a male power elite to dominate society. The rule of the Republic was too short lived to create any linkage between its past and present or to provide any linkage with the modern day. Yet modernization of the Chinese arbitral process has been—and still is—taking place. Where did China look for guidance and direction? With whom is China's arbitral chain linked?

# Notes

1. *Cracking the China Market*, Wall Street Journal, Dec. 10, 1993, R1, cited in G. Dernelle, *Direct Foreign Investment and Contractual Relations in the People's Republic of China,* 6 DEPAUL BUS. L. J. 331, 333 at Fn. 13 (1994).

2. Statistics are from the U.S. State Department's *Background Note: China,* at http://www.state.gov/r/pa/ei/bgn/18902.htm (last visited on December 5, 2006).

3. Source: Ministry of Foreign Trade and Economic Cooperation, cited at the US-China Business Council website http://www.uschina.org/statistics/economy.html (last visited on December 5, 2006).

4. Source: http://www.uschina.org/info/chops/2006/china-economy.html (last visited December 5), 2006.

5. *FDI Confidence Index*, A.T. Kearney Global Business Policy Council 2005 Volume 8, *available at* http://www.atkearney.com/main.taf?p=5,3,1,140,1.

6. Source: http://www.uschina.org/statistics/fdi_cumulative.html (last visited December 5, 2006).

7. Source: Press Release August 8, 2006, *available at* www.china-embassy.org/eng/xw/t268200.htm (last visited December 5, 2006).

8. Source: Press Release January 26, 2006,*available at* www.china-embassy.org/eng/gyzg/t233179.htm (last visited December 5, 2006). The yuan-to-dollar exchange rate hovers in the 8-to-1 range.

9. From materials provided by Deloitte Development LLC during the Santa Clara University seminar, *New Perspectives: Re-Examining Your China Strategy,* held January 17, 2006.

10. *Quarterly Update*, World Bank Office, Beijing, November 2006.

11. P.K. Chew, *Political Risk and U.S. Investment in China: Chimera of Protection and Predictability,* 34 VA. J. INT'L L. 615, 682-3 (1994).

12. Minxin Pei, *The Dark Side of China's Rise*, FOREIGN POLICY, March/April 2006.

13. W. Alford, *On the Limits of "Grand Theory" in Comparative Law,* 61 WASH. L. REV. 945, 947 (1986).

14. http://lawprofessors.typepad.com/china_law_prof_blog/2006/12/blocked_again.html (last visited December 7, 2006).

15. Source: http://www.usc.edu/libraries/archives/arc/libraries/eastasian/china/toqing.html.
16. D. BODDE & C. MORRIS, LAW IN IMPERIAL CHINA, 3-4 (U of Pennsylvania Press 1973).
17. L. LADANY, LAW AND LEGALITY IN CHINA, 42 (U of Hawaii Press 1992). *One acre is equal to about 6.6 mou.*
18. DANIEL CHOW, THE LEGAL SYSTEM OF THE PEOPLE'S REPUBLIC OF CHINA, 45 (Thompson West 2003).
19. CHOW, at 46.
20. BODDE, at 184.
21. CHOW, at 53-54.
22. Shin-yi-Peng, *The WTO Legalistic Approach and East Asia* . . . 1 APLPJ 13:1, 8 (2000).
23. *Youngstown Sheet & Tube Co. v. Sawyer*, 343 U.S. 579, 655 (1952).
24. J. Cohen, *Chinese Mediation on the Eve of Modernization,* 54 CAL. L. REV. 1201, 1213 (1966).
25. R. Brockman, *Commercial Contract Law in Late Nineteenth-Century Taiwan*, 84-85, found in J. COHEN, ET. AL., EDS., ESSAYS ON CHINA'S LEGAL TRADITION, (Princeton U Press 1980).
26. C. WANG & X. ZHANG, INTRODUCTION TO CHINESE LAW, 6 (Sweet and Maxwell 1997).
27. K. ZWEIGERT & H KOTZ, AN INTRODUCTION TO COMPARATIVE LAW, 291 (Oxford University Press, 3rd Ed. 1998).
28. J. Cohen, *Chinese Mediation on the Eve of Modernization,* 54 CAL. L. REV. 1201, 1206, (1966).
29. Cohen, at 1212.
30. Cohen, at 1215.
31. Brockman, at 85-7.
32. Dean Kyong-Whan Ahn of the Seoul National University, College of Law and Visiting Professor to Santa Clara School of Law in a note to the author dated April 4, 2005.
33. Hugh Scogin, *Between Heaven and Man: Contract and State in Han Dynasty China,* 62 S. CAL. L. RVW. 1325, 1372-75 (1990).
34. Scogin, at 1375.
35. J. Mo, INTERNATIONAL COMMERCIAL LAW 13 (Lexis-Nexis Butterworth's Australia 1997).
36. Mo, *id.*
37. R.P. Anand, *Maritime Practice in South-East Asia Until 1600 A.D. and the Modern Law of the Sea,* 30 INT'L & COMP. L.Q. 440, 444 (1981).
38. C. Shi, *Commercial Development and Regulation in Late Imperial China: An Historical Review,* 35 HKLJ 481, 482 (2005).
39. W. Howell, Book Review of *Maritime Sector and Sea Power of Premodern China by Gang Deng,* JOURNAL OF THIRD WORLD STUDIES, Fall 2002.

40. Anonymous, *Chinese Imperial Law*, found at http://www.daviddfriedman.com/Academic/Course_Pages/legal_systems_very_different_06/final_papers_04/anon_china.htm (visited December 11, 2006).

41. R. Lakritz, *Taming a 5000 Year-Old Dragon* . . . 11 EMORY INT'L L.REV. 237, 246 (1997).

42. Shi, at 484-5.

43. C. WANG & X. ZHANG, at 6.

44. Scogin, at 1400.

45. Scogin, at 1401.

46. Scogin, at 1375-78.

47. M. ZHANG, CHINESE CONTRACT LAW, 27 (Martin Nijhoff 2006).

48. L. LADANY, LAW AND LEGALITY IN CHINA, 33 (U. of Hawaii Press 1992).

49. Brockman, at 82.

50. Brockman, at 83.

51. Brockman, at 84.

52. Shi, at 488-9.

53. Shi, at 491.

54. See Ladany generally at 33-36.

55. Derek Roebuck & K. Wong, *Rapid Change and Traditional Morality-Enforcement of Foreign Arbitral Awards in the People's Republic of China*, 5 AUSTRALIAN JOURNAL OF CORPORATE LAW 342,354 (1995) cited by Wong at 10.

56. Anonymous, *China, The Hundred Schools of Thought*, Library of Congress found at http://lcweb2.loc.gov/cgi-bin/query/r?frd/cstdy:@field(DOCID+cn0016) (last visited December 7, 2006).

57. Anonymous, found at http://www.ibiblio.org/chinesehistory/contents/02cul/c04s02.html (last visited December 11, 2006).

58. Anonymous, *China* . . . , supra, n. 56.

59. D. BODDE & C. MORRIS, LAW IN IMPERIAL CHINA, 11(U of Pennsylvania Press 1973).

60. BODDE, at 11.

61. Anonymous, http://www.ibiblio.org/chinesehistory/contents/02cul/c04s02.html (last visited Dec. 11, 2006).

62. R. Lakritz, *Taming a 5000 Year Old Dragon* . . . , 11 EMORY INT'L L. REV. 237, 245 (1997) citing D. Forte, *Western Law and Communist Dictatorship*, 32 EMORY L.J. 136, 148 (1983)

63. Lakritz, at 245.

64. J. Ge, *Mediation, Arbitration and Litigation: Dispute Resolution in the People's Republic of China*, 15 UCLA PAC. BASIN L.J. 122, 133 (1996) citing Cai Faband, *A Course in Civil Procedure Law* 37 (1984).

65. JOHN W. HEAD & YANPING WANG, LAW CODES IN DYNASTIC CHINA, 63 (Carolina Academic Press 2005).

66. D. BODDE & C. MORRIS, LAW IN IMPERIAL CHINA, 19 (U of Pennsylvania Press 1967).

67. K. ZWEIGERT & H. KÖTZ, AN INTRODUCTION TO COMPARATIVE LAW, 290 (Oxford U Press 3rd ed.1998).
68. Lakritz, at 246.
69. Lakritz, at 243.
70. Bodde & Morris, at 29.
71. The following discussion is based on readings of K. Zweigert & H. Kotz, *supra* note 67; R. Thirgood, *A Critique of Foreign Arbitration in China,* 17 JOURNAL OF INTERNATIONAL ARBITRATION 3, 89-102 (2000); Bobby Kwok Yuen [B K Y] Wong, *Dispute Resolution by Officials in Traditional Chinese Legal Culture,* 10 MURDOCH UNIVERSITY ELECTRONIC LAW JOURNAL 2 (2003); and R. Lakritz, supra note 41, at 237-266.
72. Lakritz, at 244.
73. Cited by Wong *supra,* note 71, at 3.
74. Wong, *supra* note 71 at 12.
75. Wong, *supra* note 71, at 6 citing *Mi Ging Shu Pan Qing Ming Ji,* Vol. 2, 393-4.
76. BODDE & MORRIS, AT 27-8.
77. HYUNG KIM, FUNDAMENTAL LEGAL CONCEPTS OF CHINA AND THE WEST, 117, (Kennikat Press 1981).
78. Chin Kim, *The Chinese Legal System,* 61 TUL. L. REV., 1413, 1430 (1986-7).
79. Pei, at 13:13.
80. Mo, at 14.
81. Pei, at 13:12
82. Ge, at 133.
83. *Law of Civil Procedure of the People's Republic of China,* (Adopted by the Fourth Session of the Seventh National People's Congress, April 9, 1991, promulgated by the Order No 44 of the President of the People's Republic of China, and effective on the date of its promulgation).
84. Cohen, at 1205.
85. *id.*
86. Cohen, at 1225.
87. Stanley Lubman, *Bird in a Cage: Chinese Law Reform after Twenty Years,* 20 Nw. J. Int'l L. & Bus. 383, 396 (Spring 2000). For an interesting discussion of the interplay between *quanxi* and the legal system, see P. Potter, *Guanxi and the PRC Legal System,* in T.GOLD, D. GUTHRIE, & D. WANK, EDS., SOCIAL CONNECTIONS IN CHINA, (Cambridge U Press 2002).
88. P. CORNE, FOREIGN INVESTMENT IN CHINA, 15-16 (Hong Kong University Press, 1997).
89. CHOW, *supra* note 18, at 62-3.
90. Amendment Three (adopted in March 15, 1999) of the *Constitution of the People's Republic of China,* adopted December 4, 1982.

91. CHOW, at 115-6.
92. STANLEY LUBMAN, BIRD IN A CAGE, LEGAL REFORM IN CHINA AFTER MAO, 126 (Stanford University Press 1999).
93. LUBMAN, *supra* note 92, at 130.

# Chapter Six

# The Modern PRC and the Arbitral Chain

## Does Modern Chinese Arbitral Practice Point to the Existence of an Arbitral Chain?

China entered the modern arbitral world when its Arbitration Act was adopted in June 1994 and enacted in September 1995.[1] Hereinafter referred to in text and footnotes as *the CAA*, the provisions of this Act purportedly reflect a substantial influence of the United Nations Commission on International Trade Law (UNCITRAL) Model Law on International Commercial Arbitration.[2]

Prior to the adoption of the Arbitration Law, no PRC statute had been specifically enacted to regulate arbitration with foreign parties. Rather, arbitration was regulated by a combination of central government decrees, statutes referring to arbitration, regulations enacted by arbitration authorities, and common practice.[3] The arbitral system was Lego-like. There were fourteen acts, eighty administrative regulations, and approximately two hundred local regulations that contained provisions regarding arbitration.[4] After the Arbitration Act went into effect, the arbitral formulary was narrowed as arbitral matters were considered within the Civil Procedure[5] and Contract Law[6] amalgam. Along with enacted legislation, the formulary continued to include both the judicial interpretations of the PRC Supreme Court, as well as such international treaties as the New York Convention.

Since the Chinese Arbitration Act lays down legal principles under which arbitration takes place in China, it is a good place to start our quest for the arbitral chain. If, as we saw, an arbitral chain was not forged in pre-modern China, is the arbitral chain of recent vintage? If so, with whom is it linked? The Arbitration Act is also a good place to start since a business person/lawyer negotiating a commercial arrangement in the PRC should be aware of the law(s) that might affect future dealing with his or her PRC business partners.[7]

Again, the reader is reminded that the purpose of exploring the canvas of China's arbitral landscape is not to make the reader an expert on Chinese law, but to glean those principles embedded within Chinese arbitral law that will help lead to the existence or lack of existence of the arbitral chain. As will be seen, not all arbitral law will come under the glare; rather the spotlight will shine only on those topics which will render the best opportunity to bring closure to our arbitral search.

We shall see throughout this chapter the assertion that China permits commercial parties the freedom to contract, particularly in matters arbitral. However, investors should always heed the popular Chinese metaphor, "bird in a cage." The term received some notoriety when used by the Chinese economic planner, Chen Yun, to describe the Chinese economic model wherein the state functioned as a cage and defined all business activities (the birds). In a word, freedom to contract goes only to the boundaries established by the state. It must always be remembered that in China a right or a freedom is granted, not inherent.[8]

When and to whom does the Arbitration Act apply? First, the Act does not apply to matters generally falling under the umbrella of family law, labor disputes, and disputes that by law must be adjudicated by administrative agencies. For example, by law, trademark disputes must be taken up with the Trademark Review and Adjudication Board.[9] In fact, if parties attempted to include a trademark dispute as an arbitral matter, Article 17 of the CAA would void the arbitration agreement as one that went beyond the scope of legally specified arbitral matters. Capacity and coercion also void an agreement under this Article. Family, labor, and administrative law matters are simply not arbitrable by Chinese arbitration commissions.

As for what disputes may be arbitrated, Article 2 of the CAA speaks generally to the arbitration of "Contractual disputes and other disputes concerning property rights and obligations between citizens, legal persons and other organizations of equal stature . . ." A September 2006 promulgation by the PRC Supreme Court was both specific and expansive in its approach as to what were arbitral matters including but not limited to disputes arising from contract formation, validity, modification, assignment, performance, liability for a breach of contract, interpretation and rescission of a contract.[10]

An issue embedded within Article 2 that might give us a hint as to the presence or absence of an arbitral chain and about which there is surprisingly little material, is whether a contract between a state entity and a private person is a contract between parties of equal stature. Typically, in the international commercial arena, a state that acts *de jure gestionis* stands on equal footing with its contracting party. The Roman contractual principle of *obligatio* laid the predicate that private law be applied horizontally; public law is applied vertically. China has maintained that any foreign investment dispute that implicates Chinese sovereignty be litigated in the Chinese courts under Chinese law.[11] Professor Zhang posits that the PRC Contract law would require that "[I]f the State or a state agency or a state owned enterprise is engaged in a civil activity, it shall be deemed as the same as a regular party and shall have no privilege over any other party."[12] I discussed this matter with a Chinese arbitral official, a China-based foreign lawyer (pseudo-named *Thirteen*), and a Chinese lawyer (pseudo-named *Eleven*). The arbitral official smiled and said, "Of course the state would stand on the same footing as the private party. That is the law." The nature of the smile was perplexing: was it to send a subtle message? Or on the other hand, was it a condescending dismissal of a perceived naïve question? *Thirteen* said, "Think about it. I know back home if the Feds litigated in the county courthouse who would win. Same here." *Eleven* said that "China would adhere to the international principle and not seek refuge in its court system." That China would look to international principles for guidance and not rely on *jure imperii* is revelatory, for certainly Mao and pre-Mao law would not have done the same.

Commercial arbitration in China is bifurcated into domestic disputes and foreign disputes (our focus). The Arbitration Law applies to both branches.[13] Any provision of the Arbitration Law that is silent as to whether it applies to foreign or domestic disputes should be considered as applying to both. Article 65 demonstrates the law's specificity as it applies to foreign arbitration.

> The provisions of this Chapter shall apply to the arbitration of disputes arising from economic, trade, transportation and maritime activities involving a foreign element. For matters not covered in this Chapter, the other relevant provisions of this Law shall apply.[14]

The Chinese Arbitration Act kicks off arbitration in China by requiring that to be valid, an arbitration agreement must be in writing, defined as a visible recording, as well as "electronic documents."[15] The written agreement must include: 1) an expression of intention to apply for arbitration; 2) the matters to be referred to arbitration; and 3) the specific designation of an arbitration commission.[16] In fact, Article 18 of the CAA holds that if the disputants have not selected an arbitration commission, their agreement will be void unless an arbitration commission is included in what the Article refers to as a "supplementary agreement."

Two cases illustrate the seriousness with which the courts have interpreted this requirement regarding the naming of an arbitration commission.

1. The Haikou Peoples Court invalidated an arbitration clause which called for a dispute to be settled "under the Rules of Arbitration of the International Chamber of Commerce. The place of arbitration is London."[17] The court held the clause invalid since no arbitration institution was designated. The ICC Rules are not used exclusively by the ICC.
2. The Guangzhou Maritime Court ruled similarly holding that while a) the ICC Rules were cited in the arbitration clause, b) the place of arbitration was to be the defendant's domicile and c) the parties expressed their intent to arbitrate disputes, no specific arbitration commission was named. The People's Supreme Court upheld the decision by the Maritime Court that declared the arbitration clause invalid.[18]

A softening of this provision was made in a recent PRC Supreme Court promulgation in which the Court determined that an arbitration agreement would be valid if the arbitral institution could be "ascertained pursuant to the arbitration rules which have been agreed to be applicable."[19] To clarify: if an arbitration agreement between the parties indicated that an arbitration should be held under the auspices and rules of the arbitration commission housed in the Zhaoshang Building, on Jian Guo Road, in the Chaoyang District of Beijing, and whose telephone number is (010) 65668077, and whose Secretary-General is Wang Hongsong, then the likelihood is that a court, following the Supreme Court's pronouncement, would hold that even though the commission was technically unnamed, the parties could have only meant that the Beijing Arbitration Commission was their selected arbitral institution.

There is no ad hoc arbitration in China. An October, 2006 People's Supreme Court decision is the most recent affirmation of that Chinese principle.

In March 2000, a Malaysian Airlines ("MAS") Airbus A330 was declared a constructive total loss following leakage of a dangerous chemical described as general cargo. The International Airline Transport Association (IATA) Agreement provides for the resolution of disputes by arbitration, with the parties left to appoint one or more arbitrators who would settle the dispute.

The People's Supreme Court issued a judgment declaring the IATA arbitration provision invalid as the parties had failed to reach an agreement (at the time of contract or subsequently and before the court action) on the hearing of any dispute at a permanent arbitration tribunal.[20] So while the Arbitration Law does not explicitly ban ad hoc arbitration, it is however, implicitly discouraged since parties are required to reach agreement on the selection of a "designated Arbitration Commission" (Articles 6 and 16). Where the parties cannot reach clear agreement on the arbitration organization, the arbitration agreement shall be deemed void (Article 18).

Even before the Court's ruling, China-based domestic and foreign lawyers confirmed that the requirement of Article 16—that an arbitration agreement be in writing and designate an arbitration commission—is one section of the Arbitration Act that the Chinese arbitral officials take quite seriously. The written agreement might be come about after the dispute comes to a head, but in writing it must be! Furthermore, inasmuch as Article 16 requires that an arbitration commission be specifically designated, this section of the CAA, arbitral officials agree, precludes ad hoc arbitration. An official with one of the Chinese arbitration commissions took the matter a bit further. "Candidly," the official said in an affectatiously inclusive manner, "the Chinese have always trusted the institution over the individual. This is really why you don't see ad hoc arbitration in China." Rather than be argumentative, I mentally filed the comment until I could memorialize it. Had the arbitral official been more in tune with Chinese history, the official might have realized that rarely were there opportunities throughout Chinese history providing individual access to freely chosen arbitral venues.

The slice of legal pie known alternatively as Conflict of Laws/Choice of Law/Private International Law, or simply as "Conflicts," has received and continues to receive an unfortunate subjugation to 'sexier' courses taught in law school. As a result, lawyers, law students, *et al.*, have never studied, hence, have little appreciation for, the importance their choice of law can have on their commercial venture. It is maddening to see choice of law provisions relegated to the back of an agreement where the legal boilerplate resides. Parties to any business arrangement, especially an international venture—and even more especially a Chinese commercial venture—must consider which *laws* will be applied when the inevitable dispute arises. And it is, indeed, *laws*, in the plural, for the legal calculus must include the substantive law governing the agreement, the law governing the arbitration agreement itself, and the law governing the arbitral proceedings.

Article 145 of the PRC's Civil Law[21] permits the parties to a contract involving foreign interests to choose the law they deem applicable to handling of disputes arising from their contract, except otherwise stipulated by law. Furthermore, those parties may, under Article 128 of the PRC Contract Law, choose an arbitral venue either in China or have their dispute decided before a foreign arbitral institution. If there is no foreign element within the commercial agreement, however, the matter must be arbitrated in a Chinese arbitral institution.[22] Under the PRC Contract Law at Article 126, contracts for Chinese-foreign equity joint ventures, for Chinese-foreign contractual joint ventures, and for Chinese-foreign cooperative exploration and development of natural resources to be performed within the territory of the People's Republic of China, shall apply the laws of the People's Republic of China and may not opt for a venue other than China.[23]

In April 2006, a seminar entitled *Arbitration in China* was held in Hong Kong during which the following example was used to illustrate and clarify this "foreign element" matter: A Singaporean investment company decided to develop a power plant in China. It formed a joint venture between its Chinese subsidiary and a Chinese energy company. The arbitration agreement reflected that fact that since both entities were Chinese; and since there was no "foreign element," only mainland Chinese arbitration was available. The fact that the subsidiary was Singaporean-owned was an insufficient "foreign element." Had the contract been negotiated and consummated outside the PRC, then, perhaps, the "foreign element" could have been invoked.[24]

It is rather commonplace for contracting parties to choose the law of the place where the contract is to be performed—the *lex loci solutionis*— as the governing law should a dispute arise. Absent a choice of law proviso, the Chinese Civil Law default is the law of the country having the closest relationship to the contract. (See also PRC Contract Law.[25]) Parties may also contract for the application of the law of the state or the law of their joint domicile rather than Chinese law, should damages for an "infringement of rights" be sought. If the parties did not provide for such a contingency, the PRC's Civil Law default is the law of the place where the infringement occurred.[26] The PRC is in lockstep with the international community by providing that, in the case of real property, the law of the place where the property is situated (*lex loci rei sitae*) shall apply.[27]

As is the case throughout the international arbitral world, the law chosen by the parties cannot be one that is inimical to the public interest of the PRC.[28] The PRC's adoption of this rule is consistent with international norms as the classical *ordre public* clause.[29]

However, to just select the law that will substantively govern the arbitration is insufficient; the parties must also consider the *lex arbitri*— the procedural law governing the arbitration process. For example, a contract might provide that U.K. law shall govern the arbitral dispute; however, the non-substantive matters, the procedures, will be drawn from those of the Stockholm Chamber of Commerce. Under such an arrangement, the Stockholm Chamber's procedural law would be utilized to deal with such matters as the selection of the arbitrator(s), the language to be used, the conduct of the arbitration, etc., while U.K. law would be used to determine the substantive matters of the dispute before the arbitration tribunal. Prior to May 2005, an arbitration award obtained under such an arrangement would not have been enforced in China, given the requirement that the seat of a Chinese arbitration had to be in China. Now, however, if an award similar to the hypothetical were to be obtained in a New York Convention signatory, the award would be enforced in the PRC.

Much of the Chinese Arbitration Act contains arbitral canons and standards found in any number of national or institutional codices. Articles 4 and 5 require that an arbitration agreement be valid and if valid, courts are then precluded from exercising jurisdiction over the dispute. Under Articles 9 and 62, an arbitration award is final and judicially enforceable. The Arbitration Act charges Chinese courts with determining the validity of arbitration agreements,[30] with preserving evidence and property,[31] and with the power to set aside an arbitration award.[32]

As for evidentiary matters, the most relevant provisions are set out in Articles 43-45 of the CAA which does not impose a complex set of rules of evidence. Article 43 permits the parties to "provide evidence in support of their own arguments." However, the arbitral tribunal may, if "necessary, collect evidence on its own." Further, under Article 44 of the Arbitration Law, an arbitral tribunal may, if it considers necessary, refer an issue for an appraisal to an appraiser approved by the parties or an appraiser designated by the arbitral tribunal. Parties may, with the permission of the arbitral tribunal, request the appraiser to attend the hearing and to answer questions. Article 45 provides that evidence shall be provided during the hearing that may be questioned or substantiated by the parties. Parties will find additional procedural requirements imposed on them by the various Chinese arbitral bodies.

The PRC is a civil law country and, consequently, Chinese arbitrators more closely fit the mold of civil law judges who conduct proceedings and seek evidence in a participatory/inquisitorial manner, in contrast with the common law judge's supervision over adversarial proceedings. To stay in tune with its clients' requirements, CIETAC officials proudly assured me that their panel of arbitrators included persons capable of conducting and willing to conduct an arbitration in either manner. One rather young Chinese lawyer who was accompanying his more senior *senpai* suggested that CIETAC could conflate both the inquisitorial and adversarial, if need be. This comment received a stern facial rebuke from his "pupil master."

When all the evidence is in and considered, the arbitral award that follows must be made by a majority of the arbitrators. If the tribunal cannot reach a majority opinion, the award shall be made in accordance with the opinion of the presiding arbitrator.[33] The award must contain the facts of the dispute, the reasons on which the award is based, the result of the award, the allocation of the arbitration costs, as well as the date on which and the place at which the award is made. The facts of the dispute and the reasons may be omitted if parties so desire.[34] The award must be signed by the arbitrators. Arbitrators who dissent may choose whether to sign the award or not.[35] The issued award has *res judicata* effect. The award is final and binding upon both parties, and neither party can appeal against the decision of an arbitration tribunal once a "PRC agency in charge of arbitrating disputes involving foreigners has rendered a ruling."[36]

The Chinese Arbitration Act was purported to have been drawn from the UNCITRAL Arbitration Model Law. Yet, a close reading of both indicates some rather noteworthy differences between the two documents. That there are differences is not to suggest that one is "better" than the other. Our purpose here is not to judge the relative merits of the two approaches to commercial arbitration. Rather, it is to find the arbitral chain and perhaps, the UNCITRAL Model Law is a link. To begin, the UNCITRAL Model Law applies only to international commercial arbitrations,[37] but as we noted above, the CAA applies to both international and domestic arbitrations. Whereas the UNCITRAL Model Law serves as an off-the-shelf set of guidelines accommodating ad hoc arbitration, Chinese arbitration only permits institutional arbitration.

As for tribunals, the UNCITRAL Model Law and the Chinese Arbitration Law both read that a tribunal *may* rule on its own competence. Under the UNCITRAL Model Law, however, the tribunal's power is inherent; in contrast, a Chinese tribunal's power is delegated.[38] The UNCITRAL Model Law gives parties the flexibility to decide whether the decision of the tribunal will be either unanimous or majority driven. In China, only a majority is necessary for an award.[39] If, in China, the parties fail to agree on the composition of their arbitral tribunal, the chairperson of the arbitration commission makes the decision. Under the UNCITRAL Model Law, the parties would go to a court or to another authority and request that a tribunal be named.[40] The UNCITRAL Model Law allows the parties to select the number of arbitrators; the default is three. By law, a Chinese tribunal will be comprised of either one or three members.[41] Interestingly, in China the Arbitration Act specifically requires that potential arbitrators possess the Arthurian qualities of honesty and justness in addition to certain experiential requirements in order to qualify as an arbitrator.[42] The UNCITRAL Model Law has no such requirements.

There is one subject within the Chinese Arbitration Act that is different from other arbitral institutional rules: mediation. The CAA gives an arbitration tribunal the power to exercise mediation either *sua sponte* or at the request of the parties.[43] It is rather uniquely Chinese to include such a provision in an arbitration law. Such a proviso is not to be found in either the ICC Rules or the UNCITRAL Rules, for example. That it is part of the Chinese law at all is upsetting to the common law lawyer. A more expansive discussion of mediation in Chinese arbitration is forthcoming when the Chinese arbitral commission is explored below. Suffice to say, an arbitral official with whom I spoke agreed that U.S. lawyers, for example, always have difficulty with the ability of a tribunal to conduct mediation while the arbitration is in progress. Western-trained lawyers argue that the independence of the tribunal would be corrupted if 'confidential' material is shared during mediation. It's impossible, they argue further, for arbitrators to divorce what they heard during mediation from the properly introduced evidence admitted during the 'trial.' However, it is not an obstacle to Chinese-trained lawyers, the arbitral official opined. And every Chinese-based attorney with whom I spoke agreed that, in fact, mediation during arbitration was, in the words of one U.K.-educated Chinese lawyer, no big deal. Surprisingly, those western lawyers who had practiced for some time in China also agreed! As under the ICC Rules and the UNCITRAL Model Law, any agreement reached by the parties *before* the conclusion of the arbitration can be sanctified by an arbitration tribunal, thereby giving the award preclusive effect.[44]

Before moving on to the Chinese arbitral commission, it seems timely to reflect on the Chinese Arbitration Act, and to suggest that *no* obvious arbitral link was formed between the CAA and the rules of such extant international arbitral bodies as the American Arbitration Association, The London Court of Arbitration, the Stockholm Chamber of Commerce, as examples. One Chinese scholar has maintained that when compared with the previous PRC arbitration legislation, the Chinese Arbitration Act represented an improvement towards the accepted international practice in arbitration. The basic framework and procedure had been influenced by the UNCITRAL Model Law. "But, the overall assessment of the Arbitration Law will show that the law is too much influenced by local standards."[45]

China's best-known arbitral face and scholar, Wang Sheng Chan, likewise failed to find an arbitral link: "The UNCITRAL Model Law on International Commercial Arbitration, which has not been adopted in China, served as a guide in the course of drafting the Arbitration Law of the PRC which was enacted on 1 September 1995."[46] There seems little disagreement based on my research and discussions with a variety of Chinese and Chinese-based lawyers, that while China looked westward for general guidance as to the development of its arbitration act, what came out in the end was a legal omelet—ingredients from both Chinese and non-Chinese sources blended together to create an edible product consumable by a wide variety of the legal world's arbitrally malnourished. No arbitral link here, but perhaps some clues will be forthcoming as we now continue the quest for the arbitral chain by turning to the body that administers the bulk of international arbitrations in China.

A recognizable, legalized form of arbitration commenced in the early 1900s with the promulgation of the *Constitution for Business Arbitration Office*, followed by the *Working Rules for Business Arbitration Office* in 1913. Under the 1913 rules, arbitration awards were not binding on the disputants unless the parties had previously agreed to be bound. Absent mutual agreement, litigation followed.[47]

Until the founding of the PRC in 1949, little progress had been made toward the institutionalization of dispute resolution. Arbitral systems for both foreign and domestic parties came into being as mere 'in-house' arbitration tribunals that adjudicated the disputes of their affiliated parents.[48] The trade commissions heard cases involving economic contracts, labor matters, patents, property rights, etc., with their jurisdiction limited to disputes between Chinese legal and natural persons. Foreign Investment Enterprises (*FIE*s) were considered Chinese legal persons and, therefore, subject to the exclusive ambit of the domestic arbitration system.[49] Internal industrial contract disputes were channeled primarily, but not exclusively, to an administrative hierarchy for resolution which, if proven ineffective, could be taken to the people's courts. A contract supplement illustrates that dispute settlement in the early 1950s was carried out within ministerial hierarchies, "If in executing the contract . . . serious disputes occur before state arbitration organs have been established, the parties may report to their superiors for arrangement (*t'iao-ch'u*) and decision (*chieh-chüeh*)"[50]

In 1954 the new Communist state was still at the toddler stage with everything starting anew. The Soviet model served as the basis for the whole foreign trade system.[51] Foreign trade was at insignificant levels and commercial dealings were, in the main, consummated with Soviet bloc countries. This Sino-Soviet trading regime served as the impetus by which foreign commercial arbitration took root in China. In 1950, an arbitration protocol between the USSR and the PRC was realized.[52] The protocol provided that any dispute involving a Soviet respondent would be arbitrated in the USSR. Conversely, a Chinese respondent's case would be heard in the PRC. To implement the protocol, a distinct arbitral body was required that was separate and distinct from the extant domestic arbitration regime. The arbitral body that was created foreran the subsequent establishment of what is known today as The Chinese International

Economic and Trade Arbitration Commission or simply by the acronym *CIETAC*.

CIETAC's establishment in April 1956 came about during the height of the Cold War. Investment in the PRC from other than Soviet sources was almost non-existent.[53] During this era, PRC courts were preoccupied with criminal matters; thus whenever trade disputes came about, they were shuttled off to CIETAC.[54] Between 1956 and the early 1980s, CIETAC handled no more than a few dozen cases, all involving disputes between the PRC and Eastern European countries. In addition, the entire arbitration system was virtually shut down during the Cultural Revolution (1966-1976).[55] Indeed, "between 1949 and 1978, Chinese legal scholarship subsided . . . and went underground only to be reborn after the demise of Chairman Mao and the Gang of Four."[56] A rebirth did not come about until after a three-decade slumber.[57]

What then was the impetus behind the renascence of CIETAC—its phoenix-like rise from the ashes, so to speak? Professors Tao's & Chen's writings suggest a bit of chicken and egg. Tao, in a rather formalistic/legalistic approach, suggests that the revival of the arbitration system in the PRC came about with the passage of the *Economic Contract Law* of 1982 that established the basic legal framework for contractual relationships between domestic entities within the PRC. This was followed in 1983 by the State Council's promulgation of *The Regulation on Contract Arbitration for the People's Republic of China*[58] mandating that economic arbitration be handled by dedicated contract arbitration commissions. Later that year, the State Administration of Industry and Commerce issued *The Organizational Rules of Economic Contract Arbitration Commission* requiring that the aforementioned arbitration commissions base their decisions on the *Regulation on Economic Contract Arbitration of the People's Republic of China.*[59]

On the other hand, Chen views CIETAC's renascence as "a happy coincidence" of increased Sino-foreign trade disputes, national economic reforms, and a general distrust of the judiciary that "turned CIETAC's obscurity into an unexpected advantage."[60] The populace's distrust of the judiciary, Chen observes, was, in general, exacerbated by its lack of competence in commercial dealings, the poor quality of judges, and the then held view that the judiciary "was an extension of the government in its adjudication function."[61] It is striking how the popular views of the judiciary in both the pre- and post-Mao regimes were remarkably similar. It is also telling that neither Tao nor Chen suggest that those responsible for the creation of China's arbitral system ever sought instruction from China's past to guide the development of China's arbitral future. Regrettably, China's arbitral past would have provided little inspiration, given the corrosive effects of local protectionism, a judiciary incapable of enforcement, more communal mediation than arbitration, and a Soviet model as its guiding light. Cleverly, the parent China Council for the Promotion of International Trade (CCPIT)[62] and its arbitral progeny were distanced from the judiciary and anointed as "private institutions" that were headquartered in Beijing and organizationally centralized, thus giving the appearance of an organization capable of implementing consistent national arbitral procedures.

The Chinese Arbitration Act gives the former CCPIT, now legally designated as the China International Chamber of Commerce, authority to establish arbitration commissions for the resolution of foreign disputes.[63] The CCPIT's new name has never taken hold and within arbitral circles the organization is still better known by its former acronym. The charter of the CCPIT has changed over time; its primary mission now is to promote foreign investment in China, but it still maintains a close relationship with CIETAC. The CCPIT appoints the CIETAC commission and arbitration panel members, CIETAC officials may hold concurrent positions both within CIETAC and the CCPIT, and the CCPIT retains responsibility for formulation of rules that govern foreign related arbitrations.[64] CIETAC remits an amount of its revenue to the CCPIT. CIETAC officials maintained to me their independence from the CCPIT on the day-to-day functional running of the organization. But, during their protestations of independence, my colleague *Lee*'s comments were never far from my thoughts, "Art, you must remember that the history of China is the history of small groups. China has always been governed or greatly influenced by small groups. Focus on this and your research on arbitration will be more meaningful."

As part of its emergence from dormancy, CIETAC underwent a series of name changes. Before 1980, CIETAC was known as the Foreign Trade Arbitration Commission (FTAC).[65] Reflective of China's early reliance on the Soviets for arbitral guidance, the Chinese arbitral body carried the same name as its Soviet model, also FTAC, which had, however, been created decades earlier.[66] FTAC, under the auspices of the CCPIT, was given jurisdiction to resolve foreign and only foreign trade disputes relating primarily to contracts. An FTAC decision was to be considered final and enforceable in Chinese courts. The CCPIT, later the FTAC, maintained a list of arbitrators from whom the parties could select. Still in its arbitral infancy, FTAC arbitrated only thirty-eight cases and mediated sixty others between 1956 and 1979.[67]

In 1980, FTAC's name was updated to the Foreign Economic and Trade Arbitration Commission (FETAC). Neither FTAC nor FETAC were truly independent arbitral bodies, however. Rather, they were administrative commissions upon whom authority was granted to hear foreign trade related disputes. FETAC's charter was broadened permitting it to arbitrate disputes arising from a variety of economic cooperative ventures with foreign entities.[68]

In June 1988, FETAC was privatized as an arbitration institution and was renamed the China International Economic and Trade Arbitration Commission—or CIETAC, as we now know it.[69] Once CIETAC's brief was broadened to cover all international disputes arising from international economic and trade disputes, CIETAC was considered competent *ratione materiae* to resolve economic and commercial disputes and stood, consequently, on equal footing with other world arbitral bodies such as the International Chamber of Commerce and the Stockholm Chamber of Commerce.

If we might be allowed to jump forward to 2005 for a moment, the number of cases heard by CIETAC compared to the Hong Kong, ICC, and Singaporean tribunals validate that CIETAC should have been compared to the world's major arbitral bodies since it has, indeed, surpassed them in activity.[70]

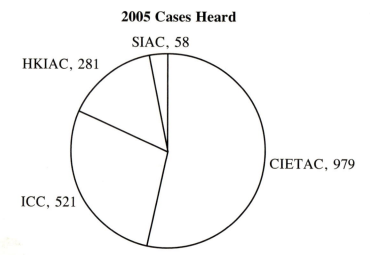

**2005 Cases Heard**

Not content simply with privatization and the window dressing of name changes, CIETAC has undergone six rule changes since its founding. CIETAC's original 1956 rules were generally copied from those of the Soviet Union and stayed in effect for some thirty-two years until it adopted new rules in 1988.[71] The 1988 reforms[72] rendered, *inter alia*, that: 1) arbitration hearings would be held in closed session; 2) CIETAC's panel of arbitrators could include foreign nationals; 3) conciliation could be a form of dispute resolution with the conciliation agreement forming the basis of a subsequent arbitral award; 4) related disputes subject to arbitration could be consolidated; 5) the presiding officer of an arbitration tribunal would be appointed by the Chairman of CIETAC rather than elevated by the two-party appointed arbitrators; 6) parties could submit evidence in support of their claims; and 7) CIETAC's jurisdiction would expand to include not only foreign trade disputes but any dispute arising from a contractual matter, as well. This self-extension of jurisdiction also came about to "meet the competition" in view of the State Council's decision in 1988 to vest domestic arbitration commissions with authority to hear foreign cases, as well as domestic cases.[73]

The 1988 Rules that permitted the Chairman of CIETAC to name the chief arbitrator were not only a departure from its 1956 rules but, more importantly, the change was a substantial departure from international practice.[74] It has been suggested that the rules were changed to ensure that there would be a majority of Chinese arbitrators on a tribunal that included a foreigner![75]

The 1994 reforms expanded CIETAC's jurisdiction to cover all types of commercial, international disputes, not just contractual disputes between Chinese and foreign parties. In addition, the reforms permitted languages other than Chinese to be used in arbitration proceedings; provisions were added to ensure principle of severability; a section dealing with summary proceeding was added, as well as provisions to regulate the use of information and evidence gathered independently by the arbitrators.[76]

CIETAC came into being and grew into legal adolescence as the result of a series of forces external to the arbitration world: China's history and comfort with extra-judicial dispute resolution; trade with the Soviet bloc; a judiciary with a reputation for incompetence; and the foresight of post-Mao leadership to recognize the potentially invigorating effects of foreign investment on China's economy. CIETAC matured thanks to post-Mao Chinese law that favored CIETAC as the setting for international commercial dispute resolution. Couple this legal preference with a) an increase of foreign transactions and b) the Chinese businesspersons' preference for CIETAC, and it understandable why CIETAC matured so well and so quickly. But it did so with no discernible link to its arbitral past or in the words of this book, without forming an arbitral chain.

CIETAC's jurisdiction was further expanded in 1998 to cover disputes between foreign investment enterprises and domestic companies, as well as disputes arising from the tender, construction, financing, bidding, construction, and other activities conducted by domestic companies through the utilization of capital from foreign countries. In 2000, CIETAC's jurisdiction over domestic arbitral disputes was expanded and in 2003 CIETAC created a new set of rules for the resolution of financial disputes.[77]

May 2005 brought major changes to CIETAC's rules.[78] By their own admission, CIETAC is sensitive to criticism by the arbitral world; otherwise, it would not have instituted the changes that it has. On one hand, credit is due CIETAC for its recognition of the need to adapt to an increasingly sophisticated arbitral world. On the other hand, the 2005 rule changes reflect CIETAC's modest, incremental, almost cautious approach to major institutional change. The major recent changes include:

1. The parties now have the option of choosing the rules for their own arbitration unless those rules cannot be enforced or are in conflict with the law of the place of arbitration. Chinese lawyers with whom I spoke saw this change as fundamentally cosmetic. Lawyer *Eight*, who represents primarily U.S. clients, pointed out that the change may hold some meaning for the future. As for now, Chinese partners hold the balance of power in commercial negotiations and they prefer Chinese arbitration and rules. For example, while UNCITRAL arbitrations may be permitted under the new rules, I was cautioned not to expect to see many, if any, very soon.
2. Parties are now free to appoint arbitrators other than those on CIETAC's panel, subject to the confirmation of the CIETAC Secretariat.

3. CIETAC *may* delegate to the arbitral tribunal the authority to determine the question of jurisdiction. Nevertheless CIETAC retains the right to make the ultimate decision. More on this subject in the following section.
4. The time limits for certain procedures were amended, *e.g.*, the award must be determined within six rather than nine months.
5. The restriction imposing an award limited to 10% of a winning party's costs was removed.
6. As long as the arbitration agreement contains a foreign element, the place of arbitration or "seat" of arbitration may be different from the venue or place of the "oral" hearing.[79] This is a substantial rule change permitting a CIETAC arbitration to be held almost anywhere in the world. There are still questions to be answered definitively as to how the Chinese courts will treat judgments obtained in a foreign country. This change was viewed by lawyers in China in a way similar to the change made to the adoption of rules referred to above. While it might appear that party autonomy has been enhanced, in fact, given the leverage enjoyed by Chinese commercial parties, CIETAC arbitration under CIETAC rules in China will be arbitral *modus operandi* for the foreseeable future.

CIETAC's jurisdictional charter gives it competence over the resolution of: 1) international or foreign-related disputes; 2) disputes related to the Hong Kong Special Administrative Region (SAR), the Macao SAR, and the Taiwan region;[80] and 3) domestic disputes.[81] Prior to the 2005 Arbitration Rules,[82] CIETAC[83] did not accept cases relating to marital, adoption, guardianship, support and succession disputes. Now, however, if the parties wish such matters arbitrated outside the PRC, they are free to do so. CIETAC arbitration tribunals do not have jurisdiction over infringements of patents or trademarks. As a matter of information, the PRC's Trademark and Patent Laws[84] reserve jurisdiction over such matters to the appropriate governmental agency or to the court system. In 1998, China established the State Intellectual Property Office (SIPO) with the notion that it would coordinate China's IP enforcement efforts by merging the patent, trademark and copyright offices under one authority. However, this has yet to occur. Today, SIPO is essentially China's

Patent Office.[85] China's enforcement of intellectual property matters is essentially two-track: the first is administrative, whereby an IP rights holder files a complaint at the local administrative office; the second is judicial, whereby complaints are filed through the court system. (China has established specialized IP panels in its civil court system throughout the country.) Unfortunately for foreign investors, jurisdiction of IP protection is diffused throughout a number of government agencies and offices, with each typically responsible for the protection afforded by one statute or one specific area of IP-related law.[86]

Beyond the legalisms which define an arbitral body's charge, there is, in International Law, general acceptance of the principle of *Kompetenz-Kompetenz* under which a judicial or an arbitral body has the authority to rule on its own jurisdiction. This is not the case with respect to arbitration in the PRC. Under its rules, it is the CIETAC, and not the arbitrator, nor the tribunal, that, ultimately, has "the power to determine the existence and validity of an arbitration agreement and its jurisdiction over an arbitration case" subsequent to a challenge by one of the disputants. In May 2005, the rule was modified permitting CIETAC to delegate the decision regarding jurisdictional power to an arbitral tribunal "if necessary."[87] What circumstances make the delegation "necessary" is unclear. Keeping the jurisdictional issue at the Commission level may lead, in the words of one commentator, to an arbitrator's "being unduly dependent on the CIETAC Commission, and to doubts arising about the impartiality and independence of CIETAC's empanelled arbitrators."[88] *Lee*'s admonition rings true again, "Art, you must remember that the history of China is the history of small groups. China has always been governed or greatly influenced by small groups."

The 2003 award in the arbitration between Yaung Chi OO Trading Co. and the Government of Myanmar reflects the standard for determining an arbitration tribunal's jurisdiction. The facts of the case are not particularly important to this illustration; suffice to mention that the dispute centered on a foreign investment. The President of the arbitration tribunal, Prof. S. Sucharitkul, on the question of the tribunal's jurisdiction, ruled:

> The tribunal accordingly concludes that neither the absence of prior contractual relations between the Parties nor the non-exhaustion of local remedies excludes its jurisdiction in the present case or renders the claim inadmissible as such. It notes that similar conclusions have

uniformly been reached by tribunals under other bilateral and regional investment treaties as well as under the ICSID Convention.[89]

My research in China revealed a disconnect between academic writers and practicing China-based attorneys on the issue of an arbitral tribunal's jurisdiction. Academic writers, in the main, follow Professor Suchartikul's beacon light and navigate heartily to the principle of *competence-competence*. Likewise, the UNCITRAL Model Law upon which some in China suggest served as a guide for the Chinese Arbitration Act, requires that "The arbitration may rule on its own jurisdiction, including any objections with respect to the existence or validity of the arbitration agreement."[90]

Yet, Chinese arbitration officials and China-based lawyers who litigate before CIETAC, to a person declare this jurisdictional issue to be of little concern. As I was escorted around the offices of a CIETAC location and shown the mounds of case files on the desks of members of the Secretariat, such visual evidence was clearly meant to cement the notion that CIETAC's mounting arbitral activities precluded its involvement in jurisdictional issues. As we went on, I was reminded that while there is little scrutiny given by the people's courts after an international dispute was resolved, this was not the case when it came to domestic awards between domestic parties. A People's Court may only review a foreign-related award for procedural errors. The rules for domestic awards are different, however. A People's Court may refuse to recognize a domestic award if the court found errors of law—in other words, the court can review substantive matters. Furthermore, rather than in the mid-level courts where enforcement is sought for a foreign award, enforcement of a domestic award can be in the courts of first instance of which there are substantially more. Consequently, judges were constantly in CIETAC's offices pouring over the arbitral material of domestic cases and, generally, taking up the Secretariat's time, energy, and effort. I was assured that should CIETAC be called upon to make a jurisdictional decision it would, undoubtedly, consider the opinions of its tribunal prior to any decision being made.

The practicing lawyers agreed. "They just leave it to the arbitrators to figure it out," was the consistent comment I received. Nonetheless, as CIETAC was considering how best to internationalize its rules, it could have taken an even larger step forward, in the minds of the arbitral academy, by harmonizing its jurisdictional requirements with those of the international arbitral world. Early in the preceding chapter, we made reference to a comment by a former CIETAC arbitrator, *Lee*, who said that the history of China was the history of small groups. This clinging to its *de jure* jurisdictional power by CIETAC is reflective of *Lee*'s admonition.

In China, unless the arbitration agreement calls for a sole arbitrator, each party appoints an arbitrator from a panel of CIETAC-provided arbitrators.[91] The presiding arbitrator is appointed by agreement of the parties. Absent an agreement, and under authority granted by the parties, the Chairman of CIETAC will then select the presiding arbitrator. It is also provided in the Arbitration rules that should the parties fail to decide upon the composition of the tribunal or fail to choose an arbitrator, the Chairman of CIETAC shall make the choice.[92]

The May 2005 rule changes significantly modified the way parties may select their tribunal. While the above option remains open to them, the parties may, additionally, choose arbitrators from other than the CIETAC panel, subject to confirmation by the Chairman of CIETAC.[93] CIETAC officials deny the confirmation is simply an institutional control issue; there is a real desire, they suggest, to ensure that the qualifications of the non-CIETAC arbitrators are on par with those of the CIETAC arbitrators.

CIETAC has organized its arbitral body into seven functional panels consisting of over 1000 arbitrators of which more than 200 come out of Hong Kong SAR, Macau SAR, Taiwan and other foreign countries.[94] The new rules permit parties to select from these 1000+ persons or to go off the list to other competent arbitrators. The party autonomy offered in the CIETAC selection process is commendable. Practically, lawyers representing Western commercial interests seem convinced that while this rule change "looks good," more likely than not, given the preference of Chinese commercial interests, parties will wind up with CIETAC arbitrators. Nonetheless, kudos should be given where deserved.

When drafting an arbitration clause, a foreign party would be wise to include in its written arbitration agreement wording as to the selection of the presiding arbitrator. Under the May 2005 rules, if the parties have not jointly agreed on the presiding arbitrator, the parties give CIETAC a common name list. Each party names three arbitrators and if there is one common name, then that person becomes the presiding arbitrator. There appears to be no bar to the parties' agreeing that the presiding arbitrator shall be other than a PRC national. If there is no common name then the Chairman of CIETAC appoints the presiding arbitrator.[95]

Foreign lawyers have suggested to me that it is more likely than not that the Commission will select a Chinese presiding arbitrator, leading to a Chinese majority on the arbitration panel which may not, ultimately, be in a foreign party's best interests. And, since CIETAC staff members also serve on CIETAC's panel of arbitrators, the person chosen may be a CIETAC staff member! The potential influence of the CIETAC staff member on the tribunal is obvious. A CIETAC official with whom I met assured me that, in practice, a CIETAC staff member would only be appointed by consent of the parties. Of course, this situation might be avoided if the parties initially agree in their arbitration agreement that the presiding arbitrator will not be of the same nationality as either of the parties. There is an additional hurdle in the selection of foreign arbitrators, however, and that is the arbitrator's remuneration. Prof. Chua has written and my research bears out his observation that, "foreign arbitrators may be reluctant to accept a CIETAC appointment because remuneration is much lower than in other international arbitrations. This is something to bear in mind before deciding on CIETAC arbitration as the venue for dispute resolution. This issue has not been addressed in the 2005 Rules."[96] One of the reasons, I was told by both foreign and Chinese lawyers, that they advise their foreign clients to use the Hong Kong arbitral system, is that while an arbitrator might be on both the CIETAC list and the HKIAC list, there is a better chance of securing the talents of the desired arbitrator from the HKIAC list since the arbitrator's fee is more substantial.

Included in the 2005 changes to the Arbitration Rules was one of which CIETAC officials were quite proud. There had been some criticism of CIETAC that because China was a "civil law" country, common law lawyers and clients were disadvantaged. Arbitrators may now, at the parties' option, act either inquisitorially or adversarially in the conduct of the dispute proceedings. Of course, the parties need to be selective to assure that the arbitrator/civil lawyer can, in fact, change his/her spots and act as a common law adjudicator.

In any arbitration, the selection process is important; more so in China where an arbitrator/tribunal may make an award not only as the adjudicator, but also after having served as the parties' conciliator! The Chinese word for conciliation is *tiaojie* which can also be translated *mediation*—mediation and conciliation referring to the same procedure under

PRC law. To illustrate his point, Prof. Tao points to the Beijing Conciliation Commission being equally known as the Beijing Mediation Commission.[97]

For parties who wish to avoid arbitration and seek resolution of their dispute by mediation/conciliation only, the China Council for the Promotion of International Trade/China Chamber of International Commerce (CCPIT/CCOIC) is the permanent conciliation center in China which purports to independently and impartially resolve international commercial disputes. With over thirty conciliation centers throughout the PRC, the CCPIT/CCOIC has also branched out internationally. The Center has established cooperation agreements with the AAA and the London Court of International Arbitration as well as a bi-lateral cooperation agreement with Germany.

As to the use of mediation/conciliation in arbitral proceedings, Professor H. Tang, Vice Chairman of the Beijing Conciliation Center and Law Professor at People's University of China suggests that parties to an arbitration will "often at the end of the first stage or in the middle of the second stage . . . become aware of where they are and voluntarily ask the arbitral tribunal to conciliate the case. Or, the arbitral tribunal finds a possibility of resolving the case by conciliation and takes the initiative to ask the parties whether they are willing to settle their dispute through conciliation to be conducted by the arbitration tribunal."[98] It seems unlikely that parties who intend to soon "divorce" or parties who are bound by a "one shot" synallagmatic contract would view mediation as a viable method to resolve their dispute, however.

Even though an arbitral tribunal may play the role of a conciliator in the midst of arbitration proceedings, there is little guidance given to the arbitrator/conciliator as to how the combined role is to be carried out. CIETAC's Article 40 (3) simply provides that the arbitration tribunal may conduct conciliation "in the manner it deems appropriate." Should the parties reach a conciliation-assisted resolution, their agreement will then serve as the basis of a subsequent arbitral award in order to bring enforceable closure to the matter.[99]

Certain fundamental principles have been followed, however, when combining arbitration with conciliation. Conciliation is an option for the parties and not a required mandatory procedure of arbitration; conciliation must be based upon the absolute free will of the parties; either party or the arbitration tribunal itself may terminate the conciliation if it appears that continuing on the conciliative path is futile.[100] Confidentiality is mandated upon all parties; hence, any information obtained during conciliation that is adverse to the opposing party may not be invoked in subsequent arbitrations or judicial hearings.[101] The *Ethical Rules for Arbitrators*, likewise, provide that the arbitrator(s) maintain confidentiality "of all information revealed during the case. . . ."[102]

But Article 19 of the *2000 Conciliation Rules of CCPIT/CCOIC* permits a conciliator, in the absence of contrary instructions by a party, and at the conciliator's discretion, to disclose information received during conciliation to the opposing party.[103] Nonetheless, these confidentiality requirements, on balance, give the Chinese process a distinct advantage over litigation in the court system wherein similar requirements for confidentiality are not subscribed to, given the public nature of the court system.

If the conciliation were properly conducted, then the parties fully aired their views and shared the weaknesses and strengths of their case with the conciliator/arbitrator. Should the conciliation subsequently fail, it becomes arguable that the arbitrators can simply "switch hats" and once again impartially resume their arbitral role without having had their impartiality affected by knowledge obtained during the course of their *ex parte* discussions. Former Justice Hunter of the Hong Kong Supreme Court dismisses this concern an "intuitive reaction of the western adversarial lawyer. . . . it seems to me that he (the arbitrator) is more, not less likely, to produce an award which both parties will recognize as fair and just."[104]

It is, of course, the issue of confidentiality that most upsets Western-trained common lawyers. They argue, and perhaps with some justification, that matters discussed during conciliation cannot be extirpated from the brain of the tribunal. *Ex parte* discussions are not evidence, it is maintained, yet those discussions may, in fact, influence the outcome of arbitration. CIETAC officials and Chinese-trained lawyers scoff at such allegations and are resolute that the CIETAC arbitrators can take off their conciliator's hat as easily as they put it on. After all, I was told repeatedly that mediation and conciliation are almost part of the Chinese genetic makeup. Mediation is part of Chinese culture. But as I listened to one of the few references to China's dispute resolution past, I could not help but think of a highly compelling article written by Prof. Neil Damant of Tel Aviv University on the subject of mediation in the PRC.[105] Prof. Damant is especially hard on Wall and Blum, who in a 1991 article in the *JCR* puts forth the notion that China is "the most heavily mediated nation on earth" and that "all disputes there . . . are mediated." Damant calls their work that of "lumpers"—writers who want to put all the boxes together in one neat bundle. He, on the other hand, is, by his own admission, a "splitter"—one who points out divergences and draws distinctions. Damant argues that based on archival sources and his interviews with urban and rural officials, one should subscribe to a disaggregated notion of conflict resolution in the PRC. Rather than constituting a national pattern, preferences for dispute resolution, in fact, vary substantially by region, class, and gender. To the extent it was practiced at the grassroots level, mediation was/is only one method of dispute resolution; others include collective action, interpersonal violence, and even feigned suicide. Damant maintains that once scholarly recognition of how disaggregated dispute resolution is in the PRC, then—and only then—will practical applications for improvement to the system be meaningful.

Once again, we are reminded that when choosing an arbitrator or a tribunal or a presiding arbitrator, how important the selection process is; one might very well wind up with an arbitrator cum conciliator.

The Chinese Arbitral Act mandates that an arbitrator decide a dispute "fairly in accordance with truth and in compliance with the law."[106] CIETAC rules require the tribunal to make an award, "in compliance with the principle of fairness and reasonableness."[107] This ability to decide a dispute *ex aequo et bono* is somewhat anomalous, especially when an arbitrator is given discretion that is seemingly unbounded. Typically, in civil law countries and under the UNCITRAL Model Law,[108] arbitrators may act as *amiable compositeurs,* but *only* with the consent of the parties.[109] How China came to include these provisions in its arbitral law is difficult to ascertain. Is it, once again, the CIETAC compulsion for institutional dominance? We see this proclivity repeated as it applies to an arbitration award, as well.

There is an underlying concern regarding the institutional oversight by CIETAC of an arbitration tribunal's award, or in international law parlance, the *droit de regard*. While the rules of CIETAC pronounce that an arbitration tribunal shall act independently,[110] the rules go on to require a tribunal to submit "its draft award to the CIETAC for scrutiny before signing the award. The CIETAC may remind the arbitration tribunal of issues in the award on condition that the arbitration tribunal's independence in rendering an award is not affected."[111] Couple this rule with Chen's assertion that not all CIETAC arbitrators write their own awards. Awards might be drafted by the CIETAC Secretariat staff and approved by the Secretary-General or one of his deputies before being sent on to the arbitrators. Why? Chen suggests that, "CIETAC likes uniformity for the sake of uniformity . . . the general cultural sentiment in the chinese [sic] society [is] that uniformity is always preferred even if it does not serve an obvious purpose."[112]

CIETAC's superintendence over arbitration awards is quite similar to my research regarding the jurisdiction of CIETAC tribunals. As with tribunal jurisdiction, there is dissonance between academicians who write about arbitration in China and those who are engaged in arbitration "on the ground," so to speak. CIETAC officials, as well as practitioners, both agree that CIETAC is far too busy to bother writing or reviewing arbiters' awards. Then why keep such language in CIETAC's rules, they were asked. The typical response I received mirrored Chen's observation about uniformity and repeated the suggestion that the Chinese trust institutions over the individual. How casually my host lawyers could ascribe a cultural attribute to over a billion people was revealing as to the stereotypes Chinese lawyers held of the Chinese populace.

## Beijing Arbitration Commission

In addition to CIETAC, there are some 180 arbitral commissions in China that are located in key provincial cities whose main responsibility is the arbitration of domestic disputes. But these commissions are also authorized to hear foreign-related disputes as well as international disputes (if the parties agree).[113]

One that deserves special mention is the Beijing Arbitration Commission (BAC). I had the opportunity to spend time with BAC's Secretary-General Wang Hongsong and a BAC official, Chu Cong Yan. Both parties are named because Ms. Wang eschewed any notion of anonymity. Whatever she had to say would be on the record. Both women were aware that I was taking notes during our conversation.[114]

Ms. Wang was asked what in her opinion made Chinese arbitration different from arbitration in other parts of the world. She unhesitatingly replied that it was the widespread use of arbitration throughout the country. In few places in the world were arbitral commissions as readily available to the populace as existed in China. The proliferation of arbitration in China was an obvious source of pride.

It is not difficult to be impressed with the BAC. Ms. Wang offers creative, dynamic, and forward thinking leadership. It is also an organization that markets itself well—from an impressive lobby to a well done website; from accessibility to scholars to marketing materials wrapped up in a DVD. Ms. Wang is clearly proud of BAC's independence as a non-governmental institution which she sees as a major difference between BAC and CIETAC's susceptibility to CCPIT influence. Arbitrators serve three year terms, are not employees of the BAC, and produce awards in an average of seventy days. Importantly, the BAC enjoys an excellent reputation within the legal community I visited—substantially more so than CIETAC.

BAC's leadership and growing reputation had seen its utilization steadily increase from a low of 12 cases in 1995 to close to 2000 cases in 2006; the amount in dispute will exceed one billion U.S. dollars. While the BAC has cognizance to hear international cases, most of its arbitration thus far has been domestic cases; but, the BAC will have heard 44 international cases in 2006 (compared to CIETAC's 958 concluded cases in 2005).[115]

The BAC is not without rebuke, however. Among the criticisms it receives is the BAC's Article 22 provision allowing the BAC to remove an arbitrator who is not performing to BAC standards. Of course, the BAC suggests that the issue is quality control and it is simply putting in its rules what is the typical Chinese practice. But by international standards, this provision is an anomaly and runs counter to the BAC's marketing efforts as a forward looking commission employing the best international arbitral standards. Additionally, the BAC markets its international commitment and its utilization of only high grade arbitrators. Yet, the BAC website portrays a table of its arbitrators of whom 285 were Chinese (including Hong Kong and Taiwan) and only 9 were non-Chinese.[116]

No doubt in an effort to stay abreast of a perceived competitor, a number of the CIETAC May 2005 rule changes, in fact, mirror provisions that were already in place at the BAC. For example, we pointed out that prior to May 2005, under CIETAC's rules, a tribunal's competence was determined at the Commission level. After May 2005, CIETAC's amended rules permit the matter of competence to be delegated or, in the words of the BAC Rules, the tribunal may be "authorized" to rule on jurisdictional objections.[117] Notwithstanding this letting out of the tether, ultimately, the matter of arbitral jurisdiction in both organizations sits at the Commission level to be doled out as the Commission deems appropriate.

When I asked Secretary-General Wang why there must be this insistence upon institutional control, she explained that historically Chinese people have had more trust in the "institution than they had in individuals." A light went on! No Confucius. No suggestion of the supposed Asian proclivity for extra-judicial dispute resolution. Just a reference to the same Chinese preference for institutional dispute resolution that was given to me by those at CIETAC.

Ms. Wang's comment required validation. I made it a habit of asking every lawyer with whom I spoke about this alleged socio-cultural propensity of the Chinese people. To a person they agreed. Chinese people, it was repeated, tend more toward institutional rather that individual trust. But, what about—I would ask purposefully—the matter of Chinese history and the ideals of Confucian dispute resolution. The Chinese lawyers were a bit put off initially by the question and then, as if trying to reaffirm their history, averred that Confucianism, certainly, played into the dispute resolution system—but not the arbitral system. Foreign lawyers admitted they had never heard Chinese lawyers speak of their arbitral history in Confucian terms. The question must then be pondered: If no one knows history, does it exist? And, if it does exist, does it exist within the context of arbitration? Thus far, neither the Chinese arbitral laws nor the CIETAC/BAC rules have revealed an arbitral chain. We turn now to the enforcement of arbitration awards in China as the last unexplored arbitral cave.

# Notes

1. *Arbitration Law of the People's Republic of China*, (Adopted at the 9th Session of the Standing Committee of the 8th National People's Congress of the People's Republic of China, and promulgated by the President, on August 31, 1994, effective, September 1, 1995). Hereinafter: *CAA*.

2. *UNCITRAL Model Law on International Commercial Arbitration* (1985) (as adopted by the United Nations Commission on International Trade Law, June 21, 1985).

3. G. Liu & A. Lourie, *International Arbitration in China . . .* , 28 J. MARSHALL L. REV. 539, 540 (1995).

4. Hu Li, *Enforcement of the International Commercial Arbitration Award in the People's Republic of China,* 16 JOURNAL OF INTERNATIONAL ARBITRATION 4, 1-40, 42 (1999)

5. *Civil Procedure Law of the People's Republic of China,* (Adopted at the 22nd Meeting of the Standing Committee of the Fifth National People's Congress and promulgated by Order No. 8 of the Standing Committee of the National People's Congress, March 8, 1982, and implemented on a trial basis, October 1, 1982).

6. *Contract Law of the People's Republic of China,* (Adopted at the Second Session of the Ninth National People's Congress, March 15, 1999). Hereinafter, *Contract Law.*

7. This section, dealing with the *CAA*, is an amalgam of various authors' thoughts on the formation of the arbitration agreement; notably: M. Chao, I. Seow, J. Tan and P. Wang, *White Paper-Arbitration in China,* Jones Day Publications (March, 2004); M. Kidwell & J. Brown, *China: A Perspective on International Arbitration in China, Recent Developments; CIETC Arbitration,* 20 CONSTRUCTION JOURNAL 5, 253-261 (2004); and *A. Shields, China's Two Pronged Approach to International Arbitration, New Rules and New Law,* 15 JOURNAL OF INTERNATIONAL ARBITRATION 2, 67-84 (1998).

8. MO ZHANG, CHINESE CONTRACT LAW, 60, ( Martin Nijhoff 2006).

9. See Chapter Five of the *Trademark Law of the People's Republic of China,* adopted at the 24th Session of the Standing Committee of the Ninth National People's Congress, October 27, 2001.

10. Article 2, *Interpretation of the Supreme People's Court on Certain Issues Relating to the Application of the Arbitration Law of the People's Republic of China* issued Sept. 8, 2006. NOTE, hereinafter : *SPC Interpretation.*

11. Li Mei Qin, Attracting Foreign Investment into the PRC. . . . , 4 SING. J. INT'L & COMP. J. 159, 186 (2000).

12. MO ZHANG, at 73.

13. The May 2005 changes in CIETAC's rules have somewhat blurred the distinctions.

14. *CAA*, Chapter VII, Art. 65.

15. *Contract Law*, at Article 11.

16. *CAA*, at Article 16.

17. Yang Hong Zhi, *Can ICC Arbitration be Conducted in Mainland China,* 12 HELLER EHRMAN ASIA PRACTICE BULLETIN, December 2005.

18. Zhi at 12.

19. *SPC Interpretation,* at Article 4.

20. P. Coles, *Supreme Court Of China: Ruling On Arbitration Clause In IATA Ground Handling Agreements,* 2006 WLNR 17752847, 10/11/06 MONDAQ BUS. BRIEFING.

21. *Civil Law of the People's Republic of China,* adopted April 12, 1986 by the 4th Session of the 6th National People's Congress.

22. Article 178 of *the Supreme People's Court Opinion on Certain Issues Relating to the Full Implementation of the PRC General Principles of Civil Law* provided that a contract will have a foreign element when: (a) one or both

parties to the contract are foreign or stateless parties; (b) the subject matter of the contract is located in a foreign country; or (c) the act which gives rise to, modifies, or extinguishes the rights and obligations under the contract occurs in a foreign country.

23. I agree with Eu Jin Chua, *The Laws of the People's Republic of China* . . . , 7 CHI. J. INT'L L. 133, 144 (2006) that the question of whether a domestic arbitral matter held before a Chinese arbitral body outside of China is valid has still not entirely answered.

24. Conference materials, *Arbitration in China*, KEY MEDIA INTERNATIONAL, Hong Kong, April 11, 2006.

25. Article 126 of *The Contract Law of the People's Republic of China*, effective October 1, 1999.

26. *PRC Civil Law* at Article 146.

27. *PRC Civil Law* at Article 144.

28. *PRC Civil Law* at Article 150.

29. Art. V ¶ 2 ,*The United Nations Convention on the Recognition and Enforcement of Foreign Arbitral Awards* (New York, June 10, 1958) (hereinafter, the " *New York Convention* ").

30. *CAA* at Article 20

31. *CAA* at Articles 48 & 28.

32. *CAA* at Article 58

33. *CAA* at Article 53.

34. *CAA* at Article 54

35. *CAA* at Article 54

36. Article 259, *Law of Civil Procedure of the People's Republic of China*— 1991 (Adopted by the Fourth Session of the Seventh National People's Congress, April 9, 1991, promulgated by the Order No 44 of the President of the People's Republic of China, and effective on the date of its promulgation)

37. Article 1, *The United Nations Commission on International Trade Law: Model Law on International Commercial Arbitration*, (A/40/17, Annex D). Hereinafter *UNCITRAL Model Law*

38. *UNCITRAL Model Law,* at Article 16 & *CAA* at Article 20

39. *UNCITRAL Model Law,* at Article 29 and the *CAA* at Article 53.

40. *CAA*, at Article 32 and the *UNCITRAL Model Law* at Article 11.

41. *UNCITRAL Model Law,* at Article 10 and the *CAA* at Articles 30-32.

42. *CAA*, at Article 13.

43. *CAA*, at Article 51.

44. *ICC Rules of Arbitration,* at Article 17, *UNCITRAL Model Law* at Article 30, *CAA* at Articles 51-2.

45. Gu Weixia, *Recourse against Arbitral Awards: How Far Can a Court Go?* . . . , 4 CHIN. J. INTL'L L. 481, 499 (November 2005).

46. Wang Sheng Chang, *Resolving Disputes Through Conciliation and Arbitration in the Mainland China*, 2 ANN. 2000 ATLA CLE 1643 (2000).

47. J. TAO, ARBITRATION LAW AND PRACTICE IN CHINA, See generally Chapter One, *History of Arbitration in China*, 1-32 (KLUWER LAW INTERNATIONAL, 2004).
48. TAO, at at 3 .
49. TAO, at 2.
50. Stanley Lubman, *Studying Civil Law*, 248 CONTEMPORARY CHINESE LAW (Jerome Cohen, ed. HARVARD U PRESS 1970).
51. L. Chen, *Some Reflections on International Commercial Arbitration in China*, 13 JOURNAL OF INTERNATIONAL ARBITRATION 2, 121-162, 122 (1996).
52. TAO, at 3.
53. Chen, at 123.
54. Chen, at 123.
55. Chen, at 123.
56. S. Sucharitkul, *Rebirth of Chinese Legal Scholarship, with regard to International Law,* Vol.3, No.2 LEIDEN JOURNAL OF INTERNATIONAL LAW 12 (April 1990).
57. Sucharitkul, at 11.
58. *Regulations of the People's Republic of China on the Arbitration of Disputes Over Economic Contracts* (Promulgated by the State Council on August 22, 1983).
59. All citations are found in TAO at 2-3.
60. Chen, at 122-3.
61. Chen, at 122-3.
62. Now the China Chamber of International Commerce.
63. Article 66 of the *CAA*.
64. R. Peerenboom, *The Evolving Regulatory Framework for Enforcement of Arbitral Awards in the PRC*, ASIAN-PACIFIC LAW & POLICY JOURNAL, 1 APLPJ 12: 1,3 (2000).
65. Concurrent with the founding of CIETAC, an arbitral body was established for the resolution of maritime disputes, now known as CMAC (China Maritime Arbitration Commission). No further discussion of CMAC will be made in this book.
66. A. Yakren, ed., A LEGAL GUIDE TO DOING BUSINESS IN RUSSIA AND THE FORMER USSR, 144 (American Bar Asscoc. 2000).
67. G. Liu & A. Lourie, *International Commercial Arbitration in China. . . . ,* 28 J. MARSHALL L. REV. 539, 540-1, (Spring 1995).
68. Liu & Lourie, at 541.
69. PITMAN B. POTTER, FOREIGN BUSINESS LAW IN CHINA, 70-71 (The 1990 Institute, 1995)
70. Source from Conference materials, *Arbitration in China*, KEY MEDIA INTERNATIONAL, Hong Kong, April 11, 2006.
71. Chen, at 126.
72. Chen, at 126.

73. Robert Morgan, *Book Review*, 32 HKLJ 3, 730-34, 730 (2002).
74. Article 14, *Arbitration Provisions of the China International Economic and Trade Arbitration Commission Act,* Sept. 12, 1988.
75. Liu and Lourie, at 547.
76. Li Hu, *Enforcement of the International Commercial Arbitration Award in the People's Republic of China*, 16 JOURNAL OF INTERNATIONAL ARBITRATION 4, 1-40, 5 (1999).
77. *Financial Disputes Arbitration Rules of the China International Economic and Trade Arbitration Commission—CIETAC (2003)* (Adopted, April 4, 2003, by the China Council for the Promotion of International Trade / China Chamber of International Commerce, Effective, May 8, 2003). The financial disputes arbitration process will not be discussed in this book.
78. *CIETAC Arbitration Rules (2005)*, (Revised and adopted by the China Council for the Promotion of International Trade/China Chamber of International Commerce on January 11, 2005. Effective, May 1, 2005). Hereinafter, *CIETAC Rules*.
79. *id.*
80. TAO at 172-8. With the 1997 transition of sovereignty, something of a legal vacuum arose in the PRC in that the legal basis (the New York Convention) for enforcing, theretofore enforceable Hong Kong arbitration awards was no longer available. Hong Kong had continued to recognize PRC awards, however. Return to the *status quo ante* was restored in 2000 with the *Arrangement Concerning Mutual Enforcement of Arbitral Awards Between the Mainland and the Hong Kong Special Administrative Region*. See TAO at 172-3. In 1998, a similar but less extensive recognition of Taiwanese arbitration awards was instituted via the *Supreme People's Court's Recognition of Civil Judgments Made by Courts in Taiwan Region*. See TAO at 176-8.
81. *CIETAC Rules*, at Article 3.
82. *CIETAC Rules,* at Article 2.
83. In the Arbitration Rules, CIETAC is referred to as the Arbitration Commission
84. *The Trademarks Law of the People's Republic of China* ,amended version adopted October 22, 2001; *Patent Law of the People's Republic of China,* amended version adopted August 25, 2000.
85. See SINO's website at http://www.sipo.gov.cn/sipo_English/gysipo_e/default.htm.
86. U.S. Embassy Beijing China, *Protecting your Intellectual Property Rights (IPR) in China*, December 2005 found at http://beijing.usembassy-china.org.cn/protecting_ipr.html. (last visited December 1, 2006).
87. *CIETAC Rules,* at Article 6 .
88. Shields, *supra* at n.7.
89. *Yaung Chi OO Trading PTE Ltd. v. Government of the Union of Myanmar*, ASEAN I.D. Case NO. ARB/01/1

90. *UNCITRAL Model Law,* at Article 16.
91. *CIETAC Rules,* at Article 20.
92. *CIETAC Rules,* at Article 22.
93. *CIETAC Rules,* at Article 21 (2).
94. From the *News* section at CIETAC's website, http://www.cietac.org.cn/english/news/news6.htm (last visited January 1. 2007).
95. *CIETAC Rules,* at Article 22 (3).
96. Eu Jin Chua, *The Laws of the People's Republic of China: An Introduction for International Investors,* 7 CHI. J. INT'L L. 133, 145-6, (2006).
97. TAO, at 120, n.193
98. H. Tang, *Is There an Expanding Culture that Favors Combining Arbitration and Conciliation or Other ADR Procedures?,* ICCA CONGRESS SERIES NO. 8 (Seoul/1996), 101-120.
99. *CIETAC Rules,* at Article 40 (6).
100. *CIETAC Rules,* at Article 40. See also Wang Wenying, *The Role of Conciliation, in Resolving Disputes: a P.R.C. Perspective,* 20 OHIO ST. J. DISP. RESOL. 412, 440, (2005).
101. *CIETAC Rules,* at Article 40(8).
102. *Ethical Rules for Arbitrators,* Revised Version dated May 6, 1994.
103. TAO, at 122, n. 197.
104. R. Thirgood, *A Critique of Foreign arbitration in China,* 17 JOURNAL OF INTERNATIONAL ARBITRATION 89, 94 (2000).
105. N. Damant, *Conflict and Conflict Resolution in China,* 44 JOURNAL OF CONFLICT RESOLUTION 4, 523-546 (August 2000).
106. *CAA,* at Article 7.
107. *CIETAC Rules,* at Article 43.
108. *UNCITRAL Model Law,* at Article 28 (3).
109. For an interesting perspective on this matter, see H. Li, *Arbitration ex aequo et bono in China,* 66 JOURNAL OF CHARTERED INSTITUTE OF ARBITRATORS 3 (Aug. 2000)
110. *CIETAC Rules,* at Article 43.
111. *CIETAC Rules,* at Article 45.
112. Chen, at 136.
113. *Notice of the General Office of the State Council,* June 8, 1996, cited in D. Howell, *Developments in Arbitration Law and Practice in Asia,* found at http://www.fulbright.com/images/publications/03312006HowellArbitration.pdf.
114. The matters regarding the BAC are taken either from my notes from my meeting of October 26, 2006 or from *The Beijing Arbitration Commission Arbitration Rules* (Revised and adopted at the Fifth Meeting of the Third session of the Beijing Arbitration Commission on September 16,2003. Effective as from March 1. 2004.) Hereinafter referred to as the *BAC Rules.*

115. Zhao, Xiuwen and L. Kloppenberg, *Reforming Chinese Arbitration Law and Practices in the Global Economy,* 31:3 UNIVERSITY OF DAYTON LAW REVIEW, 421, 425-6, (2006).

116. http://www.bjac.org.cn/en/organise/report2.htm (last visited January 3, 2006).

117. *BAC Rules*, Article 6.

# Chapter Seven

# Chinese Arbitral Enforcement Practices and the Arbitral Chain

## Does a Study of the Enforcement of Foreign Arbitration Awards Lead to an Arbitral Chain?

In the final analysis, there is no sense expending the time, money, and effort arbitrating a dispute if, in fact, the dispute is resolved within a legal system that precludes the enforcement of the obtained award. Therefore, the subject for this chapter is the unfolding of China's enforcement mechanisms in order to determine if those mechanisms, or the lack thereof, provide insight into the existence of a Chinese arbitral chain. Since various references in this section will be made to the courts in the PRC and their role in the arbitration process, it might be useful, at this juncture, to provide a brief description of the Chinese judiciary.[1]

The 1982 PRC State Constitution and the Organic Law of the People's Courts[2] created for a four-level court system. The Supreme People's Court sits in Beijing at the apex of the judicial system, while the Higher People's Courts reside in the provinces, autonomous regions and special municipalities. Intermediate People's Courts are found at the prefecture level and also in parts of provinces, autonomous regions, and special municipalities. Basic People's Courts populate the counties, towns, and municipal districts. Special courts have been created to handle matters affecting military, railroad transportation, water transportation, and forestry.[3]

On its website, the Supreme People's Court portrays itself as the highest trial organ in the country [exercising] its right of trial independently. It is also the highest supervising organ over the trial practices of local people's courts and special people's courts at various levels. It reports its work to the National People's Congress and its Standing Committee. The right of appointment and removal of the president and vice presidents as well as members of the trial committee of the Supreme People's Court lies with the National People's Congress.[4]

A top-line organization chart of the Court is shown:[5]

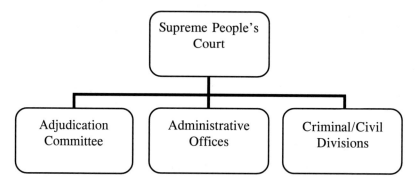

An organization chart reflecting the Chinese judicial system is provided.[6]

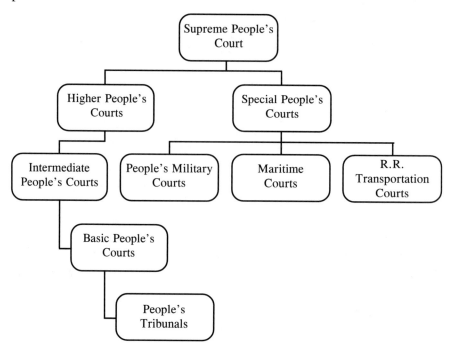

Lest the common lawyer assume that the Chinese judiciary is a co-equal branch of government, it certainly is not. Nor is it the equivalent of a judiciary within a civil law or common law parliamentary system. The Chinese judiciary is not a partner in a scheme of constitutional separation of powers. On the contrary, the constitutional basis of the Court is that of an administrative organ under the guidance of the Standing Committee of the National People's Congress. The Standing Committee is the organization constitutionally charted to interpret the Constitution.[7]

Clarke writes,

> As it rejects the notion of vertical separation of powers, the PRC also rejects the notion of horizontal separation of powers between different branches of government (for example, the traditional troika of legislative, executive, and judicial branches). A necessary separation of functions is acknowledged, but constitutionally speaking the National People's Congress (in form, a legislature) sits at the apex of China's political power structure. In reality, that position is occupied by the Standing Committee of the Politburo of the Chinese Communist Party, but both form and reality share the rejection of multiple power centers.[8]

Prof. Brown elaborates and writes of a distinct socialist origin of Chinese law as displayed through the interaction between Party and government in the administration of law.[9] The political realities are that of Party influence on the policy directions of the Court within a political system that subordinates the Court to the National People's Congress and the agencies of the State Council.[10] One foreign lawyer based in Shanghai told me that the Chinese Supreme Court tended to smell the Party scent in the wind and voluntarily move in the direction of the scent lest the Court be involuntarily moved in that direction.

In a tad lengthy—but highly revealing—excerpt, the Court's "2005 Work Report" is illustrative of its legal fidelity. Xiao Yang, president of the PRC Supreme People's Court, delivering the work report of the Supreme People's Court at the 4th Session of 10th National People's Congress, stated:

> Now, on behalf of the Supreme People's Court, let me report the work of the court for deliberation by the session.
>
> Under the leadership of the CPC Central Committee with Comrade Hu Jintao as its general secretary and guided by the Deng Xiaoping theory

and the important thinking of the "Three Represents," the Supreme People's Court in 2005 fully implemented the scientific development concept, enforced in depth the work principles of "fair adjudication" and "serving the people wholeheartedly," carefully implemented the demands made by the 3d Session of the 10th NPC, and conscientiously fulfilled the duties entrusted to it by the constitution and the laws.

During the past year, the Supreme People's Court, proceeding from the big picture of promoting socioeconomic development, maintaining social stability, and building a harmonious socialist society, consistently did a good job in the administration of justice and enforcement work.[11]

Both the common and civil lawyer would be hard pressed to take the above quote, substitute the names of his/her country's then prevailing political party and head of state, and then suggest that such a predicate would be found in the work report of its national court.

The logical extension of the subordination of the court system to the political system is that "PRC courts are much weaker institutionally and judges and the judiciary have a much lower stature than in the United States or even civil law countries."[12] Furthermore, courts are financially reliant on their corresponding level of government for salaries, housing, and benefits. There is no security of tenure to fall back on. Judges, according to Peerenboom, are beholden to their government counterparts and, in spite of a proclaimed formality of judicial independence in adjudication, contacts between judges and government officials is routine.

The constitutional incongruity is manifest: Article 126 of the PRC Constitution reads, "The people's courts shall, in accordance with the law, exercise judicial power independently and are not subject to interference by administrative organs, public organizations or individuals." Yet, Article 128 organizationally subordinates the courts, "The Supreme People's Court is responsible to the National People's Congress and its Standing Committee. Local people's courts at different levels are responsible to the organs of state power which created them." And since, the people's congresses appoint judges and many of the congress persons are Party officials, there is a further ratcheting down of the independence of the courts. Many senior judges are Party members who might well discuss a difficult or controversial case with their appropriate Political-Legal Committee.[13] As we explore the matter of enforcement further, we will see how this mutualism is played out in local protectionism, ofttimes to the detriment of the non-local compliant party.

In China, one must look under many tents to find the appropriate law(s) that govern the enforcement of arbitration awards. In addition to the Chinese Arbitration Law, there are the Civil Procedure Law, the Contract Law, the Civil Code; and laws governing foreign investment enterprises, such as the Sino-Foreign Equity Joint Venture Law[14] and the Sino-Foreign Cooperative Joint Venture Law.[15] An illustration of arbitration in the Joint Venture Law is found at Article 25 which provides that, absent an agreement by the board of directors to resolve their differences by consultation, the dispute should be submitted to a Chinese arbitration institution.

There are Interpretations and Promulgations of the Supreme People's Court concerning arbitration that must be put into the enforcement equation.

And as for foreign awards, China is a signatory to the New York Convention and has, as have many other nations, acceded to the Convention subject to the reciprocal and commercial reservations that permit

> any State may on the basis of reciprocity declare that it will apply the Convention to the recognition and enforcement of awards made only in the territory of another Contracting State. It may also declare that it will apply the Convention only to differences arising out of legal relationships, whether contractual or not, which are considered as commercial under the national law of the State making such declaration.[16]

China has implemented the New York Convention through a 1986 Standing Committee Decision, as well as a 1987 Supreme Court Notice.[17] China has also entered into an international convention with the United States in which there is strong support for private commercial arbitration.[18]

For those who have studied law in general, and arbitration in particular, it is conceded axiomatically that situations will occur whereby a party on the losing end of an arbitration will resile from an award or judgment that went against him/her. In such a circumstance, the compliant party may apply to the appropriate People's Court for enforcement, subject to any application by the non-compliant party for setting aside the award.

For disputes involving a foreign element and adjudicated by a Chinese arbitral body, China's Civil Procedure Law requires that

> In a case in which an award has been made by an arbitral organ of the People's Republic of China handling cases involving foreign element, the parties may not bring an action in a people's court. If one party fails to comply with the arbitral award, the other party may apply for its enforcement to the intermediate people's court of the place where the party against whom the application for enforcement is made has his domicile or where his property is located.[19]

For an award obtained outside the PRC, China's Civil Procedure Law provides a similar enforcement mechanism.

> If an award made by a foreign arbitral organ requires the recognition and enforcement by a people's court of the People's Republic of China, the party concerned shall directly apply to the intermediate people's court of the place where the party subjected to enforcement has his domicile or where his property is located. The people's court shall deal with the matter in accordance with the international treaties concluded or acceded to by the People's Republic of China or with the principle of reciprocity.[20]

Whether the foreign-related award was obtained in China or in a New York Convention signatory state, the compliant party is required to seek enforcement in the jurisdiction of one of the some 400 Intermediate People's Courts, specifically, the Intermediate Court where the non-compliant party is domiciled or his/her assets are located. If this court of first instance determines it has grounds to revoke the award, it must refer its decision to the next higher Court, and ultimately, to the Supreme People's Court for approval. The Supreme People's Court must agree to the non-enforcement of a foreign-related arbitral award. Without the consent from the Supreme Court, a lower Court is, technically, powerless to reject the award. Rather than set aside an award, the People's Court may, if it considers it appropriate, suspend its activity and notify the arbitral tribunal to re-arbitrate the dispute. If the arbitration tribunal refuses to re-arbitrate the dispute, the Court will resume the process to set aside the award.[21]

As for setting aside an award, Article 70 of the CAA and Article 260 of the Civil Procedure Law need be read in tandem to understand the bases for setting aside a foreign-related arbitral award.[22] Legal persons must file an application to set aside an arbitral award within six months after receipt of the award[23] The award may be set aside by the People's Court if:

- The parties have neither included an arbitration clause in their contract nor subsequently concluded a written arbitration agreement;
- The non-moving party was neither notified to appoint an arbitrator nor to take part in the arbitration proceedings, nor was the non-moving party able to present his case due to reasons for which he is not responsible;
- The formation of the arbitration tribunal or the arbitration procedure was not in conformity with the rules of arbitration;
- The matters decided in the award exceeded the scope of the arbitration (the award was ultra vires); or
- The award was against the public and social interest of China.

A glaring example of the last point dealing with the public and social interest provision is the case of *Dongfeng Garments Factory and others v. Henan Garments Import & Export.*[24] The case serves as a wake up call to remind the foreign investor of what he or she might face in the Chinese courts. In *Dongfeng*, damages were awarded to the claimants in a CIETAC arbitration arising from a breach of a joint venture contract. The claimants, the respondents and one other party were engaged in a joint venture for the manufacture of garments. The claimants applied to the local Intermediate People's Court for an enforcement of the award against the respondents. The local court refused to entertain the application for enforcement of the award. It did not contest the findings of the CIETAC's arbitration tribunal. It rejected the application on the ground that it would be harmful to the "economic influence of the State and the public interest of the society and adversely affect the foreign trade order of the State." The defendant was a major local economic force. Its decision was overturned upon appeal to the Supreme People's Court.[25]

While the enforcement provisions on paper appear to be structurally and procedurally sound, in reality, there has been a substantial amount of criticism of the arbitral enforcement mechanisms in the PRC. Critics point to the refusal of regional courts to enforce foreign arbitration awards against local economic interests.[26] Such refusal has caused commentators to suggest that CIETAC awards are "paper tigers" and that CIETAC had made promises that the courts will not keep.[27] One observer characterized enforcement as "spotty at best."[28]

Every judicial system wishes there was one, or perhaps more than one, case that was never litigated, never decided upon, and whose judgment never reached the light of day. Chinese lawyers, from academia to private practice to officialdom would agree that case is *Revpower Ltd v. Shanghai Far East Aerial Technology Import and Export Corp. Revpower Ltd.* has, unquestionably, become the poster child for the lack of Chinese court enforcement of foreign awards. Forbes magazine described the *Revpower* fiasco.

> Robert Aronson . . . runs Revpower, based in . . . Fla. A decade ago he signed a joint venture deal with the Shanghai Far East Aero-Technology Import & Export Corp. to develop a battery factory. Revpower would provide the know-how and distribute the product. The Chinese would organize the plant. In 1989 the Chinese imposed . . . a price hike of 40%, purportedly because of higher utility costs. Aronson terminated the deal and started arbitration proceedings in Stockholm. Aronson won a $5 million award, which, with interest, comes to $8 million. But Aronson's award could be enforced for only six months, and the Chinese courts stalled recognition of it. After the U.S. government applied diplomatic pressure on the Chinese to get on with it, the Shanghai Intermediate People's Court finally recognized the award. In 1996 Aronson discovered that most of the assets of his Chinese partner had been transferred elsewhere. Aronson went home empty-handed, having learned too late about doing business in the world's hottest economy.[29]

Peerenboom's view of *Revpower* is that "many of the most extreme claims about the hazards of enforcing arbitral awards in China have been largely based on a single widely reported case, the Revpower case, and are grossly overstated."[30]

It seems appropriate having just cited Peerenboom, to discuss his research on Chinese enforcement for it bears on our search for the arbitral link(s).

Oft mentioned during my research in China, in scholarly arbitral materials, and during a recent ABA tele-seminar,[31] was a survey completed concerning the enforcement of CIETAC and foreign arbitral awards conducted by the highly regarded Prof. R. Peerenboom. Quantitatively, the survey is rather sparse. One suspects that it was the reputation of the maestro behind the survey that drove its qualitative notoriety. Only 72 cases were included in the survey. The judiciary's enforcement of the awards was almost evenly split between awards that were enforced and awards that were not enforced.[32]

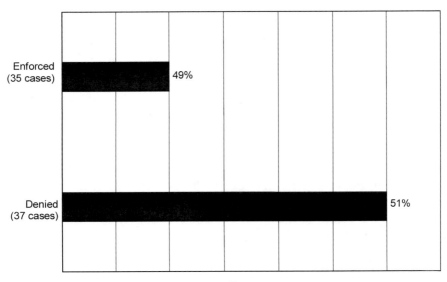

Of the thirty-five awards that were enforced, the amounts recovered by claimants varied. In only one-third of the cases did a party receive all that was due; in one-third of the cases the enforcing party received less than half than the award for which enforcement was sought.[33]

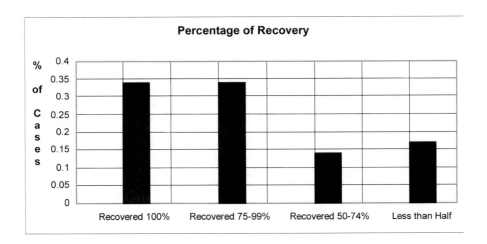

As to why awards were not enforced, Prof. Peerenboom's findings were, initially, unexpected. The largest obstacle to enforcement that Prof. Peerenboom found, by far, was the insolvency of the respondents accounting for 43% of all non-enforcement cases.[34]

On reflection, I recalled that two counsels during the ABA tele-seminar commented on the difficulty of enforcing judgments against state or locally owned enterprises if the enforcement of the arbitration award would have a negative impact on the local economy.[35] How much of the insolvency found by Prof. Peerenboom was due to the "Revpower-like" shifting of assets is unknown. But, two leading arbitral practitioners during the ABA tele-seminar suggested it might very well be the case. The other overarching reason for lack of enforcement was the finding of procedural violations by the court such as faulty appointment of an arbitrator, the tribunal's exceeding its authority, *etc.*[36]

My own discussions and research support that of Prof. Peerenboom. He and I both found that in many instances, arbitration awards, once obtained, were complied with, or, if the award was abjured, a Chinese court enforced the award. Full stop, end of story. The below three cases reflect this observation.

1. In November 2003, the Heifei Intermediate People's Court refused to enforce an arbitral award issued by HKIAC dated June 28, 1997, holding that the parties had not entered into an arbitration agreement. In fact, one party had reached the arbitration agreement in the name of a third entity but had not been duly authorized to do so. After review by the High Court and the Supreme Court, the award was not enforced.
2. In July 2003, the Beijing No.1 Intermediate People's Court refused to enforce an arbitral award issued by the Sugar Association of London (SAL) dated August 6, 2001, holding that the award had acknowledged a foreign options transaction agreement which had not been approved by the Chinese government. The Supreme Court overturned the refusal, stating that the agreement did not violate public policy, regardless of the flaws in the transaction agreement.
3. In 1998, the Guangzhou Maritime Court refused to enforce an arbitral award issued by the Lloyd's Salvage Arbitration Branch in London dated August 29, 1995, holding that the

application for enforcement had exceeded the time limit of six months from the issuance of the award.[37]

But it is the all-too-many exceptions that challenge the rule. A claimant can surely expect to encounter resistance to enforcement, I was told, if a state-owned enterprise was involved and/or if the enforcement was sought in the rural areas of China versus its more urbane coastal cities.[38] The above cases are rather simple and straightforward. And the cases involve either the People's Supreme Court or the court in a major Chinese city.

Reinstein's research parallels my own. She interviewed Dean Wang Chenguang of Tsinghua University and member of the Adjudication Committee of the Supreme People's Court. Dean Wang confirmed that courts in the coastal cities were "more highly developed" given the higher education obtained by the area's judges and lawyers, to say nothing of the higher interaction with foreigners. The rural areas, Dean Wang explained, suffer a higher attrition rate as students leave the countryside to pursue their education and careers in coastal cities. The rural court system is then left with an inadequate legal system and personalities to deal with the enforcement of foreign disputes.[39]

The term "local protectionism" is often bandied about by arbitral observers as an impediment to enforcement in China. But to what the term precisely refers can cause one to wander down a number of analytical paths. Prof. Chen, for example, ascribes the existence of local protectionism to governmental/structural deficiencies. A local court might exhibit a reluctance to enforce a CIETAC award because of its subordination to the local government which, in turn, has an interest in local/regional economic health. In my conversations with Chinese lawyers, Chen's observations were supported, especially when the losing party was a state-owned enterprise. My hosts felt, most assuredly, that local government officials would resist the enforcement of any award that would result in layoffs or bankruptcy that, in turn, would deleteriously impact the local economy.

The direct influence by local officials is compounded by judicial insufficiencies: enforcement matters are subordinate to civil & criminal cases and enforcement divisions are inadequately funded.[40] Heye describes China's enforcement apparatus as "The weakest prong of the Chinese court system. . . ."[41] Enforcement is not considered a prime assignment for judges. Those with the least amount of training are typically assigned to enforcement duties which are far less intellectually stimulating than work on other benches.[42] "The enforcement department of the judiciary is generally considered to be the worst assignment for judges. . . . [T]he execution chamber is the refuge of the tired, mediocre, and the uneducated."[43] One Chinese lawyer likened the enforcement power of the court to the musculature of a young lady. Pointing to his biceps, Lawyer *Four* said, "Their enforcement is like a little girl's muscle. Very, very weak. . . ." Prof. Clark likens the courts' enforcement orders to those of "just another bureaucracy with no more power to tell banks what to do than the Post Office."[44] One lawyer on the ABA tele-seminar related the experience of her Japanese client who had received a five million dollar award in Stockholm against a Chinese company. The award was not enforced for over five years!

As if the above were insufficient to jeopardize Chinese courts' repute for judicial independence, further opprobrium comes from the fact that there sits along side most Chinese courts an Adjudication Committee composed of the court's administrative leaders who "decide sensitive or complex cases behind closed doors after only listening to a report from the judge in charge of the trial. Outside agencies—including higher courts as well as local and central Party apparatus—frequently influence rulings behind the scenes."[45] Reinstein depicts the Adjudication Committee system as a further detraction from judicial independence.[46]

The lack of prestige and the resultant inadequate funding for the enforcement divisions can lead to situations frightfully disconcerting to the foreign investor. Bersani cites an instance wherein court personnel from the place where an enforcement application was submitted had to travel to a non-performing party's local court. The per diem provided to the court personnel was so meager that the foreign company was asked to cover travel expenses. Since rail travel is lengthy, the foreign company was also asked to pay air travel expenses, as well. For a U.S. businessperson to risk a violation of the Foreign Corrupt Practices Act or risk the loss of an arbitration award already secured is a choice no party to a judicial proceeding should face.[47]

There are additional problems when attempting to enforce an arbitral award in local courts. A foreign party seeking the enforcement of an arbitration award must retain local counsel to bring the request for enforcement to the intermediate people's court located where the party against whom enforcement is sought is either domiciled or has property located. Foreign lawyers may not practice law in Chinese courts as Chinese law requires that "When foreign nationals, stateless persons or foreign enterprises and organizations need lawyers as agents *ad litem* to bring an action or enter appearance on their behalf in the people's court, they must appoint lawyers of the People's Republic of China."[48] On the other hand, CIETAC Rules permit a foreign citizen to represent his/her client before a CIETAC tribunal.[49] However, the foreign lawyer may not give advice or comment during the course of the arbitration on Chinese law and the issues surrounding Chinese law. What happens, practically, is that the foreign party will include a Chinese lawyer as part of his/her legal team, obviously causing legal fees to increase.

In fact, in mid-2006, the Shanghai Lawyers Association issued a memorandum decrying what it called the unauthorized practice of law by foreign law firms in China and calling for a crackdown by the authorities in order to "put in order, regularize and purify the Shanghai foreign legal services market [which] is crucial to the majesty of our nation, justice, independence, and economic safety."[50] Lofty words, indeed! Prof. Clark dismissed the hue and cry of the Shanghai lawyers: "This is about protecting Shanghai lawyers from competition, not about protecting the public or the clients of the foreign lawyers."[51] My research in China confirmed the requirement for the use of Chinese lawyers. All the foreign lawyers with whom I spoke had, in fact, set up a relationship with a Chinese law firm so each could benefit reciprocally. But the time and expense required by the successful compliant party is obvious.[52]

Once in court, the enforcing foreign party faces a judicial system slighted and, perhaps, even antagonistic toward a CIETAC arbitration award, given the "official" preference for arbitration over judicially-based dispute resolution. Adding coals to the fire are the "marketing" efforts of CIETAC who, while boasting of their competence and independence, imply criticism of the judiciary. Thus, the foreign party may find itself confronted by a local court system "skewed against strangers . . ." with local protectionism being "the decisive factor in decisions by the courts." The possible result: "The arbitration award is merely a piece of paper, dependent for execution on the often elusive cooperation of local officials."[53]

What is the impact of the foreign anxiety with Chinese enforcement mechanisms? One result is the below letter that one of my foreign-based hosts shared with me. Asked to provide a perspective on PRC arbitration by a client, my host suggested that the PRC be avoided all together and that the client opt for Hong Kong. Lawyer *Fifteen* wrote:

_____ has a great reputation for its international banking practice, but I would be of a different mind on interpreting/addressing certain PRC-specific issues, such as this one. There are numerous reasons to avoid choosing CIETAC, including the fact that CIETAC arbitrators are inexperienced with these types of issues.

Other reasons include:

(1) All provisional remedies must go through CIETAC and not directly to court. ICC/HKIAC (and other international institutions) allow the parties to go directly to the court to request provisional remedies. If one must first go through CIETAC, a key aim in pursuing provisional remedies may be defeated.

(2) CIETAC can make decisions based upon reasonableness and therefore can ignore the contract/law.

(3) In choosing the tribunal, the presiding arbitrator is almost always a local and someone connected with CIETAC.

(4) Earlier this year, CIETAC's management was detained and removed for corruption. These events have put the future stability of CIETAC in question.

Typically, we have found that conducting arbitration in Hong Kong using the Hong Kong International Arbitration Center ("HKIAC") is a satisfactory solution to the Chinese counterparts with whom our clients are negotiating. We will typically provide that the arbitrator(s) will not be a PRC national, nor a national of the country where our client is from. The arbitration can be conducted in Chinese and in English. These requirements are fair to both parties.

Cheers,

Arguably, this letter represents one lawyer and one client. But one needs to take pause when foreign arbitration participants reflect similar views in a survey conducted by the American Chamber of Commerce in the PRC. The response from the participating membership was not flattering toward Chinese arbitration. The participant population, however, was far too sparse for one to make any overall conclusions or generalizations. Perhaps most telling were the comments, made independent of the survey, by an unnamed U.S. Embassy official. The official was not particularly flattering either about the conduct of arbitrators ("[T]hey don't follow procedures, they violate confidentiality, they lack ethical standards, there have been charges of corruption. . . .") or the arbitration process, maintaining that the process is so transparent that what should be judged in the criminal courts is being decided in arbitration.[54]

During the previously-mentioned ABA tele-seminar, a number of lawyers based in Hong Kong and the PRC spoke to the subject of enforcement. Their views were telling. I report their comments from notes taken during each one's presentation. The counsel for GE in Hong Kong shared her preference for arbitration in Hong Kong given that the Hong Kong courts will "more readily" enforce an arbitration award than will PRC courts. Her "largest problem" with arbitration in China was the identification of assets against which to enforce a judgment. The counsel in Beijing, a noted arbitral scholar in her own right, commented that foreign parties had experienced "mixed enforcement" in the PRC and while there were still problems, she felt the enforcement issues were "changing slowly for the better." She also explained that corruption, while abating, is still a live issue in the Chinese courts. During the tele-seminar she reflected the GE counsel's concern about asset identification and spoke to a case wherein a tipster in a court alerted the local losing party of an anticipated enforcement order, prompting the losing party to move assets away from the local bank.

Lest it be surmised that complaints about enforcement of arbitral awards emanate exclusively from the disgruntled and those who comment on the disgruntled, no less a person than the President of the PRC's Supreme Court wrote in 2004 that, "The difficulty of executing civil and commercial judgments has become a major chronic ailment often leading to chaos in the enforcement process; there are few solutions to the problem."[55]

As for the future of arbitral enforcement by the courts in the PRC, one observer suggests that "In the foreseeable future, the weakness of the judicial system will contribute considerable uncertainty to an already uncertain business environment. Chinese legality will remain weak, and so will the Chinese state as well."[56]

The former President of the American Chamber of Commerce in China, Sally Harpole, is a bit more sanguine, opining that there has been "significant progress" by Chinese arbitration authorities in recent years. Her optimism is reinforced by her observation that CIETAC hears some 900 arbitrations each year and there have been "dozens and dozens of precedents where the Chinese courts have recognized and enforced a CIETAC arbitration decision."[57]

While there is certainly enough criticism to go around for the way arbitration is conducted in the PRC, since its inception, CIETAC has, in fact, more or less successfully maneuvered through the choppy waters of institutionalization. From its beginnings as a Soviet clone, CIETAC now handles more international disputes than any arbitral body in the world. Its panel of arbitrators is multi-national in nature and its rules are, by and large, comparable with those of other major international arbitral institutions. Given CIETAC's success at adapting to the challenges it has confronted, the likelihood of success is high. But, CIETAC can't do it alone. Enforcement reform within the court system must be carried out, as well, if the PRC is to become a truly attractive international arbitration venue.

And while all the above gives clues as to the modern arbitral system in China, nowhere do we see a linkage to China's legal past. The enforcement mechanisms are of recent vintage and trace their origins to post-revolutionary times. The one tenuous link that might be associated with an arbitral chain is the similarity between the dynastic propensity for the centralization of things legal that is likewise reflected by CIETAC and the BAC. Courts were weak under the emperors; they remain weak when viewed alongside their legislative and Party counterparts. Having concluded the enforcement portion of our quest for China's arbitral chain, we move from our arbitral journey to the following chapter wherein we provide our observations and conclusions of the journey.

## Notes

1. R. BROWN, UNDERSTANDING CHINESE COURTS AND LEGAL PROCESS, see Chapter 3 generally, 51-54 specifically, (Kluwer 1997).

2. *Constitution of the People's Republic of China* (Adopted at the Fifth Session of the Fifth National People's Congress and Promulgated for Implementation by the Proclamation of the National People's Congress, December 4, 1982); *Organic Law of The People's Courts of The People's Republic of China,* (Adopted at the Second Session of the Fifth National People's Congress, July 1, 1979, and revised according to the Decision Concerning the Revision of the Organic Law of the People's Courts of the People's Republic of China adopted at the Second Meeting of the Sixth National People's Congress, September 2, 1983).

3. The court system is mirrored by an organization of prosecuting entities called People's Procuratorates headed by the Supreme People's Procuratorate. No additional references will be made to this organization given the focus of this book.

4. Found at http://english.gov.cn/links/supremecourt.htm (last visited January 2, 2006).

5. BROWN, at 43.

6. Found at http://www.china.org.cn/english/Judiciary/31280.htm (last visited January 6, 2007).

7. PRC Constitution, at Article 67 (6) and (1) respectively.

8. D. Clarke, *The Chinese Legal System,* (July 2005) found at http://docs.law.gwu.edu/facweb/dclarke/public/ChineseLegalSystem.html (last visited January 15, 2005).

9. BROWN, at 7.

10. BROWN, at 35.

11. *Supreme People's Court Work Report for 2005, found at* http://lawprofessors.typepad.com/china_law_prof_blog/files/spc_work_report.html *(last visited December 25, 2006).*

12. R. Peerenboom, *The Evolving Regulatory Framework for Enforcement of Arbitral Awards in the PRC*, 1 APLPL 12:1, 8, (2000).

13. Perenboom, at 9.

14. *Law of People's Republic of China on Sino-Foreign Equity Joint Ventures,* (Adopted July 1, 1979 at the 2nd Session of the 5th National People's Congress. Amended April 4, 1990 at the 3rd Session of the 7th National People's Congress in accordance with the Decision to Revise the Law of the People's Republic of China on Sino-foreign Equity Joint Ventures, Amended March 15, 2001 at the 4th Session of the 9th National People's Congress in accordance with the Decision to Revise the Law of the People's Republic of China on Sino-foreign Equity Joint Ventures).

15. *Law on Sino-Foreign Cooperative Joint Ventures,* (Adopted April 13, 1988 at the 1st Session of the 7th National People's Congress, Revised October 31, 2000 at the 18th Meeting of the Standing Committee of the National People's Congress by the Decision on the Revision of the "Law of the People's Republic of China on Sino-foreign Co-operative Enterprises").

16. New York Convention, at Article 1 (3).

17. *Decision of the Standing Committee of the National People's Congress on China Joining the Convention on the Recognition and Enforcement of Foreign Arbitral Awards* (1986) and *The Supreme People's Court Notice on the Implementation of China's Accession to the Convention on the Recognition and Enforcement of Foreign Arbitral Awards* (1987).

18. *Agreement on Trade Relations between the United States and the People's Republic of China*, (July 7, 1979).

19. Article 259, *Civil Procedure Law of the People's Republic of China* (Adopted at the Fourth Session of the Seventh National People's Congress on April 9, 1991, promulgated by Order No. 44 of the President of the People's Republic of China on April 9, 1991, and effective as of the date of promulgation).

20. PRC Civil Procedure Law, Article 269.

21. CAA, at Article 61.

22. Article 58 of the CAA, lays out different criteria for the setting aside of a domestic arbitration award.

23. Article 59 of the CAA, Given the logistical hurdles to overcome (translation, hiring Chinese lawyers, etc.) six months seems to be far too short a limitations period.

24. This case was unreported, but has been cited in numerous secondary sources as in Qiu below.

25. Xiaowen Qiu, *Enforcing Arbitral Awards Involving Foreign Parties . . .* 11 AM. REV. INT'L ARB. 607, 612, (2000).

26. For the enforcement of foreign-related awards, application is made to the People's Intermediate Courts (Articles 259 and 269 of the Civil Procedure Law).

27. M. Bersani, *The Enforcement of Arbitration Awards in China*, 10 JOURNAL OF INTERNATIONAL ARBITRATION 2 (1993), 47-54, 47.

28. G. Rushford, *The Rushford Report*, THE ASIAN WALL STREET JOURNAL, Nov. 29, 1999.

29. James Zirin, *Confucian Confusion*, FORBES, Feb. 24, 1997.

30. Perenboom, at 2, n.3.

31. *"China: The New Frontier in Arbitration,"* a tele-seminar conducted by the American Bar Assoc, October 10, 2006. My notes serve as the basis for my observations.

32. Source from R. Peerenboom, *Seek Truth From Facts: An Empirical Study of Enforcement of Arbitral Awards in the PRC,* 49 AM. J. COMP. L. 249, 263, (2001). Hereinafter referred to as *Enforcement* to distinguish this source from other Peerenboom sources.

33. Peerenboom, *Enforcement*, at 264-5.

34. Peerenboom, *Enforcement*, at 265.

35. *"China: The New Frontier in Arbitration,"* a tele-seminar conducted by the American Bar Assoc, October 10, 2006.

36. Peerenboom, *Enforcement*, at 266.

37. From a presentation by Susan Munro at an International Bar Association seminar entitled *International Arbitration and China: recent developments and current issues*, held in Shanghai, Feb. 2006.

38. Peerenboom, *Enforcement,* at 271.

39. E. Reinstein, *Finding a Happy Ending for Foreign Investors . . .* , 16 IND. INT'L & COMP L.REV. 54 (2005).

40. Chen, at 134 .
41. W. Heye, *Forum Selection for International Dispute resolution in China* . . . 27 HASTINGS INT'L & COMP. L REV. 535, 537 (Spring 2004).
42. Perenboom, at 10.
43. Heye, at 538. The author is contrasting the execution chamber with the more prestigious adjudicatory chamber.
44. D. Clark, *Power and Politics in the Chinese Court System* . . . , 10 COLUM. J. ASIAN L. 1, 56 (1996).
45. Jerome Cohen, *China's Legal Reform at the Crossroads,* FAR EASTERN ECONOMIC REVIEW (March 2006) found on the website of the Council of Foreign Relations.
46. Reinstein, at 37, 49.
47. Bersani, at 50.
48. PRC Civil Procedure Law, Article 241.
49. CIETAC Rules, Article 16.
50. *Shanghai Lawyers Association News Brief*, No. 9, April 17, 2006.
51. China Law Prof Blog, May 15, 2006, found at http://lawprofessors.typepad.com/china_law_prof_blog/2006/05/complaints_abou.html (last visited January 8, 2006).
52. J. TAO, ARBITRATION LAW AND PRACTICE IN CHINA, For enforcement of foreign arbitral awards, see generally Chapter VI (Kluwer Law International, 2004).
53. C.K. Harer, *Arbitration Fails to reduce Foreign Investors' Risk in China*, 8 PACIFIC RIM LAW AND POLICY JOURNAL 2, 393-422, 417-18 (1999).
54. Views *of American Companies Regarding Arbitration in China*, an American Chamber of Commerce survey dated May 30, 2001.
55. Quoted in an undated, uncited article by Sidney Lubman entitled *Law of the Jungle,* e-mailed by Prof. A. Han to the writer.
56. *Ibid.*
57. Rushford, *supra* at n.51.

# Chapter Eight

# The Sinicization of the Expedient

There is no arbitral chain. If an arbitral scholar or attorney expects to understand Chinese arbitral law in the context of an historical continuum, there will be disappointment, indeed.

As dynasties changed, so did dynastic law. Positive law was whatever the then Emperor's law was determined to be. Civil law was either underdeveloped—in the hands of the extended agrarian community leadership—or administered by local "courts" as agencies more often shunned than utilized. Dispute resolution was practiced by community members as an instrument of peaceful coexistence.

Additionally, the post-revolutionary forces of China have ensured that whatever pre-revolutionary arbitral law or notions of ADR that might have been embedded in history have been discredited. The Communist Party has execrated Confucius, the Tao, and Buddhism. Post-Maoists have denounced Mao. The contributions of post-Mao arbitral thought incorporate very little originality. Certainly, one can fairly point to the Confucian "legacy" of settlement of disputes through mediation, to the Confucian emphasis on harmony, and to a general historical aversion to litigation. But it should be recalled that the emphasis on harmony and the use of mediation in dynastic days was as much a contribution to the stability of a communal-agrarian life style as it was a response to a belief system. Courts were distant and travel to them was expensive. Local dispute settlement by an elder was quicker and cheaper even though there was rarely a clear-cut winner and loser. More typically, compromise to save face on both side of the issue was required. After all, once the dispute had been "adjudicated," the parties and their families would go on living side by side for generations. My notions of the social aspects of dispute resolution in pre-modern China were reinforced by an observation that was shared with me by one of my Chinese host lawyers. While lunching and talking about China's arbitral antecedents my colleague reflected that "Chinese arbitration came out of a social system and not out of a legal system." It was unlikely, I was cautioned, that I would find modern links to a dynastic dispute resolution system that had been utilized, more or less, by an agrarian population that was fixed both geographically and socially. It is, in addition, understandable that this pre-modern "socio-meditative" approach to dispute resolution was preferred over litigation given the incompetence of the courts and the emphasis of dynastic law on criminal rather than civil matters. Taking one to court was essentially to criminalize the defendant and the delict. Face, so important, would be lost.

While the Confucian values of righteousness and kindness have held up well for years, other tenets ascribed to dynastic Confucianism do not, in today's commercial world, hold up as well. The Confucian maintenance of a hierarchical social order by a small group of men who required the subordination of individual rights to family/community groupings might find sympathy in authoritarian political systems but not at the table of the world's modern commercial economies. To her credit, China recognized that portions of her pre-modern legal heritage needed revision. China's Arbitration Law and its subsequent amendments are attestations to China's attempts at arbitral modernity by recognizing the voluntary submission of a dispute by the disputants to a neutral third party for resolution. In Chinese international arbitration the parties stand on equal footing before an arbitral "court" chosen by them. The Confucian hierarchical system at arbitration has been discarded. And, in a one hundred eighty degree turnabout from the male dominated Confucian society, all the major parties and their counsel may be women. Wisely, China understood that states, regardless of their power, must comply with norms that, while not necessarily in their short term interests, reflect long term trade and commercial aspirations.[1] But this is modern Chinese thinking. It is not based on its historical past. As earnestly as one might want such a past to exist—as this writer did—there simply is insufficient evidence of arbitral links between modern commercial arbitration and Confucian thought.

The Chinese arbitral system reflects, in some way, the cultural transition that is taking place in China. In the creation of Chinese commercial law, there was no legal compass, no legal gyroscope, no legal directional signal that guided the development of the legal system, in general, or the arbitral system, in particular. There were no arbitral links. It is not unfair to suggest that even the commercial catechisms of the modern Communist Party have given way to the capitalist urge to make money—and to make money now! Perhaps China's legal development will be akin to that of South Korea, Taiwan, and Singapore where the rule of law was at first subordinated to economic interests; over time, however, democratic institutions became incorporated into the political weave.

As for today, however, China is undergoing a massive economic facelift. Infrastructural construction is so pervasive that the Chinese have jokingly designated their national bird as the crane (the construction crane)! Whether these facelifts will cause a similar reconstruction of the legal landscape is yet to be seen. If, as Prof. Sylvester suggests, the West both influences and creates other cultures and that non-western societies judge themselves by western standards,[2] then additional changes may well be in store. For while credit must be given to the Chinese for the legal and arbitral transformation that has taken place from the nineteen mid-seventies onward, the fact is that, consistent with Prof. Sylvester's view, Chinese arbitration systems, when judged against those of the West—and judged against the West they are—are deficient even in view of attempts at modernization.

That there exists an arbitral deficiency when China's arbitral system is juxtaposed with Western arbitral systems is not to be dismissed as a mere academic observation of no commercial consequence. Academics and practitioners alike should come to realize that a commercial arbitration system has implications beyond the immediacy of merely resolving a dispute between two parties to a contract. Benson's observations on this point are worthy of elucidation and elaboration.

Benson posited, in reliance on Hayek, that the *jus gentium,* the law merchant and the practice of the ports and fairs were steps in the evolution of law that ultimately permitted the creation of open societies.[3] We demonstrated in previous chapters that an arbitral chain had been forged between the legal eras to which Benson and Hayek refer. The U.K. and U.S. systems give substance to their thesis that the beneficial attributes of an open mercantile regime are observable in "open societies."

We do not suggest that an arbitration system in step both with a nation's and with the international community's commercial needs inevitably leads to an open society. But it does suggest that if China's merchant class (broadly defined) were to form arbitral links with the medieval law merchant, the benefactions of that formation might contribute to a more open and liberal system in the PRC.

Admittedly, the prospects for such an occurrence are remote, especially when it has recently been reported that a senior Party official—mirroring President Hu Jintao's position—described the westernization of China's legal system as the infiltration of "enemy forces." Judicial officials, according to Luo Gan, a member of the nine-person Politburo Standing Committee, had the responsibility to prevent western infiltration and that the position of the legal system should recognize that "The correct political stand is where the party stands."[4] Perhaps recognizing the international implications of his statement, Luo attempted to balance his remarks by urging the courts to protect the foreign and nongovernmental organizations operating legally within China. Luo was firing a shot across the bow of the courts while assuring his nation that the CCP was not going to play the *erhu* while Beijing was ideologically burned down.[5]

There are so many, perhaps too many, forces at work in China. Party discipline is corrupted by capitalist influences; the legal structure is warned of western "enemy forces" while arbitration tribunals struggle mightily to wobble into modernity. CDs by Madonna occupy music store shelves next to those of the Beijing Opera. I was drawn into this whirlpool of legal-social abstractions as one morning I stood in the middle of Tiananmen Square with a young Chinese friend. I asked my friend what she knew of the Tiananmen event in 1989. "I'm 28," she replied. "That was a long time ago. I don't remember anything at all." If it were not for the contact she had with foreigners, the 1989 Tiananmen event might have never reached her memory banks. It was never taught in school. It was never discussed in her household.

Looking straight on, I saw the Forbidden City, the remembrance of a demised system that once served as the locus for the imperial, dynastic rule that gripped China for centuries. I looked over my shoulder to the right and saw a line of people queued up to visit the Mao Zedong Memorial Hall. The average age of the visitors was well over sixty years. Over my other shoulder stood the Great Hall of the People in which meetings of today's legislators of China are conducted, subject to their adherence to the real locus of political power: the Communist Party's Politburo Standing Committee.

At no other time have I ever stood in one place and viewed architectural symbols representing governing systems so diverse and so legally disjoined. And what made the illusion even more impactful was that each system conjured was in place and functioning at some time within the past 100 years! Of course, there was no monument to the Nationalist regime that was part of the 100-year time span. The high turnover of this or any nation's legal/arbitral system makes it virtually certain that links to preceding historical eras are not forged. The law and arbitral systems are born in something of an historical vacuum. The expedient is imported, legislated and implemented.

An illustrative contrast to the expediency of legal development is Justice Joseph Story's masterful *Commentaries on the Conflict of Laws*, in which citations to Roman law, as well as common and continental law, were referenced in both French and Latin. Reading Story is to almost physically and parapsychologically touch and feel the chain linking one generation with its successor; ultimately leading to modern Conflict of Laws. We demonstrated that such a chain existed with respect to common and civil arbitration—the Greeks linked to the Romans and then to Law Merchant, the common law and, lastly, the link to U.S. arbitral law. We are unable to demonstrate such a Chinese chain. Tsing Hua University's Prof. Peng might well agree that "settling disputes through a legalistic adjudicatory system never became rooted in Chinese thinking. The term 'rule of law' therefore is a foreign concept to Chinese society/thinking and the Chinese are still in the process of learning this new vocabulary."[6] Nowhere is my and Peng's contention more illustrative than in China's approach to intellectual property.

For years it has been frustratingly difficult for foreign commercial enterprises to see their trademarks and patents flagrantly displayed and copied in China. Walking the streets of Beijing and Shanghai is an adventure for those who are apparently non-natives. From Rolex watches to Louis Vuitton handbags, from Mont Blanc pens to Nike sneakers—all are available for prices that approximate lunch for two at one's favorite fast food establishment. However, it must be realized that, for years in pre-modern China, there was never a proscription against appropriation of intellectual property by the Chinese from other Chinese. In fact, copying was a testament and complement to the talents of the copied artist. So to offer foreigners a protection unavailable to the citizenry fell—and in no small measure continues to fall—on deaf ears.[7] The "new vocabulary" Prof. Peng wrote of has been developed; whether it will "stick" is still an open question. So too with arbitration.

One of the delights of studying the history of law, in general, and of a nation's legal evolution in particular, is the ascertainment of the legal links between that nation's legal past and its legal present. This task is difficult when attempting to link China's legal/arbitral past with its legal/arbitral present. Certainly, the maintenance of a powerful non-democratic legal center is traceable from past to present. That the court system was underdeveloped and underutilized can, likewise, be traced from past to present. But, as we have seen in previous chapters, the arbitral tracings are tenuous, at best, and, as a result, the foundations on which the legal/arbitral practices rely are the products of expediency. Absent its own arbitral chain that links to its dispute resolution past, China has picked and chosen swatches from the international arbitral quilt and simply sinicized them. What has taken place since the import of soviet style arbitration into China has been *the sinicization of the arbitral expedient*.

One should not take this comment as a criticism. As China's economic fortunes increased, laws were needed by which to superintend the economic effects of this boom on the nation. China had to build a legal system with no historical references to rely on. She had no choice but to look to the common and civil systems, take what was expedient for the time, and then—for the sake of practicality—sinicize the expedient. While there is still criticism among lawyers with whom I spoke about the professionalism and legal aptitude of the Chinese judiciary, a much better job, it was reported anecdotally, was done with the importation of arbitral law, regulations and practices. Still, the lack of a legal core in China's arbitral history is seen in its kaleidoscopic sources of arbitral law. Bits and pieces of multi-colored arbitral glass are found by turning the eyepiece around a floating center. In a wonderful turn of a phrase, Duke's Prof. Bernstein characterized the codification of Chinese law as being drafted, "first retail and then wholesale."[8] The courts and the arbitral commission staffs in China are attempting to deal with an arbitral law that is new, has been subject to revisions, may or may not be enforced in the local courts, and is moderated by a number of other civil laws, such as the Contract Law and laws dealing with establishment of Sino-foreign enterprises.

There may be no better way to illustrate this author's notion of the sinicization of the expedient than to put Chinese arbitration graphically

|  | Offshore Arbitration: ICC, HKIAC, SIAC | CIETAC | Beijing Arbitration Commission (BAC) |
| --- | --- | --- | --- |
| PRC Judicial System | Jurisdiction | Available only with "Foreign related" contracts | Int'l and Domestic Commercial Disputes |
| Int'l and Domestic Commercial Disputes | By contract or based upon jurisdictional rules | Panel of Arbitrators | Advisory or recommended panels |
| Until recently, panel was required | Panel is required | N/A | Discovery |
| None but parties and tribunal frequently suggest/choose IBA Rules of Discovery | None | None | None |
| Provisional Remedies | May pursue in any court of competent jurisdiction per rules | Provisional remedies may only be pursued by and through Commission | Provisional remedies may only be pursued by and through Commission |
| Provisional remedies available but courts do not have powers of contempt | Powers of Tribunal | Tribunal is required to base decision on facts/contract/law and not based on equity unless parties agree | Tribunal may make a decision based upon reasonableness or equity |

|  | **Offshore Arbitration: ICC, HKIAC, SIAC** | **CIETAC** | **Beijing Arbitration Commission (BAC)** |
|---|---|---|---|
| *Advantages* | • Well established and respected<br>• Perception of fairness<br>• Arbitrators paid fairly for time | • Cost effective<br>• Well established and respected in China<br>• Follows procedural due process | • Cost effective<br>• New facilities<br>• Financially supported by Beijing Municipal Government<br>• Commission will not select Commission staff as arbitrators (problem with CIETAC) |
| *Disadvantages* | • Relatively expensive in terms of fees<br>• Location of arbitration raises costs<br>• Chinese parties frequently refuse to select forum outside of China | • Perception of home town advantage<br>• Facilities in Beijing are aged and low tech<br>• Presiding arbitrator frequently a narrow group of "professional" arbitrators or CIETAC staff<br>• PRC arbitrators receive low pay | • Supported by Beijing Municipal Government<br>• Perception of unfairness<br>• PRC arbitrators receive low pay |

*Source*: James Zimmerman of Squire and Sanders, Beijing China. Presentation to the European Chamber of Commerce-China April 27, 2006.

side by side so that the reader may observe an international practice and observe how China has put its own spin on the practice.

When viewed side by side, China's arbitral approach confirms an observation made to me by a CIETAC official with whom I met. The official described the importation of arbitral rules into Chinese arbitral practices as an attempt "to harmonize international rules with Chinese minds." Perhaps this is the reason that only "halfway" measures are frequently taken when Chinese officialdom agrees to amend the Chinese arbitral law. For example, when CIETAC issued its May 2005 amendments, many of which are praiseworthy, it could just as easily have emulated the Beijing Arbitration Commission and proscribed the use of its own staff as arbitrators. It could just as easily have emulated international practice and put the matter of jurisdiction in the hands of the tribunal. It could just as easily have emulated the customs of the major arbitration associations by permitting ad hoc arbitration and foregoing the option of reviewing arbitrators' decision before publication. It could have 'beefed up' its ethical rules and cast a wide disclosure net mandating that all real, potential, and perceived conflicts of interest be disclosed to the disputants.

The experience of Prof. Cohen illustrates the need for full disclosure of any conflicts of interest by CIETAC arbitrators. In a CIETAC case, Cohen was on the losing side of a dispute in which he served as the advocate for a foreign party. Cohen felt the arbitrator's decision was particularly unfair. A week after the award, Cohen discovered that the advocate for his opponent had become a Vice-Chair of CIETAC *before* the hearing—a fact not disclosed! The presiding arbitrator was, in fact, the subordinate of Cohen's opponent. This impropriety caused CIETAC to replace the presiding arbitrator and rehear the case. The damage to CIETAC's reputation had been done, however, and the additional expense to both disputants was substantial.

Enforcement of arbitration awards, while improving, is still a problem for China. My conversations with various practicing lawyers in Beijing and Shanghai confirm that enforcement in the courts of the major 'coastal' cities stands head and shoulders above enforcement elsewhere in China. But, local protectionism, the *quanxi* reliance on relationships for success, CCP interference on the local judicial level, a judiciary that is still in the process of transforming itself, and allegations of judicial corruption,[9] all give the foreign investor cause for concern when scanning the Chinese arbitral enforcement scheme. Perhaps these shortcomings, in a rather convoluted and negative way, create something of a link to Chinese dispute resolution history. Many of the criticisms regarding modern arbitral enforcement were, it will be recalled, characteristic of dispute resolution within dynastic China. But the mission of this book was to find links that forged and became an arbitral chain—to look to China's arbitral past for keys with which to unlock China's arbitral future. Alas, China's arbitral future will not be a reflection of its dispute resolution past. Rather, one might expect to see the continuation of China's sinicizing those international arbitral issues that will make it more attractive to the international community and yet stay within the four walls of Party ukases.

Understandably, one might ask why China continues to enjoy an inflow of foreign capital if there is, as suggested, a positive correlation between a sound arbitral system and foreign investment. My research suggests a few reasons. First and foremost, it is the perceived opportunity to make money. From a sales and marketing standpoint, the vast market of China makes it an attractive place in which to sell. Furthermore, there is the likelihood of sustained sales increases given China's expected future growth hovering in the 5-10% range in a low inflation environment. In addition, special economic zones and "open cities" have been established by the Chinese government in order to attract foreign investment by ensuring a favorable economic environment, an established infrastructure, and a variety of special economic policies. The calculus used by foreign investors indicates to them that the perceived financial rewards outweigh the potential risks of China's arbitration system. Lawyers advising foreign investors in China were remarkably consistent in describing the optimistic outlook of their clients regarding the further liberalizing effect of commerce on China's political system. Whenever I heard this recital, I could not help being reminded of Prof. Chew's admonition that China was like a chimera providing whatever face to the investor that the investor wished to see. There is a wonderful expression in Chinese, "Same bed, different dreams" (*Tong chuang yi meng*). Investment might put foreign and Chinese parties in the same bed, but how they resolve their disputes need not create nightmares.

The arbitral process in the PRC reflects a system colored by "new law" and "old custom." On one hand, various Chinese arbitration laws and CIETAC's rules attempt to mirror rules and regulations of the world's foremost arbitral bodies. On the other, pre-Mao practices, such as *quanxi*, local protectionism, and an emerging judiciary take away from the effectiveness of arbitral law in China. But nowhere in this scheme does an arbitral chain emerge. Even so, arbitration in China, in general, and CIETAC, in particular, has—in fairness—rather successfully maneuvered through the choppy waters of institutionalization, even in the absence of historical roots. In half a century, China has gone from a Maoist state with a xenophobic and ubiquitous central authority, to a country, still dominated by the Chinese Communist Party, but more receptive to international arbitral systems. CIETAC now handles more international disputes than any arbitral body in the world. Its panel of arbitrators is multinational in nature and, while still having some distance way to go, its rules are somewhat comparable with those of other major international arbitral institutions.

China has enacted a viable—albeit poorly constructed—Arbitration Act, possesses a Supreme Court vocally in support of enforcement, and has established a commercial arbitration organization that touts its independence. Enforcement of foreign awards will continue to be spotty, however, as long as the influences of *quanxi* and local protectionism continue. Through state persuasion and education, local courts must come to the realization that short term advantage gleaned for their localities will, in the long run, prove to have deleterious effects for the Chinese economy overall by making China a less attractive place to invest and do business.

This criticism is echoed by no less a personage than a former Vice-Chair of CIETAC, "To [sic] much judicial or governmental interference will adversely affect the healthy development of international arbitration. It does no good to the healthy development of the economy either."[10]

It is difficult to comprehend why a system so committed to international arbitration would bar ad hoc arbitration and permit CIETAC to be subject to international criticism by its withholding from its arbitrators the *competence de la competence* to decide their arbitral jurisdiction. It is even more curious that CIETAC continues to be out of step with the rest of the world by superintending arbitrators who pen their own awards. In the overall arbitral scheme, these are not insurmountable obstacles, but should be dealt with so that China's arbitral dignity is enhanced.

Given CIETAC's success at adapting to the challenges it has confronted, the likelihood of success is good. After all, CIETAC successfully underwent major structural and substantive reforms in 1988, 1994, 2000, and 2005. But CIETAC can't do it alone. Reform within the court system must be carried out as well if the PRC is to flourish as a first-class, attractive, international arbitration venue.

## Notes

1. Sophie Clavier, *Contrasting Perspectives on Preemptive Strike* . . . , 58 MELR 566, 585 (2006).
2. Jon Sylvester & Ruth Gordon, *Deconstructing Development*, 22 WIS. INT'L L. J. 1, 74 (Winter 2004).
3. Bruce Benson, *Law and Economics*, 574-589 THE ELGAR COMPANION TO PUBLIC CHOICE, W. Shughart & L. Razzolini, eds. (London: Edward Elgar 2001).
4. J. Kahn, *Chinese Official Warns Against Independence of Courts*, NEW YORK TIMES, February 3, 2007.
5. The metaphor is taken from R. Peerenboom, *Seek Truth From Facts* . . . , 48 AM. J. COMP. L. 249, 319 (2001).
6. Shin-yi-Peng, *The WTO Legalistic Approach and East Asia: From the Legal Cultural Perspective*, 1 ASIAN-PACIFIC LAW & POLICY JOURNAL 13:13 (2000).
7. For a wonderful look at China's approach to intellectual property, see W. ALFORD, TO STEAL A BOOK IS AN ELEGANT OFFENSE (Stanford U. Press 1995).
8. H. Bernstein, *The PRC's General Principles From A German Perspective*, 52 LAW & CONTEMP. PROBS. 117, 121 (1989).
9. Jerome Cohen, *Opening Statement Before the First Public Hearing of the U.S.-China Commission*, June 14, 2001.
10. Wang Sheng Chang, *The Globalization of Economy and China's International Arbitration*, [2003] ASIAN DR, 187, 188, cited in Maniruzzaman, A., *Arbitration of International Oil, Gas, and Energy Disputes in Asia* . . . , 1 OIL GAS, AND ENERGY LAW INTELLIGENCE (March 2003).

# Table of Public Laws/Statutes and Rules

*An Act for the Further Amendment of the Law, and the Better Advancement of Justice*, 3 and 4 William IV c. 15 (1833).

*An Act for determining differences by arbitration*, 9 and 10 Wm. III c. 15 (1698).

*Arbitration Law of the People's Republic of China*, (Adopted at the 9th Session of the Standing Committee of the 8th National People's Congress of the People's Republic of China, and promulgated by the President, on August 31, 1994, effective September 1, 1995.)

*Arbitration Provisions of the China International Economic and Trade Arbitration Commission Act* (Sept. 12, 1988).

*Agreement on Trade Relations between the United States and the People's Republic of China*, (July 7, 1979).

*Beijing Arbitration Commission Arbitration Rules* (Revised and adopted at the Fifth Meeting of the Third session of the Beijing Arbitration Commission, September 16, 2003. Effective, March 1, 2004.).

*CIETAC Arbitration Rules (2005)*, (Revised and adopted by the China Council for the Promotion of International Trade/China Chamber of International Commerce, January 11, 2005. Effective, May 1, 2005.).

*CIETAC Ethical Rules for Arbitrators,* Revised Version dated May 6, 1994.

*Civil Law of the People's Republic of China,* adopted April 12, 1986 by the 4th Session of the 6th National People's Congress.

*Civil Procedure Law of the People's Republic of China,* (Adopted at the 22nd Meeting of the Standing Committee of the Fifth National People's Congress and promulgated by Order No. 8 of the Standing Committee of the National People's Congress, March 8, 1982; implemented on a trial basis, October 1, 1982).

*Constitution of the People's Republic of China* (Adopted at the Fifth Session of the Fifth National People's Congress and Promulgated for Implementation by the Proclamation of the National People's Congress, December 4, 1982).

*Organic Law of The People's Courts of The People's Republic of China,* (Adopted at the Second Session of the Fifth National People's Congress, July 1, 1979, and revised according to the Decision Concerning the Revision of the Organic Law of the People's Courts of the People's Republic of China adopted at the Second Meeting of the Sixth National People's Congress, September 2, 1983)

*Contract Law of the People's Republic of China,* (Adopted at the Second Session of the Ninth National People's Congress, March 15, 1999).

*Constitution of the People's Republic of China,* adopted December 4, 1982.

*Convention on the Settlement of Investment Disputes between States and Nationals of Other States,* commonly called the 1965 ICSID Convention or the Washington Convention.

*Decision of the Standing Committee of the National People's Congress on China Joining the Convention on the Recognition and Enforcement of Foreign Arbitral Awards* (1986).

*English Arbitration Act*, 1889, 52 and 53 Vict. c. 49 .

*English Arbitration Act,* 1950, 14 & 15 Geo. 6 c. 27

*English Arbitration Act,* 1979, 53 & 53 Vict. c. 49.

*English Arbitration Act,* 1996, 1996 Chapter 23.

*English Statute of Fines and Penalties,* 8 & 9 Will. III c. 11 §. 8 (1687).

*Federal Arbitration Act,* 43 Stat, 883 (1925), 61 Stat. 669 (1947), codified as 9 U.S.C. §§1-16.

*Financial Disputes Arbitration Rules of the China International Economic and Trade Arbitration Commission - CIETAC (2003)* (Adopted April 4, 2003 by the China Council for the Promotion of International Trade / China Chamber of International Commerce, Effective, May 8, 2003).

H.R. Rep. No. 68-96, at 1 (1924).

*International Chamber of Commerce Arbitration Rules,* 1998.

*Interpretation of the Supreme People's Court on Certain Issues Relating to the Application of the Arbitration Law of the People's Republic of China* issued, Sept. 8, 2006.

*Law of Civil Procedure of the People's Republic of China,* (Adopted by the Fourth Session of the Seventh National People's Congress, April 9, 1991, promulgated by Order No 44 of the President of the People's Republic of China, and effective on the date of its promulgation).

*Law of People's Republic of China on Sino-Foreign Equity Joint Ventures,* (Adopted July 1, 1979 at the 2nd Session of the 5th National People's Congress. Amended April 4, 1990 at the 3rd Session of the 7th National People's Congress in accordance with the Decision to Revise the Law of the People's Republic of China on Sino-foreign Equity Joint Ventures. Amended March 15, 2001 at the 4th Session of the 9th National People's Congress in accordance with the Decision to Revise the Law of the People's Republic of China on Sino-foreign Equity Joint Ventures).

*Law on Sino-Foreign Cooperative Joint Ventures,* (Adopted April 13, 1988 at the 1st Session of the 7th National People's Congress, Revised, October 31, 2000 at the 18th Meeting of the Standing Committee of the National People's Congress by the Decision on the Revision of the "Law of the People's Republic of China on Sino-foreign Co-operative Enterprises").

*Magna Carta or The Great Charter of King John Granted June 15th, A.D. 1215, In the Seventeenth Year of His Reign.*

*N.Y. Arbitration Law*, ch. 275, §§ 1-10 (Cahill 1923) (repealed 1937).

*Ordinance and Statute of the Staple* (1353).

*Patent Law of the People's Republic of China,* amended version adopted August 25, 2000.
*Permanent Court of Arbitration Optional Conciliation Rules, July 1, 1996.*

*Regulations of the People's Republic of China on the Arbitration of Disputes Over Economic Contracts* (Promulgated by the State Council, August 22, 1983).

*Supreme People's Court Notice on the Implementation of China's Accession to the Convention on the Recognition and Enforcement of Foreign Arbitral Awards* (1987).

*Supreme People's Court Opinion on Certain Issues Relating to the Full Implementation of the PRC General Principles of Civil Law*, passed January 26, 1988.

*Supreme People's Court Work Report for 2005 found at* http://lawprofessors.typepad.com/china_law_prof_blog/files/spc_work_report.html.

*Trademark Law of the People's Republic of China . . . ,* adopted at the 24th Session of the Standing Committee of the Ninth National People's Congress, October 27, 2001.

*U. K. Arbitration Act,* 1996 Chapter 23.

*UNCITRAL Arbitration Rules* (1976), (Adopted by the General Assembly, December 15, 1976).

*UNCITRAL Conciliation Rules*, 1980.

*UNCITRAL Model Law on International Commercial Arbitration* (1985) (as adopted by the United Nations Commission on International Trade Law, June 21, 1985).

*Uniform Arbitration Act* (adopted by the National Conference of Commissioners on Uniform State Laws in 1955, amended in 1956, and approved by the House of Delegates of the American Bar Association, August 25, 1955, and August 30, 1956).

*United Nations Convention on the Recognition and Enforcement of Foreign Arbitral Awards (New York 1958)* (The New York Convention*)*.

*UNIDROIT Principles of International Commercial Contracts,* 2004.

*The U.S. Federal Arbitration Act*, 9 U.S.C. § 1 et seq.

*WIPO Arbitration Rules*, WIPO Publication No. 446.

# Table of Authorities

*Advanced Micro Devices Inc., v. Intel Corp.,* 885 P.2d 994 (Cal. 1994) (enbanc).

*Allied-Bruce Terminix Companies, Inc. v. Dobson,* 513 U.S. 265 (1995).

*Amco-Asia Corp v. Republic of Indonesia,* 23 I.L.M. 351 (1984).

*Baravati v. Josepthal, Lyon & Ross, Inc.,* 28 F.3d 704 (7th Cir. 1994).

Bell Aerospace Co., Division of Textron, Inc. v. Local 516. . . *500 F.2d, 921 (1974).*

*Bergesen v. Joseph Muller Corp.,* 710 F.2d 928 (1983).

*Bernhardt v. Polygraphic Co. of America,* 350 U.S. 198 (1956).

*B.P. Exploration Co v. The Government of the Libyan Arab Republic,* 53 ILR 297 (1979).

*Bulgarian Foreign Trade Bank v. A.I. Trade Finance Inc.* Supreme Court of Sweden, October 27, 2000. Mealey's Int. Arb. Court Documents-Doc. No. 05-001127-101.

*Burchell v. Marsh,* 58 U.S. 344 (1854).

*The Carrier's Case,* Y.B. 13 Edw. IV (1473).

*Caven v. Canadian Pacific Railway*; 1925 CarswellAlta 100, Judicial Committee of the Privy Council (1925).

*Doctor's Associates, Inc. v. Casarotto,* 517 U.S. 681 (1996).

*Dolling-Baker* [1990] 1 WLR 1205 at 1213; [1991] 2 All ER 890 at 899.

*Esso Australia Resources, Ltd. v. Plowman* 183 CLR 10, 30 (1995).

*Europcar Italia, S.p.A. v. Maiellano Tours, Inc.*, 156 F.3d 310 C.A.2 (1998).

*Factory at Chorzow,* Judgment No. 8, P.C.I.J Series A, No. 17.

*Fertilizer Corp. of India v. IDI Management, Inc., 517, F. Supp. 948, 953 (S.D. Ohio 1981).*

*General National Maritime Transport Co. v. Societe Gotaverken Arendal* (1980), *D.S. Jur. 568 (Cour d'Appel Paris).*

*Green Tree Financial Corp. v. Bazzle, 539 U.S. 444 (2003).*

*Hamlyn & Co. v. Talisker Distillery, 21 Sess. Cas. L.R. (4th ser.) A.C. 202 (1894).*

*Harcourt v. Ransbottom, 1 Jac. & Walter 505, 512 (1820).*

*Hassneh Insurance Co. et al. v. Stuart J. Mew,* Queens Bench Division (Commercial Court), 22 December 1992. *2 Lloyd's Law Rep. 243 (1993).*

*Hide v. Petit, 1 Ch. Cas. 185 (1670).*

In re Badger, (1819) *106 Eng. Rep. 517.*

I.C.C. Awards *Nos. 2977, 2978, and 3033 (1978).*

Kill v. Hollister, *95 Eng. Rep. 532 (K.B. 1746).*

Knox v. Symmonds, (1791) *1 Ves. Jr. 369, 30 Eng. Reprint, 390.*

Table of Authorities 215

*Kulukindus Shipping Co., S.A. v. Amtorg Trading Corp.*, 126 F.2d 978, 982-85 (1983).

*Lesotho Highlands Development Authority v. Impregilo Sp A and others*, [2005] UKHL 43.

*Libyan American Oil Co. v. The Government of the Libyan Arab Republic* 20 ILM 1 (1981).

*Luke v. Lyde*, 2 Burr. 883 (K.B. 1759).

*Mastrobuono v. Shearson Lehman Hutton*, Inc., 514 U.S. 52 (1995).

*Meacham v. Jamestown*, 211 N.Y. 346 (1914).

*Mitsubishi Motors Corp. v. Soler Chrysler Plymouth* 473 U.S. 614 (1985).

*Moncharsh v. Heily & Blasé,* 3 Cal. 4th 1, 10, (1992).

*Petroleum Development, Ltd. v. The Sheikh of Abu Dhabi*, 18 I.L.R. 144 (1951).

*Pillans v. van Mierop,* 97 Eng. Rep. 1035 K.B. (1765).

*Prima Paint Co. v. Flood and Conklin Mfg. Co.,* 388 U.S. 395 (1967).

*Randell, Saunders & Co. (Limited) v. Thompson,* (1875-76) L.R. 1 Q.B.D. 748, 75-4 CA.

*Rhone Mediterranee Compagnia Francese Di Assicurazioni E Riassicurazoni v. Lauro,* 712 F.2d 50 C.A. Virgin Islands, (1983).

Rodriquez de Quijas v. Shearson/American Express, Inc., *490 U.S. 477, (1989).*

Russell v. Pellegrini, 6 E. & B. 1020, 1025 *(K.B. 1856).*

*Saudi Arabia v. Arabian Am. Oil Co,* 27 ILR 117 (1963).

*Scherk v. Alberto Culver Co.*, 417 U.S. 506, (1974).

*Scott v. Avery*, 5 H.L. Cas. 811 (1856).

*Shearson/American Exp., Inc. v. McMahon*, 482 U.S. 220 (1987).

*Sigval Bergesen v. Joseph Muller Corp.*, 710 F. 2d, 928 (C.A.N.Y. 1983).

*Southland v. Keating,* 485 U.S. 1 (1984).

Sumitomo Corp. v. Parakopi Compania Maritama, S.A., 477 F. Supp. 737, (S.D.N.Y. 1979).

Tehno-Impex v. Gebr. Van Weelde Scheepvaartkantoor B.V., *[1981] 2 W.L.R. 821.*

*Texaco Overseas Petroleum Co. v. The Government of the Libyan Arab Republic*, 53 ILR 389 (1979).

*United States v. Panhandle Eastern Corp.*, 118 F.R.D. 346 (D. Del. 1988).

*U.S. Asphalt Refining Co. v. Trinidad Lake Petroleum Co.* 222 F. 1006 (D.C.N.Y. 1915).

*Verlinden B.V. v. Central Bank of Nigeria,* 461 U.S. 480, (1983).

*Volt Information Services v. Board of Trustees of Leland Stanford* . . . 489 U.S. 468 (1989).

*Vynior's Case,* 4 Eng. Rep. 302 (1609).

*Wilko v. Swan,* 364 U.S. 427, (1953).

*Yaung Chi OO Trading PTE, Ltd. v. Government of the Union of Myanmar*, ASEAN I.D. Case NO. ARB/01/1.

*Youngstown Sheet & Tube Co. v. Sawyer*, 343 U.S. 579 (1952).

# About the Author

At the conclusion of his career in international business, Art Gemmell received his J.D. (Valedictorian), an LL.M in Comparative and International Law, and an S.J.D. in International Law. He currently serves as an International Law Scholar at Santa Clara University's Center for Global Law and Policy.

Dr. Gemmell has studied International Law at Oxford University, Aberdeen University (Scotland), and *The Institut International des Droits de L'Homme* in Strasbourg, France. He is the recipient of a Practice Diploma in International Arbitration from the College of England and Wales.

Gemmell teaches Public and Private International Law, as well as International Commercial Dispute Resolution.

He has authored writings and presented lectures on the subjects of foreign investment and international arbitration.